Global
Development
2.0

Global Development 2.0

Can Philanthropists,
the Public, and the Poor
Make Poverty History?

LAEL BRAINARD

DEREK CHOLLET

Editors

BROOKINGS INSTITUTION PRESS
Washington, D.C.

Library of Congress Cataloging-in-Publication data

Global development 2.0 : can philanthropists, the public, and the poor make poverty
history? / Lael Brainard, Derek Chollet, editors.
    p.   cm.
Includes bibliographical references and index.
Summary: "Celebrates the transformative trend within international aid of super-
charged advocacy networks, mega-philanthropists, and mass public involvement
through Internet charitable giving and increased overseas volunteering and offers lessons
to ensure that this wave of generosity yields lasting and widespread improvements to
the lives and prospects of the world's poorest"—Provided by publisher.
    ISBN 978-0-8157-1393-7 (pbk. : alk. paper)
    1. Poverty—Developing countries—Prevention. 2. Globalization. 3. Developing
countries—Foreign economic relations. I. Brainard, Lael. II. Chollet, Derek H.
III. Title: Global development two point oh.
    HC79.P6G65 2008
    362.5'52091724—dc22   2008025539

9 8 7 6 5 4 3 2 1

Typeset in Adobe Garamond

Composition by Cynthia Stock
Silver Spring, Maryland

Printed by R. R. Donnelley
Harrisonburg, Virginia

Contents

Foreword

THE EFFORT TO defeat global poverty is one of the defining causes of the twenty-first century. Victory will require robust alliances waging the good fight on multiple fronts. Thus, venture capitalists, celebrity activists, technologists, and emerging global powers must join forces with traditional bilateral and multilateral donors. Representatives of all these fields and more gathered in August 2007 in Aspen, Colorado, under the auspices of the annual Brookings Blum Roundtable. For three days, they held a focused, forward-looking, action-oriented discussion about how to convert their sizable resources and shared sense of ingenuity and optimism into new ways to alleviate poverty. This book is the result. It answers in the affirmative the question posed by its subtitle: Can philanthropists, the public, and the poor make poverty history? The contributors to this volume make the case for overcoming the once-deep divide between the public and private sectors, mobilizing public opinion and action on a scale before unseen, extending the boundaries of what impact and accountability should mean to poor people—in short, changing the face of global development. But the contributors are also candid about the complex, challenging obstacles faced by both new players and traditional donors that threaten to counteract the recent surge in funds and interest. The book thus also assesses the new development landscape in an effort to ensure that this unprecedented charitable groundswell will yield tangible improvements for the world's poor.

This volume, edited by Lael Brainard and Derek Chollet, includes chapters by Vinca LaFleur of West Wing Writers, Matthew Bishop of *The Economist,* Homi Kharas of the Brookings Institution, Darrell M. West of Brookings, Joshua Busby of the University of Texas at Austin, Ngozi Okonjo-Iweala of the World Bank and formerly of Brookings, J. Gregory Dees of Duke University, Ashok Khosla of India's Development Alternatives Group, Jane Nelson of Harvard University and Brookings, Simon Zadek of AccountAbility, Joseph O'Keefe of Brookings, and Mark R. Kramer of FSG Social Impact Advisors. As mentioned above, the chapters were commissioned for the Brookings Blum Roundtable convened at the Aspen Institute from August 1 to 3, 2007. The roundtable—hosted by Richard C. Blum of Blum Capital Partners and Lael Brainard and John L. Thornton of Brookings, with the support of honorary co-chairs Mary Robinson of Realizing Rights: The Ethical Globalization Initiative and Walter Isaacson of the Aspen Institute—explored "Development's Changing Face: New Players, Old Challenges, Fresh Opportunities."

The quality of this book owes much to the superb research, coordination, and vision of the associate director of the Brookings Blum Roundtable, Abigail Jones. Special thanks are also due to H. Zaks Lubin for his diligent research support, as well as to Ann Doyle, Raji Jagadeesan, and Amy Wong for all their help.

The editors wish to thank Alfred Imhoff for timely and precise editing, and Janet Walker and Susan Woollen of the Brookings Institution Press for their help in bringing the manuscript to publication. The authors remain responsible for the content of their chapters, including any errors or omissions.

This book, like the conference, was made possible by generous support from Dick Blum, whom all of us at Brookings are proud to have as a trustee.

STROBE TALBOTT
President

Washington, D.C.
June 2008

Global Development 2.0

Introduction

THE WORLD OF development is changing, and this book sets out to examine how and why—and to what end. This volume brings together the perspectives of new players with those of leaders in the public sector and academics involved in cross-cutting analysis. By examining the common challenges faced by all development players—accountability, the effective deployment of resources, agenda setting, and achieving scale and sustainability—these contributors' chapters aim to spur a debate as well as build a consensus on effective practices and, thus, establish foundations for collaboration among the growing number of people and organizations committed to lifting the lives of the world's poor.

Each chapter focuses on the actions of new players in the crowded development field, teasing out implications for efforts to alleviate global poverty. In chapter 1, Brookings's Lael Brainard and Vinca LaFleur of West Wing Writers provide an overview of the primary issues of the day, sketching recent trends in assistance strategies and objectives that have emerged with the advent of the new players.

In chapter 2, *The Economist*'s Matthew Bishop paints a vivid portrait of development's changing face, starting with the White House Summit on Malaria in December 2006. The then–president of the World Bank, Paul Wolfowitz, the UNICEF executive director, Ann Veneman, and the Nigerian health minister, Eyitayo Lambo, are seen mingling with the actor Isaiah Washington, the former AOL chair, Steve Case, and the senior pastor of California's Saddleback Church, Rick Warren. It is a scene that has become increasingly common; nowadays in the world of poverty reduction, billion-aires, celebrities, foundations, multinational corporations, nongovernmental organizations, preachers, and social entrepreneurs are working alongside the established multilateral and bilateral bodies that have dominated development since the 1950s.

To determine whether this new coalition of actors will become an integral part of the aid and development system, Bishop focuses his analysis on the strengths and weaknesses of one of development's newest players: the "new philanthropists"—loosely encompassing the high-net-worth individuals making inroads against global poverty. The new philanthropists are leveraging their expertise to establish foundations (like Microsoft's cofounder, Bill Gates), hybrid for-profit/nonprofit enterprises (as did the founder of eBay, Pierre Omidyar), and innovative incentive tools (like Celtel's founder, Mo Ibrahim).

Crediting the new philanthropists with market savviness and an eye for impact, Bishop makes the case that at their best, these high-net-worth individuals can "do things that others find significantly harder" for the global poor. Because these philanthropists are unencumbered by shareholders, political cycles, or excessive red tape, Bishop argues, they can think long term, make unpopular decisions, and act quickly. Coupled with their commitment to advocacy, the new philanthropists are strategically leveraging their resources to achieve maximum impact on the ground. Bishop rightly points out that individual philanthropists' resources to fight poverty, though large in aggregate terms, are usually dwarfed by the budgets of bilateral, multilateral, and corporate donors. The fortunate consequence is that new philanthropists systematically target interventions that promise the largest social return per dollar. Though their role is still taking shape and their long-term impact is equally uncertain, Bishop forecasts that the traditional aid architecture will most likely absorb these philanthropists in ad hoc, issue-driven partnerships.

In chapter 3, Brookings's Homi Kharas provides a detailed empirical map of total aid flows to the developing world. Kharas finds that of the $107 billion in official development assistance disbursed by rich countries to developing countries in 2005, only $38 billion was oriented toward long-term development projects and programs, known as country programmable aid (CPA). The remainder was tied up in special purpose funds for debt relief, technical assistance, headquarters administration, and the like. In-country administrative costs, siphoning off by elites, and corruption shrank the $38 billion even more, perhaps by half. Faced with a limited budget for long-term development projects, many poor countries find themselves hamstrung in their ability to meet pressing needs.

In response to traditional aid's weaknesses, the nature of development assistance has changed. Traditional donors are splintering into many specialized agencies—witness the Global Fund to Fight AIDS, Tuberculosis, and Malaria; and the Global Environment Facility. Large new bilaterals have emerged from the global South with their own approaches to development; Kharas estimates that these new bilaterals—including China, India, Taiwan, and Russia—gave approximately $8 billion in CPA in 2005. The number of private donors is also exploding, and the value of their donations, estimated between $58 and $68 billion in 2005, could already equal or exceed CPA. With the proliferation of development players, the new reality of aid is one of enormous fragmentation and volatility, increasing transaction costs and (potentially) decreasing effectiveness. Kharas identifies understanding the workings of coordination, information sharing, and aid delivery in the new aid architecture as a key challenge for the current era.

In chapter 4, the political scientist Darrell M. West of Brookings and formerly of Brown University turns our attention to development's most visible new player: celebrities. Though today's celebrity advocates have strong historical antecedents, West attributes the outsized nature of their contemporary voice to a number of factors. The convergence of new technologies, coupled with an exploding celebrity culture and deepening disillusionment with public officials, have thrust celebrities into the development mainstream. And given the ability of these "celanthropists" to raise money, attract media attention, and reach new audiences, they are also able to powerfully shape public opinion.

Celebrity advocates' involvement in the crowded aid and development field has its benefits and pitfalls. As West asserts, because celebrities are not bound by political constraints, they bring "independent" perspectives to our national and international dialogue. Yet in other respects, a system based on celebrity raises the risk that there will be less substance in the political process. At best, celebrities infuse poverty alleviation efforts with needed publicity and cash. At worst, civic discourse is diluted of much of its substance when star power is weighted more heavily than traditional political skills. West concludes by cautioning that at present we are dangerously close to the latter.

In chapter 5, the University of Texas political scientist Joshua Busby provides a compelling analysis of development's most celebrated advocacy movement, the Jubilee 2000 debt relief campaign. Championed by the U2 front man Bono, the campaign aimed to have the external debt of the world's poorest countries written off—and succeeded. Busby seeks to discern the roots of the campaign's success to ascertain whether other advocates can replicate such positive results.

Busby attributes the success of the Jubilee 2000 campaign to a number of interrelated factors. Unlike trade liberalization, no strong domestic constituency opposed debt relief. The costs incurred by donor nations were modest. It benefited from a message that had broad cultural appeal in strategic countries. Credible messengers, including an outspoken public and representatives across the ideological spectrum, supported the cause en masse. At the same time, savvy political insiders targeted key players on both sides of the aisle. And given its global nature, advocates utilized differentiated approaches for each national context. Going forward, Busby advises that advocacy movements remain independent from political affiliation. He also warns of an overreliance on celebrity intermediaries, echoing West's concerns about oversimplifying complex policy messages. So, though there may never be a large constituency for global poverty alleviation, advocates might emulate Jubilee's success by skillfully utilizing the mass media *and* tactically reaching out to individuals with access to policy circles.

In chapter 6, Ngozi Okonjo-Iweala, the former Nigerian minister of finance (and now managing director of the World Bank) takes an inside look at the "demand side" of Jubilee 2000: developing countries. In what reads much like a memoir, Okonjo-Iweala gives a personal account of Nigeria's successful quest for debt relief. And though Nigeria was not a direct beneficiary of the debt relief campaign, it indirectly benefited from Jubilee's success in creating an amenable environment for relief requests.

Okonjo-Iweala traces the background, elements, and enabling factors that led to the historic 60 percent write-off of Nigeria's Paris Club debt in June 2005. In December 2004, the country's external debt had stood at nearly $36 billion, 86 percent of which was owed to the Paris Club. The country's total annual debt service was about $3 billion. On the road to qualifying for debt relief, Nigeria became the first country whose homegrown economic reform program earned the endorsement of the International Monetary Fund's Policy Support Instrument. The World Bank granted the country International Development Association–only status. Nigeria regularized its debt service record. And it established that changes to the status quo were necessary to make any appreciable progress toward the Millennium Development Goals. Achieving these benchmarks with the help of academics and civil society proved instrumental in catalyzing the official talks that formalized the debt write-off, which opened doors hitherto closed for Nigeria on the investment front.

In chapter 7, J. Gregory Dees, who specializes in social entrepreneurship and nonprofit management at Duke University, investigates the phenomenon of social enterprises and sector blurring—which is rapidly sweeping through development circles. Though official donors operate almost entirely through government channels, philanthropic organizations (both established and fledgling) are increasingly looking to the power of individual entrepreneurs to transform society in a decentralized approach. These market-oriented approaches to poverty alleviation, which are essentially obscuring the lines between for-profit and nonprofit enterprises, are gradually being embraced as an integral element in creating lasting social change.

Three guiding tenets explain the growth of this social entrepreneurship approach: economic empowerment, independent innovators, and philanthropic value added. In most developing countries, serious barriers to market development prevent the poor from participating in beneficial economic relationships. Dees argues that social enterprises commonly empower economic participation and facilitate the development of nascent markets. Yet identifying ventures that promise high social returns remains a stumbling block. To fill this void, development players are increasingly looking to social entrepreneurs—those pioneering individuals on the ground who have demonstrated their ability to take risks, innovate, and adapt. Philanthropists and social investors have a pivotal role to play in financing these entrepreneurs and the worthy enterprises they champion. Going forward, Dees identifies measuring success, establishing terms of engagement, ensuring sustainability, and scaling for impact as key challenges for those interested in funding hybrid enterprises.

In chapter 8, Ashok Khosla of the Development Alternatives Group, a consortium of social enterprises based in India, builds upon these insights, reflecting further on the deep connections between sustainable development and social enterprises. Though knowledge can be a powerful tool for development, market incentives tend to stratify its benefits between the global haves and have-nots. To address this market shortcoming, Khosla looks to social enterprises, or what he calls "community ventures"—hybrid for-profit/nonprofit local enterprises that deliver basic services to the villages where they operate. As small businesses, community ventures have the potential to provide needed services while generating employment opportunities. Key to their success is the support of "network enablers," which offer the integrated services needed to help local ventures become profitable and sustainable. Drawing on extensive field experience, Khosla sees an opportunity for venture philanthropists to finance these network enablers and thus help build a small community's capacity to rise out of poverty.

In chapter 9, Jane Nelson, who focuses on corporate social responsibility at Harvard University, provides a comprehensive overview of the numerous accountability questions that have arisen as the reach, influence, number, and diversity of nonstate actors in international development have multiplied. These actors (broadly defined) range from activists and funders to emerging entrepreneurs and technologies to new sources of and models for delivering official development assistance to new initiatives and ad hoc coalitions being forged by new players. Concurrent with their rise, new players face questions of accountability and effectiveness about their governance, integrity, stakeholder participation, legitimacy, and scalability. And in reflecting on these questions, new players are increasingly imposing a certain degree of discipline on all development actors.

Nelson analyzes the implications from four primary perspectives: traditional, official donors and large corporations, civil society organizations, public-private partnerships and multistakeholder alliances, and the new bilateral donors. Some new players are imposing this discipline by filling governance and accountability gaps—monitoring and ranking the performance of traditional donors, strengthening public sector capacity, increasing public engagement, and promoting enhanced corporate social responsibility initiatives. Other new players are imposing discipline by example—pioneering legal and regulatory mechanisms, independent monitoring and ranking systems, and self-regulatory or voluntary mechanisms for oversight. Collectively, they have pushed accountability into the spotlight.

Looking to the future, Nelson believes that multistakeholder approaches to the governance and operations of development initiatives at the local, national, and global levels will become prominent. As the initial attempt to create models for mutual accountability, these collaborative initiatives grew out of the need to redefine how the development community can legitimately shape governance and accountability frameworks, and how it can effectively mobilize and deploy resources for long-term poverty alleviation. Scaling up multistakeholder initiatives (like all development interventions) will require operational models that make impact assessment, empowerment, and capacity building mutually reinforcing.

In chapter 10, Simon Zadek of the international nonprofit organization AccountAbility takes a deeper look at multistakeholder approaches to accountability. In arguing that twentieth-century accountability mechanisms are proving inadequate for today's challenges, Zadek echoes Nelson by arguing that there need to be more collaborative initiatives among public bodies, businesses, and civil society organizations. Yet he goes a step further, contending that such cross-sector networks are *the* institutional innovation of the current era, because they stand to influence all those in contact with them.

Zadek identifies three primary categories where collaborative initiatives could make the greatest impact: commercial endeavors, leveraging, and rule setting. Focusing on rule setting and on "collaborative standards initiatives"—for example, the Extractive Industry Transparency Initiative, the Kimberly Initiative, and the Equator Principles—he outlines both the benefits and risks of such endeavors. These initiatives establish standards that govern the behavior of the initiatives' signatories. As regards benefits, Zadek points to the initiatives' ability to reshape markets to value environmental and social externalities, to fill gaps in public governance, and to give voice to the communities and stakeholders active in developing the markets that affect their lives.

Yet the challenges and risks faced by these collaborative standards initiatives are not insignificant—like all new players, they have their own transparency and accountability issues. Likewise, their efforts to welcome the voice of the communities where they operate to the decisionmaking table and to align themselves with national governance systems remain haphazard at best. Free riders present an ongoing challenge, as does creating disincentives for noncompliance. Zadek concludes, therefore, by emphasizing that the efficacy of these initiatives depends on establishing robust forms of collaborative governance; only then will they become an integral part of a new multilateralism fit for this century.

Undeniably, the aid and development community has undergone sweeping changes since the emergence of the new players noted here. Today, with more than 230 actors channeling resources to the developing world, the number of donors per recipient country now averages 33, compared with only 12 in the 1960s. This proliferation presents major challenges for ensuring that assistance is coordinated. In chapter 11, Brookings' Joseph O'Keefe thoughtfully explores the development community's response to this fragmentation and proposes a way forward to ensure that more donors will mean more for the world's poor.

In recent years, the multitude of donor-driven initiatives has spurred efforts to streamline aid through a loosely tiered system of coordination known as the "Consensus Model." With this model, both aid donors and recipients stand to benefit by sharing information, establishing common objectives, and collaborating on project implementation. Yet this process is plagued with fundamental problems, which will only be exacerbated as fragmentation deepens, new bilateral donors increase their aid, borrowing from capital markets continues to grow in the developing world, and market-like competition among aid donors intensifies. For aid outcomes to improve, it will be critical for actors to adapt to this rapidly changing environment. To do so, O'Keefe recommends increasing the reach of best-practice collaborative standards initiatives, providing recipient governments with the tools needed to rate donor performance, and creating a pool of funds at the multilateral level for independent impact assessment.

In the concluding chapter 12, Mark R. Kramer of FSG Social Impact Advisors proposes a concrete plan to synergistically improve the impact of the three main aid and development sectors—government, corporate, and philanthropic. He illustrates how the different institutional cultures, technical skills, and incentive structures of each sector give rise to unique capabilities for development work. Yet these differences can leave organizations that share goals but are in different sectors at loggerheads over strategy and implementation. To alleviate this situation, Kramer argues, the three sectors could greatly benefit from a division of labor. There is already a nascent acceptance of this idea; for example, some government aid spills into philanthropic organizations, and corporate investments can leverage public expenditures. However, without a common language, cooperation among the sectors is often arbitrary.

In particular, Kramer suggests, by building a consensus on four types of impact evaluations—financial returns, socioeconomic benefits, social benefits, and environmental benefits—the development field's three sectors could promote cooperation and coordination. By evaluating all their development actions in this way, the sectors could identify their comparative advantages and form a tangible system for determining how to leverage and allocate their complementary resources. In this sense, this book ends with a meditation on how the burgeoning, diverse cast of the aid and development industry can start to act together to lift the lives of the poor.

1

Making Poverty History? How Activists, Philanthropists, and the Public Are Changing Global Development

LAEL BRAINARD AND VINCA LaFLEUR

THE INTERNATIONAL DEVELOPMENT community as we have known it for sixty years is undergoing an extreme makeover. If its roots go back to the Marshall Plan and the founding of the Bretton Woods institutions, its modern incarnation has branched both up and out—dramatically altering the landscape of humanity's efforts to alleviate poverty.

During the postcolonial era of giving in the 1960s and 1970s, roughly thirty-eight official bilateral and multilateral donors annually disbursed an average of $43 billion in assistance (in 2005 dollars). Today, hundreds of development entities are spread across a larger group of countries, annually disbursing $158 billion (net of debt relief). The fight against poverty, which was once almost exclusively restricted to aid officials and learned experts, has become one of the twenty-first century's most popular causes. And the throng of new participants is not just niche players; the scholar Homi Kharas of Brookings' Wolfensohn Center estimates that in 2005, their giving was approximately equal to official development assistance from traditional donors (figure 1-1).[1]

Broadly speaking, there are five groups of newly prominent development players. First are what might be called the "megaphilanthropists"—the modern-day Fords and Rockefellers whose breathtaking commercial achievements have afforded them the resources and influence to engage in development on a global scale. Many of these new actors—such as Bill Gates of Microsoft, eBay executives Jeff Skoll and Pierre and Pam Omidyar, Virgin mogul

The authors thank Abigail Jones for excellent research assistance.

Figure 1-1. Aid Flows to the Developing World, 2005

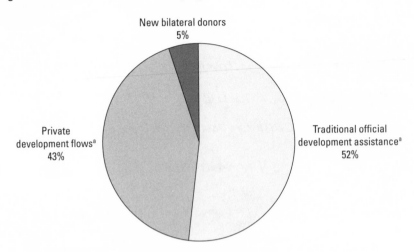

Source: Data given in chapter 3 by Homi Kharas of the present volume.
a. Members of the Development Assistance Committee of the Organization for Economic Cooperation and Development.

Richard Branson, AOL cofounder Steve Case, and Google wunderkinds Sergey Brin and Larry Page—earned their billions by pioneering transformative new information technologies. Today, they are bringing that same bold vision and creativity to their antipoverty efforts. Indeed, though the megaphilanthropists' money may have been their ticket to the development table, it is neither their only nor necessarily most important asset; they also bring to the cause convening power, an eye for breakthrough innovation, a keen drive toward efficiency, and marketing savvy.

Many of these megaphilanthropists are test driving new models of "venture philanthropy." These models seek to blend the best of the private and philanthropic sectors by investing in social enterprises that seek returns through market approaches. Others are spurring the growing interest in blending philanthropic and market investments to seed the growth of indigenous small and medium-sized enterprises (SMEs), which are too often starved for capital in poor countries.

Several megaphilanthropists are engaging in "knowledge philanthropy"— investing in the development of powerful science and new technologies to overcome the burdens of disease, malnutrition, poor water and sanitation, marginal agriculture, and unreliable power that encumber the lives of the poor. Still others, such as George Soros, are setting their sights on social and political transformation, empowering local actors who seek to transform societies in which ingrained corruption and unaccountable regimes have held back progress for generations, or in which entrenched interests have obscured growing dangers to the environment. Collectively, they represent an infusion of entrepreneurial dynamism to the development field.

The second group of newly prominent development players are from the corporate sector, which is becoming increasingly engaged. We see this in the actions of a growing number of major multinational firms that are pioneering corporate social responsibility endeavors—from corporate foundations applying what the Brookings and Harvard scholar Jane Nelson calls "a more enterprise-based and competence-led approach to philanthropy"[2] in order to advance long-term development goals, to innovative efforts to provide key services and products to the poor that encompass everything from Unilever's sales of individual shampoo sachets in India to Citigroup's thriving microfinance practice around the world.

The private sector is also fostering greater consumer involvement against poverty. (PRODUCT)[RED], for example, has reached out to consumers through brands such as Gap, Apple, Converse (owned by Nike), Motorola, and American Express. Through profits made on sales of individual company products, the (PRODUCT)[RED] organization has channeled $30 million as of July 2007 through the Global Fund to Fight AIDS, Tuberculosis, and Malaria to provide antiretroviral drugs to AIDS patients and child care to AIDS orphans in Ghana, Rwanda, and Swaziland. (PRODUCT)[RED] cofounders Bobby Shriver and Bono have created a self-sustaining campaign that promotes greater awareness of the needs of the world's poorest people while providing individuals with an avenue to make a difference by simply buying the products.

Third, more than two dozen new bilateral donors, from China to Chile to the Czech Republic, are asserting a more prominent role in providing assistance. Many of these new official donors have recently come through (or are still undergoing) the process of development themselves, and they feel they can offer more relevant advice than rich country donors. Despite being less wealthy than the traditional official donors, several of these new players are growing deep pockets. For example, China's foreign assistance already surpasses that of Australia. Estimates suggest that new bilateral donors collectively gave about $8 billion in 2005.[3]

The fourth group of unconventional development players can be broadly defined as "celebrities": high-profile individuals—from rock stars to actors, preachers, and former presidents—who are maximizing the power of their public appeal to champion global poverty awareness and activism. These celebrities bring what the Oxford scholar Paul Collier has called "development buzz" to the "development biz."[4]

Many of these well-known individuals have a demonstrated ability to raise money, attract the media spotlight, reach new audiences, and shape public opinion. And at a time when trust in government is generally low, such well-informed celebrities are injecting a dose of credibility and charisma into the foreign assistance and development debate. Indeed, several have had great success influencing official donors and government leaders. In 2005, the rock star Bono of U2 helped convince world leaders at the Group of Eight Summit in Gleneagles to forgive a portion of Africa's multilateral debts. Hollywood stars including Angelina Jolie, George Clooney, and Don Cheadle have focused public attention on humanitarian crises such as HIV/AIDS and the conflict in Darfur. And former U.S. president Bill Clinton's annual Clinton Global Initiative, which aims to tackle a range of global challenges including public health and development, mobilized almost $10 billion in pledges in its first two years alone.

The fifth significant group of new development players is the global public itself. Often fueled by celebrity appeals and the "voice" power of Internet communities, the public is making its presence known. Witness the hundreds of thousands who attended the ten "Live 8" concerts in the run-up to the Gleneagles summit, the more than 2.4 million signatures for the ONE Campaign, and the 63.5-million-strong audience for the 2007 U.S. television special *American Idol: Idol Gives Back.* These campaigns owe much to the success of the Jubilee 2000 debt relief campaign, which utilized the Internet, celebrity, and a diffuse network structure to mobilize public support and achieve its goal.

Along with lending its voice to specific issue-driven campaigns, the public has become an active participant in financing development and a growing contributor to development activities on the ground. Individual donations from the United States to the developing world have surged to approximately $26 billion a year, and innovative models promise to further facilitate this exchange.[5] Through the Internet, grassroots philanthropists can take their generosity worldwide—becoming bankers to the poor at Kiva.org, where a loan as small as $25 can help a microentrepreneur in a developing country; or browsing GlobalGiving.org's "marketplace of goodness" in search of a specific project to support. And, according to the Brookings Initiative on International Volunteering and Service, more than 50,000 Americans volunteer their time in overseas service each year, returning home with firsthand appreciation of the challenges poor communities face.[6]

How New Is New?

Critics might argue that many of these "new" development players are not new at all. After all, Audrey Hepburn was bringing attention to the plight of children in places like Sudan, Vietnam, and Somalia long before Angelina Jolie came on the scene. George Harrison and Ravi Shankar held their benefit Concert for Bangladesh fourteen years before Bob Geldof's Live Aid in 1985. Generations of Americans have trick-or-treated for UNICEF, a tradition that dates back to 1950. And U.S. foundations like Ford and Rockefeller were revolutionizing development decades before the information technology explosion that ushered the Bill and Melinda Gates Foundation and Google.org onto the stage.

But if these types of players are not new, strictly speaking, their outsized influence relative to the traditional players certainly is an innovation. The cumulative combination of enormous wealth among private donors, the messaging megaphone associated with new media and social networking, and the new flows of assistance from developing country donors and diasporas together herald a new era of global action on poverty—one that involves, as Nelson argues, "new types of cooperation and collective action across the traditional boundaries of public, private, and civil society sectors."[7]

Moreover, the increasingly competitive development field is causing established players to reexamine their role and raise their game. In 1997, the new U.K. government of Tony Blair created a cabinet-level Department for International Development with an exclusive and resolute focus on poverty reduction, fulfilling a campaign promise strongly supported by influential antipoverty groups. In 2003, U.S. president George W. Bush announced the creation of the $15 billion President's Emergency Plan for AIDS Relief, winning the support of a powerful coalition of HIV/AIDS advocacy groups. For their part, the World Bank and the International Finance Corporation are increasingly pursuing cross-sector partnerships, as evinced by their Lighting Africa Initiative, which seeks to create the market conditions needed for the supply and distribution of "green" lighting products to the 250 million people in Sub-Saharan Africa who currently have no access to electricity. Meanwhile, iconic private foundations like the Rockefeller Foundation, which in its early years spent more on foreign aid than the U.S. government, are now reorienting themselves to better leverage their intellectual and financial assets—for instance, through collaboration with the powerful newcomer the Bill and Melinda Gates Foundation.

It is fashionable to describe this ever-more-crowded development landscape as increasingly competitive, entrepreneurial, and market-led. But this new "development market" must become more effective so today's outpouring of generosity will yield sustained improvements in the lives of the world's poorest people and not succumb to the familiar cycle of activism followed by withdrawal. In a conventional market, competition drives down costs and improves offerings as producers compete to win consumer spending. But in the development market, more producers (that is, donors) do not guarantee more effective antipoverty outcomes, because the demand for results ultimately rests with donor country taxpayers and philanthropists, not poor countries.

Thus, a crucial challenge for the contemporary development community is to close the structural gap between the supply and demand sides of assistance—that is, between aid donors, activists, and service providers on the one hand and aid recipients on the other—to ensure that limited development resources go where they are needed most. Achieving this will require the engagement and creativity of both traditional and new players. *If humanity is to prevail in the fight against global poverty, the most important and empowered new actors must be the men and women of the developing world themselves—who must have more choices and a stronger voice in the decisions that affect their lives.*

Promising Arenas for Action

Having achieved success as entrepreneurs in the corporate marketplace or in popular culture, many of the new players come to the development arena with different assumptions and different skill sets. As a result, they appear more inclined to test drive unconventional approaches—such as empowering social entrepreneurs and small-scale private enterprise, advancing bottom-up technological development, and deploying messaging and social networking tools for development ends. These new actors are also freer than many official donors to work with in-country counterparts in the private sector and civil society, thus empowering a broad variety of players to stimulate development from the ground up.

Innovative Social Entrepreneurs

As the new sources of funding and advocacy-enabled public support are translated into results on the ground, the blended space where social value and market value converge is being singled out for special attention, owing in part to strong resonance with the new generation of givers and recognition of the limitations of top-down approaches to development. In the words of the Duke University scholar J. Gregory Dees, "philanthropists can add value by accelerating market development in ways that improve the lot of the poor, directing their capital and resources to the ventures most likely to engage the poor in a constructive way."[8]

Many of the new development players are casting their bets on "social entrepreneurs"—a term often credited to Ashoka founder and chair Bill Drayton. Social entrepreneurs are change agents who bring to social endeavors the same skills of innovation, leadership, team building, persistence, and implementation that are required to pioneer successful businesses. Exemplifying these qualities is Fabio Rosa, who has been an Ashoka Fellow for almost two decades. In the 1980s, Rosa developed and deployed a system that brought low-cost electricity to rural Brazilians—dramatically improving villagers' productivity and standard of living. After the privatization of Brazil's electric industry, he launched a new effort to help remote villages rent solar power equipment—a business endeavor with important social, health, and environmental benefits.

Some of the most prominent new philanthropists are looking out for more leaders like Rosa. The eBay veteran Jeffrey Skoll, for example, has devoted his Skoll Foundation to connecting and celebrating social entrepreneurs by awarding substantial prizes to "innovators who have achieved proof of concept, are poised to replicate or scale up toward systemic social change and have a message that will resonate with those whose resources are crucial to advancing large-scale, long-term solutions."[9]

Meanwhile, new intermediaries such as the Acumen Fund and the Grassroots Business Initiative are emerging to provide seed capital and managerial know-how to social enterprises. Indeed, we may be witnessing the emergence of a new market segment similar to the evolution of microfinance. Where microfinance institutions have developed to connect capital with microentrepreneurs, an intermediary philanthropic market may be emerging to serve social entrepreneurs—those whose endeavors propose large-scale social change and promise to have ripple effects throughout the economy.

In looking for worthy social development endeavors and entrepreneurs, the new philanthropists increasingly expect to apply the same notions of impact, cost-effectiveness, scalability, and sustainability demanded in corporate boardrooms. The most successful social entrepreneurs are equally pragmatic. Nick Moon is cofounder of KickStart, a nonprofit that designs and

mass markets affordable agricultural equipment to enable Africa's poorest
people to move from subsistence to commercial farming. In his words, "We
have to marry the bleeding heart with the hard head. If you can't see, quan-
tify, or measure impact, it probably isn't there."

Private donors and investors are also exploring ways to blend philanthropic and market investments to spark the growth of indigenous businesses
in the cash-strapped SME segment. Indeed, private enterprise belongs at the
very heart of the development enterprise, especially in narrowing the gap
between aid supply and demand. After all, private enterprise is the greatest
source of self-employment and jobs—the two factors poor people rank highest as having the potential to improve their lives.[10] And, given the right circumstances, the entrepreneurial spirit can be sparked within any society—a
welcome counterpoint to the culture of dependence too often associated with
foreign aid.[11]

Although some investors are convinced that there are great opportunities
to be found, there is still a need for nodal institutions or network enablers
that can act as incubators, mentors, early investors, and talent scouts for
promising SMEs, helping connect developing country entrepreneurs to
money and markets. Organizations such as Business Partners Africa and the
Small Enterprise Assistance Fund suggest that success is possible, but achieving scale and sustainability will require bridging the conventional divide
between for-profit and charitable entities. Some of the most obvious areas for
action are creating attractive exits for equity investors and exploring tax
incentives that encourage private investors to consider markets they would
otherwise deem too risky.

Some successful social enterprises may always require subsidies, but some
donors are seeking to invest in SMEs expressly to demonstrate that commercial viability can go hand in hand with the provision of socially valuable
goods and services—hearkening back to the beginning of the venture capital
industry in the wake of World War II, when firms like J. H. Whitney &
Company, Rockefeller Brothers Company, and T. Mellon & Sons actively
invested in seeding ventures with social as well as economic merit. Today,
foundations are taking the lead where angel investors fear to tread. The Shell
Foundation, for example, looks for business-focused, enterprise-based solutions with efficient service delivery, and helps seed their growth in the hopes
they can one day source capital from financial markets.

Indeed, some socially transformative enterprises have proven commercially successful (box 1-1). Celtel, for example, a wholly commercial mobile
telephony company that has built cellular networks in more than fifteen

BOX 1-1
Empowering Local Entrepreneurs

A vibrant and productive middle class is recognized the world over as an economy's primary engine of growth. That is why a vibrant SME sector is so important—accounting for 90 percent of enterprises in the world and for 50 to 60 percent of employment opportunities. In the United States, for example, small businesses provide roughly three out of four of the net new jobs added to the economy. Yet many African SMEs struggle to access capital, face high transaction costs, and frequently produce products that fail to meet importing market requirements. High levels of unemployment across the continent confirm that this sector is decidedly underperforming and citizens are looking to their governments to intervene. According to a recent NOI/Gallup Poll conducted in Nigeria, citizens unequivocally believe that their government should focus on job creation at all levels. (One-quarter of the Nigerians surveyed listed job creation as the most important issue the government should address in the next twelve months, followed by water, electricity, road system, education, agriculture, health care, corruption, violence, and the rail system. For more information, see www.noi-polls.com/index.html.)

To that end, Kenya-based KickStart develops and promotes appropriate technologies to increase the productivity and profitability of small-scale enterprises. By marketing micro-irrigation, cooking oil, construction, sanitation, hay baling, and transportation technologies to thousands of entrepreneurs in East Africa, KickStart has helped launch 50,000 new businesses as of October 2007—800 a month—which have generated $52 million a year in new profits and wages since 1991. The organization's MoneyMaker irrigation pump alone has transformed thousands of small subsistence farms into new commercial enterprises by improving farmers' productive capacity by as much as fourfold. Coupled with the fact that 4 manufacturers produce these pressure irrigation pumps in East Africa, and more than 400 retailers sell them in Kenya, Tanzania, and Mali, the MoneyMaker line has created approximately 29,000 new jobs and $37 million in new annual profits and wages. By developing affordable (under $1,000), durable, and manually operated technologies that are locally mass produced, KickStart is helping to lift thousands out of poverty.

African countries, is enabling millions of Africans to raise their living standards through the power of communication. This decidedly for-profit company may not fit preconceptions of what an organization that helps the poor should look like. But its second-largest investor was the Department for International Development's private sector investment arm, the Commonwealth Development Corporation (CDC). When the MTC Group acquired Celtel for $3.36 billion in 2005, the CDC claimed a 500 percent return;[12] meanwhile, Celtel founder Mo Ibrahim has gone on to become one of Africa's most creative philanthropists.

It is too soon to tell whether social enterprises and blended ventures will evolve sustainable models to address poverty. Many practitioners face an uphill battle in moving from startup to scale; resources for expanding "proven models" are scarce, perhaps because funders' transaction costs for rigorous evaluation are high, and the desire to fund the next new thing is more appealing than financing for scale (see below). The investor community is still waiting for signposts to navigate blended terrain; both philanthropic and private sector pioneers are still struggling to put a price tag on social value. And all involved have to grow more comfortable with the prospect of social enterprise failure if they are to take the daring risks that will spark dramatic gains.

Yet, the vigor with which entrepreneurial approaches to social change are being pursued gives cause for hope. As Dees argues, "We need better understanding of the institutional structures and supports that would allow [them] to thrive. If we can deepen our understanding in these ways, we may find a new approach to social change, one that strategically blends philanthropy and business."[13]

Knowledge for Development

The public often associates development work with saving lives. And indeed, some of humanity's greatest strides have been made in areas like child survival and life expectancy during the past fifty years. Between 1960 and 1999, life expectancy for the poorest fifth of the world increased from 53 to 87 percent of that for the richest fifth—whose own life expectancy rose from sixty-nine to seventy-six years. Child survival for the poorest fifth has reached 80 percent of that for the richest fifth. Polio has been virtually eradicated from the planet; advances are being made against other killer diseases like measles and malaria. And the caloric intake of the poorest has gone from 57 to 70 percent of the rich country benchmark over the past forty years. Though the income gap remains stubbornly persistent, it is clear that poor countries with a range of institutional capacities have achieved substantial gains in absorbing and adapting knowledge and technology in areas such as medicine, family planning, sanitation, nutrition, education, and agriculture.[14]

Although knowledge and technology can be powerful tools for development, market incentives too often tend to stratify the benefits of technology between the global haves and have-nots. Leveraging technology to improve the lives of the poor requires express efforts to promote adaptation and widespread adoption. Though some of the greatest triumphs in development have come from the systematic dissemination of technologies developed for wealthy country populations to poor communities (for example, the elimination of smallpox), others have required the creation or adaptation of technologies to the specific conditions faced by poor communities (for example, the green revolution). With much of the world's poorest population concentrated in tropical areas, there is a pressing need to develop technology specifically for those areas rather than relying on the transmission of agriculture and medicines developed for rich country markets located predominantly in temperate climates.

Developing this new technology will require changing incentives all the way through the systems for knowledge creation—from elevating the creation of solutions for the poor to a prestigious place in science and engineering curriculums in developing countries (for example, India) and rich country university systems (for example, the University of California, Berkeley; Massachusetts Institute of Technology; and Columbia University); to creating market incentives through innovations such as the Advanced Market Commitment mechanism designed by the Brookings and Harvard economist Michael Kremer and advanced by the Bill and Melinda Gates Foundation; to restoring research and development budgets and science and technology personnel in key development agencies; to involving poor communities directly in technology adaptation and uptake through organizations such as the Barefoot College run by Bunker Roy.

The entry of new players promises to breathe fresh life into this agenda. Google is designing its development program with its core competencies in mind, emphasizing areas where expanding access to information can empower poor communities. In one innovative partnership, it is deploying Google Earth satellite technology in collaboration with the U.S. Holocaust Memorial Museum to illuminate the devastation wrought in Darfur.[15] Funding from the Bill and Melinda Gates Foundation's Global Health Program has helped to seed dozens of public-private partnerships that are researching new solutions to the so-called neglected diseases that disproportionately afflict poor people. The Bill and Melinda Gates Foundation is forming a partnership with the Rockefeller Foundation in the hopes of reprising the role Rockefeller played in providing seed capital for the green revolution, with today's focus squarely on Africa. Philanthropy is helping to introduce multidisciplinary approaches to development in university settings such as the Earth Institute at Columbia University and the Richard C. Blum Center for Developing Economies at Berkeley. And forums such as the annual Technology, Entertainment, Design Conference and InnoCentive are encouraging innovative collaborations among leading entrepreneurs, corporations, philanthropists, investors, and scientists to develop new ways to deliver clean water, clean energy, and new medicines to the poor.

This new generation of social entrepreneurs and hybrid ventures will be critical in bridging the gaps among innovation, community engagement, and sustainability that too often have diminished the transformative potential of research and technology. The Nobel Peace Prize winner Muhammad Yunus has adapted the Grameen Bank's microcredit lending model to spread the power of communications technology to help lift millions out of poverty. The One Laptop per Child program led by the MIT Media Lab's Nicholas Negroponte, the PlayPumps technology that generates clean water from child's play, and KickStart's innovative approach to developing and marketing new technologies each started with the power of a compelling idea. All require the support of private philanthropy and advocacy networks, the active engagement of community organizations,[16] and ultimately support from official donors or uptake by the corporate sector to achieve scale and sustainably change the lives of the poor (box 1-2).

Policy research also has a critical role in providing rigorous assessments of the impact of innovative ventures on the well-being of the poor relative to alternative approaches, disseminating findings to facilitate replication and achieving scale, providing recommendations to fill gaps in the institutional environment, facilitating accountability, and shaping policy.

Without such critical partnerships and a favorable enabling environment, the promise of technology will remain elusive. As the Brookings and New York University economist William Easterly reminds us, "Beware of technological quick fixes. . . . Regrettably, the experience of aid is that plenty of promising technologies exist but never reach many poor people."[17]

Mobilization and Messaging: Making Hope Sell

Some of the most visible new antipoverty advocates are global celebrities who have proven extraordinarily effective at mobilizing public support for ostensibly technocratic development issues. Their efforts owe a great deal to

---

BOX 1-2
Leveraging University Assets

The Richard C. Blum Center for Developing Economies, housed at the University of California, Berkeley, is one of many new development players placing bets on the transformative potential of technologies designed to address the challenges of the world's poorest people. Along with the Earth Institute at Columbia University and the Media Lab at MIT, the Blum Center is helping to pioneer both appropriate and high technologies tailored to the developing world.

Among the challenges the Blum Center's researchers are investigating is access to uncontaminated, potable water. According to the 2006 United Nations *Human Development Report,* more than 1 billion people lack access to clean drinking water. Every day, nearly 5,000 children perish—2 million each year—and countless other people fall ill because of water-related diseases, which is curbing poverty reduction efforts and economic growth in some of the world's poorest countries. The Blum Center's potable water initiative concentrates on the development, production, dissemination, and evaluation of low-cost, small-scale water treatment systems in Bangladesh, Ecuador, Guatemala, India, Kenya, Madagascar, and Mexico.

---

the success of the Jubilee 2000 debt campaign, which the Center for Global Development economists Nancy Birdsall and John Williamson have called "by far the most successful industrial-country movement aimed at combating world poverty for many years, perhaps in all recorded history."[18] Whether rock stars, movie stars, moral leaders, or political icons, these "celanthropists" are infusing antipoverty campaigns with their own charisma and brand allure. Some are adept at crystallizing complex issues in catchy slogans like "Drop the Debt" and "Make Poverty History." Others have made energetic use of the popular media to attract new development audiences; witness MTV's *Diary of Angelina Jolie and Dr. Jeffrey Sachs in Africa.* Seasoned performers on the global stage, these development champions are eloquent and impassioned in their appeals on behalf of the impoverished—invoking emotional language and images designed to anger, engage, and inspire action. And it works. The public is answering their call in unprecedented numbers.

At the same time, this high-profile celebrity advocacy may carry some unintended consequences. Some observers worry that black-and-white storylines obscure the nuances and intricacies of development, misleading the public to believe that solving poverty is just a matter of more foreign aid. As Collier cautions, "Unfortunately, although the plight of the bottom billion lends itself to simple moralizing, the answers do not."[19] Raising public expectations too high could breed disillusionment and disengagement down the line.

The blurring of celebrity brands with social movements creates challenges for both sides. Celebrities may be understandably leery of alienating their constituencies or tarnishing their reputation, which can crimp their desire to champion complex, controversial, or less media-friendly causes. Meanwhile, some nongovernmental organizations (NGOs) may be cautious about associating the serious causes on which they have been laboring for years with celebrity advocates whose own credibility, seriousness of purpose, and staying power may be untested.

In addition, the perceived validation that high-profile advocacy grants to a development cause may inadvertently cause other worthy priorities to be neglected. In Rwanda, for example, thanks to the success of the Global Fund, $48 million a year is available for HIV/AIDS, which affects about 3 percent of the population age fifteen to forty-nine years, in contrast to only $1 million for less publicly visible maternal and child health programs.[20]

Despite these potential pitfalls, under the right circumstances, celebrity advocates and high-profile campaigns have a great deal to offer the development community. Already, their efforts have delivered important—and in some cases, long overdue—gains for poor people, from debt relief to antiretroviral medications. Looking ahead, as the celebrity and high-profile advocacy movement matures, a range of opportunities can expand and intensify its reach.

One such opportunity will be to take on some of the riskier obstacles to development. It is not surprising that advocacy networks to date have proven more effective in instances of humanitarian crisis such as the Indian Ocean tsunami or the genocide in Darfur, where the face of human suffering is beamed into our living rooms in real time, than on trade liberalization or dismantling agricultural subsidies, where domestic opposition is strong and the connection to poverty is less starkly illustrated. Grassroots donors want to feel that their contributions are making a real difference, which is easier in the case of appeals to alleviate visible catastrophes; meanwhile, celebrity and high-profile advocates are understandably drawn to black-and-white issues with a greater likelihood of success. But a future test for these advocates will be to leverage their power to mobilize the public on behalf of more complex issues that are tougher sells, such as trade and market access.

A second important opportunity is to help improve global perceptions of Africa's progress by harnessing new development actors' messaging and mobilization expertise toward a mantra of hope and partnership. Thoughtful observers have expressed concerns that some well-intentioned Western antipoverty campaigns may be inadvertently reinforcing troubling stereotypes, for instance by downplaying the agency of Africans themselves while emphasizing the role of outside actors. Though images of human misery may spur charitable donations, they also perpetuate notions of wholesale suffering and instability—dissuading potential private sector investors from giving the continent a chance. As Easterly has argued, the emphasis on war, famine, disease, and death often present in popular portrayals of Africa creates a "dark and scary image of a helpless, backward continent," when, in fact, Sub-Saharan Africa has seen its gross domestic product grow at an impressive 5 percent for the past three years, its mobile telephone and Internet usage double each year for the past seven years, and its foreign direct investment surpass foreign aid.[21]

In partnership with the increasing numbers of inspirational African leaders in government, business, and civil society, new development actors can help bring more of Africa's "good news" stories to light—and in the process, improve the investment climate and global image of many African countries—making clear that African initiative ultimately will be the critical engine for sustained growth. Already, a number of pro-poor advocates and NGOs are taking this challenge to heart. In Oxfam America's campaign against the U.S. farm bill, for example, the organization brought African farmers to the American heartland to emphasize a message of dignity, not despair. Kiva.org cofounder Matthew Flannery defines the organization's goals in terms of progress, not poverty, and describes its work as building partnerships instead of giving aid. And (PRODUCT)[RED] and DATA (Debt, AIDS, Trade, Africa, now merged with the ONE Campaign) are exploring how to use their formidable profile and savvy to help brand Sub-Saharan Africa as open for business—a region where free markets are growing, democracy is spreading, conflicts are ending, and the potential middle class could be 43 million strong by 2030, according to World Bank estimates (box 1-3).

Celebrity and advocacy movements are one of the most visible distinguishing features of the contemporary development landscape. In the months and years ahead, these new development actors should be encouraged to put their credibility, charisma, passion, and power to even greater

BOX 1-3
Africa: Open for Business!

From the HIV/AIDS pandemic, to crippling inflation in Zimbabwe, to geno-cide in Darfur, Africa's economic and development fortunes have been the subject of widespread media attention. Yet the intense spotlight generally overlooks most of Africa's successes, often overshadowing some of the most optimistic development achievements. As the region sees fewer con-flicts, more democratic elections, and economic growth rates that are now reaching those of other developing regions, many of its countries could be poised for sustained growth and development. As African Development Bank president Donald Kaberuka notes, "Africa is on the move and has the best chance in thirty years to go beyond the tipping point—to turn the tide and break out of the long economic stagnation of the 1970s and 1980s."

Some seventeen of the forty-eight countries in Sub-Saharan Africa have seen average growth rates of 5.5 percent for the last ten years, and an addi-tional seven countries have witnessed growth rates of 7.4 percent over the same period. Taken together, these represent half the countries in the region and account for 65 percent of the continent's population (World Bank, *Africa Now: Building a Better Future,* 2007, 1).

These hopeful growth rates have been accompanied by institutional and policy reforms. Though perennially tagged a high-cost, high-risk place to do business, Sub-Saharan Africa is becoming hospitable to foreign investors. According to the World Bank report *Doing Business 2007,* Africa places among the top three regions committed to private sector reform—a water-shed achievement by any measure. Previously ranked last, the region is now making remarkable changes: Two-thirds of all Sub-Saharan countries made

benefit—both in educating Western publics and policymakers about devel-opment challenges and solutions, and in amplifying the voices of the agents of change within developing countries.

More Than the Sum of Its Parts

Risk taking, empowering change agents, innovation, messaging, and public mobilization could help transform the sometimes stodgy development field. Yet there are no guarantees that the whole will amount to more than the sum positive reforms last year. Indeed, of 175 economies surveyed, Ghana and Tanzania ranked ninth and tenth in terms of breadth and depth of reform.

A new African business environment is beginning to take shape—one with simpler business regulations, stronger property rights, more sustainable tax burdens, more access to credit, and lower transaction costs. It is an environment ready for new enterprises, new jobs, and continued growth. As Mo Ibrahim, chairman of the Mo Ibrahim Foundation, notes, "Africa is open for business. Investors seeking high returns will get the highest returns in the world in Africa right now!"

Of course, this optimism is tempered by uncertainty over the sustainability and breadth of Africa's strong growth performance. Because high commodity prices—which traditionally have followed boom-and-bust cycles—are playing a disproportionate role in African growth, there is concern that the gains could prove short-lived or that growth is overly concentrated among resource-rich economies and their immediate neighbors.

To sustain and broaden growth and improve competitiveness, African economies must continue to implement far-reaching reforms, diversify production and exports, and strengthen financial markets. As one of the least internally integrated regions of the world, Africa faces a critical need to deepen regional and subregional trade and invest in cross-border infrastructure. Provided that global economic trends remain favorable while reformers invest in their continent's growing population and build its institutional capacity and infrastructure, Africa should be able to maintain its current levels of growth and investment for many years.

of its parts. Although impromptu coalitions may be the ideal mechanism for catalyzing action in a critically neglected area, unless they are institutionalized, they may fall short in delivering sustained value. Similarly, pioneering approaches will only be taken to scale and sustained if their impact can be evaluated using commonly accepted metrics, their results are widely disseminated, and they are successfully handed off to official entities. And the enthusiasm philanthropists bring to the quest for transformational breakthroughs may not always translate into the less glamorous, daily labor of building functioning, self-sustaining societies from the bottom up.

If we accept that more hands on the development deck is a powerful and positive thing, then where might those hands best apply their strength to improve the lives and prospects of the poor? Beyond improving the life chances of impoverished people, how can donors and development actors catalyze systemic social change? And what can be done to improve aid's impact and effectiveness, with a greater emphasis on meaningful input from—and outcomes for—its intended beneficiaries?

Complementing Rather Than Duplicating Aid Efforts?

Many of the newcomers to the development stage are less constrained than governments by rules and regulations, or even than their private sector predecessors by the oversight of corporate or foundation boards. The absence of such limits should free them to pioneer activities at the riskier end of the spectrum, where official agencies are often unable to operate. The proliferation and diversity of these new actors is also leading to new partnerships and coalitions to take on specific challenges such as HIV/AIDS.

Yet this burgeoning cast of characters also carries risks of duplicated effort and inefficiency. According to the Brookings expert Joseph O'Keefe, on the official side alone, the average number of donors per recipient country grew from twelve in the 1960s to more than thirty in the period 2001–05, which suggests that multiple actors are trying to address the same challenges.

The greater number of possible funders and development partners also puts greater burdens on strapped recipients—in face-to-face meetings, idiosyncratic reporting and assessment requirements, and differences in donor-driven priorities. A recent survey by the Organization for Economic Cooperation and Development (OECD) found that traditional donors reportedly fielded 10,453 missions in thirty-four countries in 2005—an average of more than 300 per country, or 1 every 1.2 days. In addition, because of the structural disconnect between supply and demand, even though more external actors are trying to make a difference, the areas they are focusing on may not reflect recipients' priorities—which can lead to mutual frustration and reduce the effectiveness of aid.

To address these problems, the last decade has seen a rising emphasis on coordination among official donors in support of "country ownership." Some successful instances have built on coordination processes led by the recipients themselves—as in Uganda and Tanzania—while others have relied on coordination mechanisms agreed upon by official donors, such as the multilaterals' Poverty Reduction Strategy Papers.

In some cases, multilaterals like the Global Fund are integrating funders into coordination processes. These donors include several large new players like the Bill and Melinda Gates Foundation, (PRODUCT)[RED] and its partners, and UNITAID. Continuing, strengthening, and deepening these efforts will be a key priority for the future, to ensure that the contributions of significant private players and new bilaterals are harmonized with the broader community's efforts, and to align donors' good intentions with beneficiaries' greatest needs.

Ultimately, such focused coordination will have to reach all the way to efforts on the ground. A recent mapping of development assistance in Ghana and Mali by Save the Children with CARE, Millennium Promise, and McKinsey & Company found hundreds of players on the field. It is high time to revisit the lessons from experience—for example, the effort to support the Bangladesh Rural Advancement Committee in the 1970s—and create systems that will enable the whole throng of development players to routinely coordinate their efforts sectorally or geographically. Other promising approaches to improving coherence and efficiency may emerge in the virtual arena, for example, through Raj Kumar's Development Executive Group (www.developmentex.com), a searchable, online clearinghouse for multiple aspects of development work—from hiring project managers to procuring engineers.

Achieving the greatest impact from the efforts of both new and old development players, however, will require going beyond *coordination* to achieving *strategic complementarity.* Though often sharing the same broad goals, private philanthropists, official donors, and corporations approach the development endeavor with different skill sets, objectives, and approaches for measuring success. They too seldom make strategic choices about how to align their efforts with other new and old actors and thus too frequently fund overlapping projects.

Private philanthropists bring considerable strengths to the table. They are often nimble, lightly burdened by oversight and strictures, and able to take risks. But they rely heavily on intermediary organizations, often have a limited presence in the field or in-house research capacity, and generally must use their smaller funding for catalytic purposes rather than to make sustained large-scale investments. Corporations often can leverage an extensive, long-term staff presence in a country along with considerable in-house skills and resources. However, their deployment is often constrained by a primary mission that is not related to development. In contrast, both newer and established official donors tend to have extensive resources and a strong field presence along with the capacity to push bilaterally and multilaterally for governance changes (see below) but are highly constrained by changing domestic political agendas.

Too often, any or all of these players might be funding the same sector or even the same project through the same NGO in a particular country without any prior consultation or coordination. Several of the large traditional official donors, in particular, have been slow to appreciate the sheer size of assistance from the private and philanthropic sectors and even slower to pursue synergies. Some of the new megaphilanthropies have been pressed to disburse funding rapidly without having the luxury of fully studying the field and identifying complementary efforts. As a result, the impact of these efforts has been less than the sum of their parts. In the words of FSG Social Impact Advisors' Mark Kramer, "The greatest impact will be achieved when each sector directs its funding to projects that it can undertake more efficiently or effectively than other sectors, but which simultaneously help support the developmental needs of those other sectors. This shift in thinking is precisely what is needed if each of the sectors is to accomplish their agendas more effectively."[22]

Despite the same broad goals—such as reducing malaria and increasing the number of girls completing primary school—new and old actors have different notions of how to achieve and assess success. Strategic complementarity will be greatly aided not only by developing a division of labor among the various players up front but also by sharing lessons informed by common metrics of assessment. The resources for development—financial, human, and political—are too scarce to be wasted repeating the same old mistakes underwritten by different types of funders.

Ultimately, the goal for donors and development service providers must be to find ways to coordinate their efforts that go beyond simply dividing up the terrain—"You take education, I'll take sanitation." The more that development strategies can be driven by beneficiaries' priorities and plans, and the more the various aid providers are strategically positioned to deliver the best outcomes for the poor, the more likely it is that the development community's efforts will breed widespread success.

Strengthening Governance: Selectivity and Accountability

If there is one universal truth in development, it is that governance and institutions matter fundamentally for the quality and durability of outcomes. Leaders from donor and recipient countries alike emphatically underscore the prerequisite of good governance for growth—to provide not only hard infrastructure like power, roads, and sanitation but also the soft infrastructure of a transparent and predictable regulatory system, voice and accountability, an independent judiciary, and the rule of law.

Traditional donors practice *selectivity* bilaterally and through multilateral channels to create incentives for recipient governments to improve policies, institutions, and overall governance (admittedly, with mixed success). World Bank and International Monetary Fund loans have long been conditioned on assessments of recipient policy environments, and traditional donors have worked through organizations such as the OECD Development Assistance Committee (DAC) to agree on common standards, such as environmental impact.

In recent years, this trend has accelerated. The new U.S. Millennium Challenge Corporation (MCC) conditions country eligibility on sixteen governance and policy indicators, ranging from voice and accountability to the number of days it takes to start a business. Countries that score well on these indicators can determine their own priorities for assistance—and the resources come in the form of grants, rather than loans to be repaid. MCC chief executive John Danilovich describes the system as granting a "seal of approval" to developing countries, which then can leverage further investment and trade from the private sector. Similarly, the European Union and the World Bank have each developed their own sets of quantifiable criteria for making aid allocation decisions.

Yet, even as established official donors work to fine-tune conditionality and selectivity, the entire system is being challenged by the emergence of new bilateral donors. The more sources of assistance there are from which to choose, and the less coordinated they are, the more tempting it is for recipients to "donor shop" to avoid the strictures of conditionality and selectivity associated with mechanisms such as the MCC and the World Bank's performance-based allocation system.

China's willingness to provide unconditional aid to various African nations is provoking particular concern in Western capitals. Officials are troubled by China's willingness to deal with unsavory regimes like those of Sudan and Angola, reducing such countries' incentive to change. Many also fear that China's voracious appetite for natural resources will result in exploitative aid-for-trade deals with developing African nations—an issue on which many Western governments have their own unfortunate histories. In addition, some experts worry that access to loans from China could undermine low-income countries' hard-won gains on debt relief. It must be noted,

BOX 1-4
The Chinese Dragon and the African Lion

In the past twenty years, China has experienced staggering growth. Its annual gross domestic product growth rates have been in the double digits for the past five years and have not dipped below 7 percent since 1991. This strong economic performance has translated into remarkable achievements in poverty reduction. Between 1990 and 2000, 170 million Chinese were lifted out of poverty. Indeed, in the past twenty years, China has accounted for 75 percent of poverty reduction worldwide.

On the basis of China's own success alone, it would be reasonable to describe the country as a beacon of hope in the developing world. Yet its impact extends beyond mere example. The demands of its burgeoning economy for resources and markets are redrawing the economic map—perhaps nowhere so consequentially as in Africa. Since 2000, China-Africa trade has quintupled, rising to $55.5 billion in 2006, and fully 30 percent of China's oil comes from Africa. Chinese demand for oil and mineral resources has pushed commodity prices up, driving African growth, while cheap Chinese consumer goods are in growing evidence across much of Africa.

In parallel with its growing clout in trade, China is building a hefty bilateral development assistance program in Africa. With major announcements at the 2005 Millennium Review Summit and the 2006 Forum on China and Africa Cooperation, Chinese officials have committed to provide $10 billion in preferential loans and preferential export credits, with $5 billion going to

however, that Western governments have been slow off the mark to welcome China into their own aid deliberations.

Moreover, even Western observers concede that China has shown a willingness to spend in sectors that traditional donors have recently neglected, including major infrastructure projects that are essential to durable growth. And African partners are quick to point out the benefits of China's interest in investment and trade. Looking to the future, an urgent challenge for Western, Chinese, and African actors alike is to fortify channels of communication, coordination, and collaboration toward development goals—so that the impact of Chinese investment in Africa is to catapult progress, not delay or undermine reform (box 1-4). More broadly, given the rising influence of

Africa in the next three years; to double aid to Africa from 2006 levels by 2009; and to establish a $5 billion China-Africa Development Fund to encourage Chinese companies' investment in African infrastructure projects.

China's insistence that aid should be unconditional is a rebuff to the conditionality practiced by the traditional club of wealthy official donors. To some, it seems that China may see development assistance primarily as a way to further its national interests or, as officials put it, pursue "harmonious development." For example, China's loans are almost completely tied to national contractors and consultants. And China tends to favor resource-rich countries, even those that, like Sudan, are in the throes of humanitarian turmoil. These inclinations are causing consternation among the traditional donors, which have developed a common set of practices and principles to guide aid allocation, to which China does not yet subscribe.

In the years ahead, it will be critical for the traditional club of bilateral donors to involve China and other new official donors, such as Russia, in deliberations and agreements on aid practices to ensure that the new donors do not repeat past mistakes—such as contributing to unsustainable debt levels and environmental damage—or undermine current joint efforts, for instance on improving governance. However, these efforts will succeed only if the traditional donors give some credit to China for its efforts and are humble about their own past mistakes in this arena as colonial or cold war powers.

other nations such as India and Brazil, it may be time for a fundamental reappraisal of who sits at the official donor table.

A range of approaches could encourage closer cooperation among old and new donors, from expanding the DAC to fostering professional contacts and exchanges among development experts around the world. But one thing is clear: With the magnitude of funding from nontraditional sources, both new and old donors will need to reach some kind of accommodation or risk undermining their own stated goals.

Although individual philanthropic resources are too small to enforce selectivity, private philanthropists are finding ways to play a catalytic role in the good governance equation. George Soros has targeted philanthropic efforts to

BOX 1-5
Building Capacity for a Brighter Future

Capacity building is critical for successful development—not only creating capable and durable institutions in a particular country but also educating, training, and supporting the people who will lead them. This builds on some of the proudest moments in the history of philanthropy. During the last half century, the Ford and Rockefeller foundations made large-scale investments throughout the developing world, supporting the creation of institutions like teacher colleges, think tanks, and institutes of development studies. For example, the Rockefeller Foundation built medical schools in China and Latin America; the Ford Foundation was invited to India by Prime Minister Jawaharlal Nehru in 1952 to help the new Indian government establish university faculties, government departments, and training centers; and the Rockefeller and Ford foundations together funded the creation of most of the leading social science and public policy think tanks throughout the developing world (Raymond Offenheiser, "Is There a Role for International Philanthropy in Addressing Issues of Global Poverty in the 21st Century?" lecture at Princeton University, May 5, 2005). In the words of the former Ford Foundation officer and current president of Oxfam America, Raymond Offenheiser, "In the 1950s and 1960s, American foundations placed a strong emphasis on working with governments to build institutions and increase capacity. For example, the Ford Foundation's dollars in India were spent on

countries experiencing democratic transitions because they are especially receptive to reform yet are often ill equipped to effectively absorb official aid. Private philanthropy, which can be more flexible and responsive than government funding, can provide the experts and technical assistance to help a new government move forward while training local civil servants to carry on after they leave. To that end, Soros's Open Society Institute (OSI), in partnership with the United Nations Development Program (UNDP), has pioneered a fellowship program for diaspora communities to take high-level jobs in Georgia, Serbia, and Montenegro to build the capacity of new democracies to make the most of their transition period. These relatively low-cost investments can pay multiple returns, as countries put in place the sound policies that attract official aid and private investment down the line.

capacity building, from establishing community development programs that financed village health and sanitation programs, to strengthening agricultural institutes that improved soil and water management, to endowing think tanks and university programs in the social sciences. Ford thought on a large scale and invested in promising ideas to strengthen strategic institutions. If you travel to the places where they had a presence, you can still see their indelible footprint some fifty years later."

Today, many low-income countries around the world are hungering for similar long-term, strategic investments in capacity building—for example, overhauling higher education systems, ramping up investments in civil service training, promoting effective teacher training, deepening local capacity for policy analysis and recommendations, and developing new curricula. Traditionally, navigating a country's social networks and promising local partners has required an extensive presence on the ground. Establishing and revitalizing those kinds of connections throughout the philanthropic community—perhaps by funding intermediary organizations or using the power of technological platforms to bridge gaps of time and distance—could help marry the current wellspring of philanthropic generosity with capable, effective developing country partners, implementers, and innovators, priming the pump for sustainable social change.

Beyond timely support for new democracies, philanthropies can bolster governance by helping build institutional, administrative, and research capacity in developing country public sectors (box 1-5). As Nelson writes, sometimes the real problem is not bad governance but weak governance: "Even when governments want to provide their citizens with transparent and readily accessible information and with reliable and efficient services, they are all too often constrained by lack of human capital, lack of modern technology, and lack of administrative capability."[23] Private and official donors alike can help address this problem by supporting public policy and research institutes, universities, and evaluation programs in developing countries themselves. Some encouraging models are the Global Development Network, a consortium of public and private research and policy institutes that aims to share and

apply locally generated research to promote development; and the Mohammed
Bin Rashid Al Maktoum Foundation, which plans to invest in universities,
research institutes, and youth development throughout the Middle East.

Ultimately, outside donors' most important contribution to good governance may be to strengthen developing countries' internal accountability
capabilities. Programs such as OSI's Revenue Watch (now the independent
Revenue Watch Institute) and the William and Flora Hewlett Foundation–
Brookings Transparency and Accountability Project aim to equip independent civil society watchdog organizations and think tanks to monitor and analyze public spending and revenues, arming the media and citizen groups with
data and analysis to demand better government performance themselves.

Another bold endeavor, the Mo Ibrahim Prize for Achievement in African
Leadership, each year rewards a former African executive head of state or government who has demonstrated excellence in leadership, based on a ranking
of governance performance as evaluated by an independent, high-level panel.
As Ibrahim has explained, "The heart of the project is the index, not the
prize"—meaning that the primary goal of the endeavor is to establish metrics
for good governance that citizens can use to evaluate their own leaders.
Though leadership deficits are hardly confined to African nations, the cost of
bad leadership in many African countries is higher because of weak institutions. Governance indices help to empower African citizens to hold their
leaders accountable and demand lasting institutional change to ensure that
growth continues well after any particular leader has left office.

The Commission on the Legal Empowerment of the Poor, sponsored by
the UNDP, aims to identify and advocate for reforms that ensure the legal
inclusion and empowerment of the poor, including property rights, legal protection of their assets, access to justice, and legal mechanisms to facilitate
informal businesses. In the spring of 2008, this high-level commission, co-
chaired by Madeleine Albright and Hernando de Soto, will release its final
report. Finding ways to support the commission's recommendations should
be a focus for development advocates and funders in the months ahead.

Service provider organizations are also taking a harder look at empowering
civil society in the countries where they operate. According to Charles Mac-
Cormack of Save the Children, 95 percent of his organization's work is done
through service delivery—yet more could be done to work with developing
country partners on advocacy in their own countries. In MacCormack's
words, "Looking forward, we need to support and fund national organizations for their in-country advocacy work. We need to move some of our philanthropic dollars to social mobilization and constituency building."

Enhancing Accountability and Evaluation for Superior Impact

More broadly, the proliferation of new actors and the dazzling growth in the volume of resources is raising new questions of accountability and democratic participation or "voice." Simon Zadek, the chief executive officer of AccountAbility, argues that accountability is the "DNA of civilized societies, and so also of meaningful development."[24] But most development accountability mechanisms were established to manage the old order dominated by governments and official donors. The question today is which new accountability mechanisms should be established, by whom and for whom. Questions of accountability are too often oriented toward the provider of funds rather than the communities the development interventions seek to serve. Who should judge success—donors or recipients? And most important, what should be assessed?

The power—some would say imperialism—of the traditional market mechanism is the reduction of billions of complex transactions into a common metric along a relatively small handful of dimensions—most notably profits, costs, and prices. Even nonmarket side effects (so-called externalities) can be addressed once monetized and integrated into the price system. No such common agreement or parsimony determines the right "bottom line" when fighting poverty with a diverse array of actors. Devising more accurate, accessible means to measure aid's impact and effectiveness—particularly from the perspective of beneficiaries—is a crucial challenge if the development market is to reach its fullest potential.

Yet, measuring the impact of particular development interventions is inherently difficult. The contributing factors are many and varied, and players coming from the corporate, nongovernmental, philanthropic, and public sectors bring with them different practices and approaches to assessment. Nongovernmental organizations are handicapped in performing long-term impact assessments because their projects are only funded for their duration. For many startup social enterprises, the relevant data are often not collected, and methodologies for analysis are often lacking even when they are. Even the most established official donors have been slow to undertake rigorous, systematic impact assessments (for example, randomized trials, control groups), even when those techniques are routinely applied to their domestic programs.

As Smita Singh of the William and Flora Hewlett Foundation points out, it is tempting to focus on inputs instead of outcomes because outcomes are inherently more difficult to measure. Counting the number of boys and girls enrolled in school is easier than determining what they have learned; tracking the number of antimalarial bed nets distributed is easier than tracking improvements in public health attributable to the bed nets. And measurement is particularly difficult when the goal of an intervention may be to prevent something from happening. How, for example, should donors evaluate an anticorruption effort—in monies that did not disappear?

In addition, the success or failure of a specific intervention may give a false impression of overall progress toward a goal. Some experts are concerned, for example, that the massive infusion of resources to tackle HIV/AIDS is leading low-income countries to focus their strapped public health systems disproportionately on this one challenge at the expense of other more prevalent public health problems.

For assessment to be meaningful, the appropriate benchmarks have to be set from the start—a task that is harder than it sounds. Olara A. Otunnu, president of the LBL Foundation for Children, points out that though the Millennium Development Goals were established with the best of intentions, the education goal is backfiring. In many countries, even as the stated goal of universal primary enrollment is being met, it is being achieved without additional investments in school facilities, teacher hiring and training, or supplies, with the result that what little adequate primary education used to exist for poor children is being eroded.

Similarly, the more ambitious an endeavor, the more difficult it is to pinpoint causality. As both old and new donors and service providers, from rich and developing countries alike, join forces in promoting broad goals, how does each organization hold itself accountable for collective results?

There is also a risk that the push toward quantifiable metrics and results will lead donors and philanthropists to demand meaningful, measurable change in ever-shorter time horizons. As Susan Berresford, the former president of the Ford Foundation, has warned, "There is a danger that some venture philanthropists will support only what can be measured or leave in frustration when results don't come quickly. Some social problems, almost by definition, are messy and so is the search for their solutions, requiring experimentation, patience, and often a leap of faith."[25]

These are thorny challenges. Yet it is clear that improving accountability for impact is one of the most pressing opportunities and obligations for the twenty-first-century development community—including by establishing a greater willingness to reward programs that work and be honest about those that do not. Indeed, the *New York Times* columnist Nicholas Kristof has suggested the need for a "Journal of Development Mistakes"—a catalogue of pro-poor endeavors that have failed to work as planned—which would enable those engaged in such work to learn not only from one another's home runs but also from missteps. Several foundations are already taking stock of their failures and disseminating their findings so that others can avoid repeating their mistakes. For example, the William and Flora Hewlett Foundation recently published an eighty-one-page analysis of its Neighborhood Improvement Initiative, a program to reduce poverty in San Francisco, which detailed how the foundation spent more than $20 million over a decade but failed to "fulfill its participants' hopes and expectations for broad, deep and sustainable community change."

On the flip side, in the push for bigger, bolder ideas and the quest for the "new new thing," both new and old development actors must take care not to neglect demonstrated solutions that could be replicated or scaled— whether indigenous technologies, service delivery models, or effective social enterprises. Indeed, some practitioners note the need for a "replication fund" precisely to ensure that proven approaches receive the necessary funding to expand, and they worry about a perceived bias in favor of funding a multitude of "pilots" that never get taken to scale (box 1-6).

It is critical not only to be clear on establishing accountability for what, but also by and to whom. AccountAbility's Zadek and the Brookings and Harvard expert Nelson suggest that traditional and new development actors should work together to achieve "mutual accountability," building mechanisms that share responsibility and empower aid recipients to be greater stakeholders in development efforts. Collective or mutual accountability starts by forging agreement among diverse actors on the goal, specifying the different contributions that each participant in a cross-sectoral partnership or network will make, recognizing their interdependence, and holding each partner responsible to the others laterally—in contrast to the conventional hierarchical approach.

Official donors are missing a critical opportunity to contribute to these efforts. Whereas donor governments have traditionally demanded accountability to their own taxpayers and parliaments, they have largely neglected empowering intended beneficiaries to hold service providers and donors accountable. Development programs do not work unless beneficiaries are engaged. Official donors should challenge themselves to build accountability systems and feedback mechanisms into their giving, creating in-country capacity that will outlive the assistance flows. One idea would be to assess innovative, field-based governance strategies such as polling and local governance report cards to see if they could play a useful role in improving impact. After all, if the United States and other bilateral donors are serious about

BOX 1-6
Replication versus Going to Scale

"Going to scale" is often seen as the holy grail in the development field, much as gaining market share or going global might be for a successful business. Canonical examples include the development and deployment of a vaccine ultimately leading to the eradication of a scourge such as smallpox or polio—or the dissemination of new seed varieties leading to markedly improved nutritional outcomes throughout entire regions. Recognizing the critical importance of scaling up, several recent efforts such as the 2004 Shanghai Conference on Scaling Up Poverty Reduction and the Wolfensohn Center for Development have begun to look for systematic evidence on what works and what does not. But the new generation of social entrepreneurs is quick to point out that for some development efforts—for instance, where the engagement of local communities is more important than new technologies—the desire is for replicability rather than scalability.

Nonetheless, despite the strong stated emphasis on replication and scale, both funders and implementers worry that these goals are not adequately supported in practice. Funders note the paucity of systematic efforts to benchmark and rigorously assess interventions with a view to providing hard evidence on the potential impact of scaling up or replication—with the result that "pilots" too frequently evolve into isolated small-scale interventions. For their part, the entrepreneurs leading these efforts complain that a general bias toward funding "new" ideas and program delivery makes it very difficult to secure funding for systematic evaluations and scaling or replication—with occasional exceptions, such as microfinance.

Hence a call for a "replication fund"—a standing fund that each year might award on a competitive basis a select set of organizations sufficient funding to expand to the next level, whether through replication or achieving economies of scale. The fund could create incentives for establishing rigorous impact evaluations of pilots by making these a central part of the criteria for eligibility.

supporting strong grassroots democratic institutions in developing countries, where better to start than by engaging the communities that their aid dollars are intended to reach in evaluating and demanding performance?

In 2005, more than 100 donors and developing countries agreed on the Paris Declaration for Aid Effectiveness, pledging a series of concrete reforms in the way aid is delivered and managed. A fundamental precept of the declaration was the need to move from "donorship to ownership"—including by strengthening developing countries' parliamentary oversight of development policies and budgets, enhancing the role of civil society, and requiring donors to rely as much as possible on country systems and procedures. The obvious next step is to craft a similar set of principles that would also involve private donors.

Going from New to Newly Effective

Many of the new development players are entering the field unburdened by the weight of conventional wisdom and are blessed with confidence in their own ability to achieve outsized results. By taking development outside the realm of the cognoscenti and bringing practices and approaches from other sectors, they are infusing the community with a healthy dose of out-of-the-box thinking and innovation.

These new players' business, financial, and media roots make them receptive to sector blurring, with financiers investing in social entrepreneurs and philanthropists looking for ways to seed indigenous business enterprises. Those who made their own mark through innovation are seeking ways to leverage science and technology to improve the lives of the poor, which will require changing incentives and participants throughout the system for knowledge creation and adaptation. Meanwhile, a growing group of philanthropists is investing in advocacy and agenda setting for social transformation rather than charity. A new generation is being drawn into the development tent, as young people heed the call of celebrity and high-profile advocates to enlist in antipoverty campaigns and engage in global service. And this proliferation and diversity of the new actors alongside the old is also leading to new partnerships and coalitions—many on an ad hoc basis—to take on specific and pressing challenges such as HIV/AIDS.

The ultimate test is whether this new marketplace of development players delivers superior outcomes. The new players differ mightily from the old ones in their specific objectives, capabilities, and metrics for evaluating success. Nonetheless, they confront the same tough challenges faced by all development players: accountability, effective deployment of resources, agenda setting, and achieving scale and sustainability. If these diverse players can learn to collaborate effectively in partnerships and networks that cross the traditional boundaries between the public, private, and nongovernmental sectors, their efforts could amount to more than the sum of the parts. But to do so will require strategically exploiting complementarities between capabilities, adopting common methods for assessing impact and disseminating lessons, supporting a shared governance agenda, and creating effective new models of mutual accountability that put poor people, communities, and nations in the driver's seat.

But if there is much to learn to ensure that this newly crowded field delivers lasting benefits to the poor, there is even more to celebrate. At the midpoint between the launch and the target dates for the world's Millennium Development Goals, the energy, imagination, and determination of the growing cast of development players gives hope that conquering extreme poverty need not be an impossible dream. As both traditional and new actors hone their ability to collaborate and coordinate on behalf of common goals, and as donors and recipients continue their journey from a relationship of aid to one of partnership, persistent problems may be transformed into fresh opportunities—and good intentions may lead to great advances for humanity as a whole.

Notes

1. See chapter 3 in the present volume by Homi Kharas.

2. See chapter 9 in the present volume by Jane Nelson.

3. See chapter 3 by Kharas.

4. Paul Collier, *The Bottom Billion: Why the Poorest Countries Are Failing and What Can Be Done About It* (Oxford University Press, 2007), 4.

5. This includes giving from private and voluntary organizations, universities and colleges, and religious organizations in 2005. Hudson Institute, *The Index of Global Philanthropy* (Washington, D.C., 2007).

6. Brookings Initiative on International Volunteering and Service, www.brookings.edu/global/volunteer/.

7. See chapter 9 by Nelson.

8. See chapter 7 in the present volume by J. Gregory Dees.

9. "Skoll Awards for Social Entrepreneurship Guidelines" (www.skollfoundation.org/skollawards/index.asp# [August 2007]).

10. United Nations Commission on the Private Sector and Development, "Unleashing Entrepreneurship: Making Business Work for the Poor," 2004.

11. See Lael Brainard and Vinca LaFleur, *Expanding Enterprise, Lifting the Poor: The Private Sector in the Fight against Global Poverty* (Brookings, 2005).

12. Sylvia Pfeifer, "Government Fund Makes Millions on African Stakes," March 4, 2005 (www.cdcgroup.com/files/NewsItem/UploadPDF/Government%20fund%20makes %20millions%20on%20African%20stakes.pdf [August 2007]).

13. See chapter 7 by Dees.

14. Lael Brainard, "Investing in Knowledge for Development: The Role of Science & Technology in the Fight against Global Poverty," AAAS Forum on Science and Technology Policy, 2005.

15. For more information, see www.ushmm.org/googleearth/projects/darfur/.

16. See chapter 8 in the present volume by Ashok Khosla.

17. William Easterly, "Four Ways to Spend $60 Billion Wisely," *Washington Post,* July 2, 2006.

18. Nancy Birdsall and John Williamson, *Delivering on Debt Relief: From IMF Gold to a New Aid Architecture* (Washington, D.C.: Center for Global Development, 2002), 1.

19. Collier, *Bottom Billion,* 4.

20. These data are from UNAIDS and the World Health Organization.

21. William Easterly, "What Bono Doesn't Say about Africa," *Los Angeles Times,* July 6, 2007.

22. See chapter 12 in the present volume by Mark R. Kramer.

23. See chapter 9 by Nelson.

24. See chapter 10 in the present volume by Simon Zadek.

25. Susan Berresford, "Philanthropy in the 21st Century," lecture at Washington University, Saint Louis, February 7, 2001.

2

Fighting Global Poverty: Who Will Be Relevant in 2020?

MATTHEW BISHOP

SAVE THE WORLD—It's not easy, Googlers, so mail your ideas

—Written on a white board in the offices of Google.org, April 2007

FOR A WHITE HOUSE summit, it was quite a party. The president was late arriving to give his concluding remarks, so his place at the podium was taken by Yvonne Chaka Chaka, an African business woman, motivational speaker, UN goodwill ambassador, and singer. As she started to sing her latest campaign song, her fellow summiteers, in their formal business attire, seemed unclear how to behave. Then an elderly lady stood up and started to dance. But would anyone join her?

Finally, a middle-aged man in a suit got up and started to waltz with the elderly lady. Then Eyitayo Lambo, the Nigerian minister of health, clad traditionally in a brightly colored robe and hat, climbed on the podium and started to dance, somewhat raunchily, with Chaka Chaka. Soon everyone at the summit was joining in, dancing, clapping, or swaying—well, nearly everyone. "Where is my dance partner, Paul Wolfowitz?" shouted Chaka Chaka.

Wolfowitz, the then–head of the World Bank, had spoken earlier on a panel with Ann Veneman, the executive director of UNICEF; Richard Feachem, the retiring executive director of the Global Fund to Fight AIDS, Tuberculosis, and Malaria; Margaret Chan, the incoming director general of the World Health Organization; and the Nigerian health minister. Their topic was "the power of public-private partnerships and multilateral efforts" in the fight against malaria. Wolfowitz said that malaria, which kills about 2,000 people a day in Africa, besides its human costs, was "a huge drain on a poor economy."

This was followed by a speech from Melinda Gates, cochair of the Bill and Melinda Gates Foundation, the world's biggest charitable foundation. Others at last December's malaria summit included the actor Isaiah Washington who served as the "master of ceremonies," America's first lady and secretary of state, representatives of the Boys and Girls Clubs of America, several professional basketball players who pledged to "slam dunk malaria," and the chair of the American Red Cross. It was her mother who started the dancing—which turned out to be with Fred Matser, a Dutch real estate tycoon turned philanthropist, who talks freely about how his life was changed by an "out of body experience."

Other philanthropists in attendance included Steve Case, the billionaire former boss of AOL, and Ray Chambers, a private equity investor who chairs Malaria No More, the nongovernmental organization (NGO) behind the summit. Accompanying him were two of the NGO's board members, Tim Shriver, a member of the Kennedy political dynasty, and Ed Scott. With Bill Gates and George Soros, Scott provided seed finance for DATA (Debt, AIDS, Trade, Africa, now merged with the ONE Campaign), the organization started by U2 front man Bono and Shriver's brother, Bobby, which generated much of the buzz about debt relief and aid focused on the 2005 Group of Eight (G-8) Summit in Gleneagles.

Stephen Phillips, the medical director of Global Issues and Projects of Exxon Mobil, told the summit that "our business presence in Africa caused us to witness first hand the devastating impact malaria has had," and that "five years ago we started to do something about it."

Mainstream religion—or, at least, Christianity—was also represented, with speeches by the president of the Episcopal Church's relief and development agency, the senior pastor of the Living Church in Kigali, Rwanda, and Rick Warren, the senior pastor of Saddleback Church, an American megachurch. Warren is almost as keen a disciple of his mentor, the late management guru Peter Drucker, as he is of Jesus. His church has struck a partnership to distribute antimalaria bed nets with the president of Rwanda (who was inspired by Warren's bestseller *The Purpose Driven Life*). At the summit, Warren complained that by talking all the time about public-private partnerships, his fellow attendees were ignoring the "third leg of the stool," the "faith sector," especially the local congregation (of whatever religion).

So it goes nowadays in the world of development and poverty reduction. Billionaires, foundations, multinational companies, social entrepreneurs, NGOs, actors, rock stars, sports stars, eccentrics, preachers—all working, or trying to work, in partnership with the established governmental bodies that dominated aid and development for most of the post–World War II period.

These new players bring to the table a remarkable variety of voices and ideas, combined with a mixture of expertise, naïveté, and occasional outbursts of joyful dancing. The contrast could hardly be starker with the somber white male bureaucrats in smoke-filled rooms who created the main pillars of the postwar aid and development system, which arguably began at Bretton Woods in 1944 with the formation of what was to become the World Bank.

Perhaps the only constant factor—for reasons that are not immediately obvious—is the celebrity economist. Bretton Woods had the great economist John Maynard Keynes, the bisexual husband of a Russian ballerina. Today, we are blessed with the prominent economist Jeffrey Sachs, the friend of Bono and Angelina Jolie, a film star who he met at the World Economic Forum in Davos—which has become a sort of annual Bretton Woods for today's global policymakers, both old and new.

Sachs is a charismatic and influential advocate for development and poverty alleviation, particularly for spending far more money on helping the poor. However, he is also at least partly responsible for arguably one of the lowest moments for the "new aid and development" movement: Madonna's visit last year to the village of Mchinji in Malawi, during which she generated headlines around the world by adopting a one-year-old boy.

This trip was intended to inform her about the Millennium Village project, a brainchild of Sachs that aims to show how bottom-up policies focused at the village level can achieve the UN's Millennium Development Goals—a strategy not obviously advanced by a policy of one child not left behind. The child turned out not to be an orphan, as first thought. His father protested, the legality of the adoption was questioned, some human rights NGOs were outraged, and there were reports of a spat between Madonna and another celebrity adopter-activist, Jolie. If any single incident captured why so many of the older players are so nervous about the growing role of at least some of the new players, this was it.

Defining the New Players

What, then, is the proper role for the new players—and, by extension, what should be the division of labor between them and the older players? Are they here to stay? By 2020, will they be an integral part of the aid and development system—assuming that such a system is still needed—or will their current frenetic activity prove to be a fad, as the traditional players reassert themselves or, perhaps, even newer players enter the field? To answer these questions requires an understanding of both the strengths and weaknesses of the new and old players, and of what needs to be done to promote development and eradicate poverty.

To further complicate this task, it is not clear who or what actually counts as a "new" player. The Rockefeller Foundation, which recently launched a partnership for a new green revolution in Africa with the Gates Foundation, was founded in 1913 and points out that for the first thirteen years of its life it disbursed more in overseas aid than the U.S. government. Many of the big development charities, such as Oxfam, have been around long enough to count themselves among the older players even though their role in the system continues to evolve. Even celebrities have been at this for awhile. The original Live Aid concert was in 1985, so Bono has now been involved in fighting global poverty for twenty-two years. George Harrison's pioneering Concert for Bangladesh took place in 1971.

Nor do the roles that the older actors, particularly governments and the multilateral aid agencies, want to play in the future necessarily bear much resemblance to what they did in the past. Ideas have evolved—on Africanization, structural adjustment, corruption, and so on. Much aid and development activity in the past was driven by political imperatives arising from the cold war and postcolonialism, less than by a concern for the poor. That is not entirely gone, and may increase again—especially in the Middle East—but it is a less significant factor today than it was for the main donor governments. Recent events at the World Bank suggest that America's grip on it is easing slightly, while market forces have caused falling demand for its loans, putting pressure on the Bank to rethink its role. At the same time, the "competitive" use of aid may be reemerging in a different guise—to woo developing countries with strategic resources, especially in energy. Now the main competitor is China not the Soviet Union. Strikingly, more African heads of state attended the 2006 China-Africa summit than the G-8 summit in Gleneagles a year earlier.

Moreover, some of the new players in aid and development involve the old players in new guises—such as advanced market commitments by governments to purchase new drugs if they are created, and the Global Fund to Fight AIDS, Tuberculosis, and Malaria, which formally integrates governments and foundations in its governance structure.

The Bill and Melinda Gates Foundation has a seat on the board of the Global Fund—one example among many of how philanthropy is starting to have a significant impact on aid and development policy. It is a presence that has not always been welcomed by the established players, many of whom are suspicious about new philanthropists and snigger behind their hands at "naive" initiatives such as "Hedge Funds versus Malaria." Indeed, many of the new philanthropists admit they have had to do a lot of learning from initial mistakes—no doubt goaded into them by the abundant supply of snake oil salesman willing to take advantage of their good intentions. Even so, the aid establishment is increasingly starting to take the new philanthropists seriously, not least because of the significant sums of money they bring.

A New Breed of Philanthropy

With assets of $30 billion and maybe a further $80 billion to come from Gates and his bridge partner, Warren Buffett, the Bill and Melinda Gates Foundation will certainly be a significant player in 2020. Indeed, it will probably be more significant than it is today, as its new program on development starts to match the momentum of its established global health program.

As my forthcoming book with Michael Green will argue, while philanthropy has something of a mixed record historically, there are good reasons to have high hopes of Gates and the current wave of "new philanthropists." This hope is increased by the embrace of the Anglo-American tradition by the newly superrich everywhere, including those in the developing world. Nowadays, to be regarded as a good billionaire, it is a necessary (but not necessarily sufficient) condition that you are a philanthropist.

One clear conclusion from past philanthropy is that charitable foundations tend to do a far better job when the founder is alive and engaged in it. That is why Buffett's gift will only continue to flow in chunks to the foundation while at least Bill or Melinda Gates is active in it. There is every reason to expect that to be so for many years, as Bill Gates, who next spring, at the age of fifty-three, will reduce his role at Microsoft to work full time at the foundation.

Active philanthropists are more likely to keep their foundation agile and creative, rather than bureaucratic—though the rapid growth of the Bill and Melinda Gates Foundation will put that theory to the test.

Emphasizing Impact

Many of today's new philanthropists are likely to be active long enough to learn from their mistakes, which is just as well. As Mario Marino of Venture Philanthropy Partners, one of America's leading venture philanthropists, points out, "The new rich have often made their money very fast, and get intoxicated with their own brilliance into thinking they can quickly achieve results in the nonprofit sector. They forget that their success may have been due to luck, and that the nonprofit sector may be far more complex than where they have come from."

"Will our first agricultural strategy be perfect? Of course not. But we will learn and learn and learn over the next few years, and over ten years we will have an impact," says Patti Stonesifer, the chief executive of the Bill and Melinda Gates Foundation.

A focus on impact is one of the most positive contributions of the new philanthropy, and it is inspiring some significant reforms at older philanthropies such as the Rockefeller Foundation (which actually regards its renewed emphasis on impact as getting back to its roots). A key element of this focus is that foundations are trying to be more businesslike in how they go about their philanthropy, from paying their staffs well to setting strategic goals and monitoring performance against them.

These goals are often big, and extraordinarily challenging. The philanthropists behind Malaria No More aim to eradicate malaria from the planet. Bono and his backers aim to "make poverty history." Google.org aims to have a bigger impact on making the world a better place than its parent, Google.com—which would be quite something.

The bigger the goal, the greater the difficulty in measuring impact. Metrics are far better for narrowly defined projects, such as vaccinating or educating a given population. But linking good performance on these metrics to progress on development and poverty can be tricky, to say the least.

The lack of good metrics increases the risk of philanthropic market failure, which is high anyway due to the absence of pressure for performance and mechanisms for holding philanthropists to account. Insofar as government regulators take an interest in the sector, it is to uncover abuses such as misusing funds. But an occasional scandal about foundation staff using corporate jets, or a donor using a foundation to further personal interests, misses what may be a far greater problem: the lack of impact of philanthropic dollars.

Because giving is voluntary, the extent to which philanthropists really try to achieve impact, as opposed to ease their conscience or boost their social standing, is also discretionary. Underperforming philanthropists do not go bust. Some experts think that philanthropy is better understood as a luxury consumer good than as the "social investment" of the new philanthropy lexicon. A big challenge, if the new philanthropy is to achieve its promise—and justify the tax subsidy that it typically receives—is to ensure that it is "instrumental" and not merely "expressive" of who the philanthropist wants to be.

Philanthropists at their best can do things that others find significantly harder. They do not face pressure from electorates or the stock market, so they can think long term, act quickly, and do things that are unpopular. They can close a failed innovation more easily than, say, a government, which often has to deal with a vocal group that benefits from the failed scheme.

Believing in Advocacy

Increasingly, the new philanthropists believe that one way in which they can, and must, achieve leverage is through advocacy to shape the political debate. "I did not realize how much advocacy we would have to do. We expected to concentrate on developing drugs and so on. We were a bunch of product development people! We assumed others would focus on getting the products out there," says Stonesifer, who admits surprise that two of the Bill and Melinda Gates Foundation's most important partners are Oprah Winfrey and Bono.

Indeed, some at the Bill and Melinda Gates Foundation cite the money they invested in seeding DATA as one of the greatest ever examples of leverage—"$50 billion in debt relief and aid for a $1 million investment." This makes a powerful case for working with "celanthropists"—or, at least, the increasing number of celebrities who do their work on good causes professionally rather than like a virgin. As well as often being serious philanthropists in their own right—Elton John has given £27 million of his own money to fight HIV/AIDS—celebrities can shape public opinion and readily access those with the power to change policy. "People take my calls," as Jolie puts it.

Conversely, those working with them must deal with the fact that often celebrities are, to put it politely, not necessarily experts or deep thinkers about the causes they advocate. Moreover, even the best of them may be doing this work in part to promote their own brand, which may not always accord with the branding and other needs of their partners in the cause.

This may be equally true of another significant new sort of celebrity philanthropist: former world leaders who set up philanthropic foundations, such as Bill Clinton, Nelson Mandela, and, no doubt before long, Tony Blair. Although they rarely bring much of their own money to the table, they do have another hugely valuable asset: convening power. Like Jolie, their telephone calls are invariably taken. This asset can be monetized. Clinton and Mandela have raised large sums of money for the foundations that bear their names. The Clinton Global Initiative, which has already become an American counterpart/rival to Davos, claimed to have elicited 215 pledges worth $7.3 billion from attendees last year.

Again, however, the role played by politicians can be controversial and complicating. Despite the attendance of First Lady Laura Bush last year, some critics describe the Clinton Global Initiative as the "next Democratic administration in waiting."

A third, rapidly evolving category of celanthropist is the working royal. The crown prince of Holland is extremely active on water issues, and his wife is an adviser to the United Nations on microcredit. Ironically, two British royals have pioneered two different sorts of celanthropy—Princess Diana, who knew how to generate publicity for a cause, and her onetime husband, Prince Charles, who has proved to be a surprisingly effective social entrepreneur.

Leveraging for Greatness

Perhaps the most important buzzword of the new philanthropists is "leverage"—getting the maximum bang for their bucks. This reflects the fact that, for all their billions, the resources of philanthropists are dwarfed by those of governments and the for-profit sector. So to have an impact, they have to do more than resource transfer; they need to think systematically and find bottlenecks or tipping points where their dollars can have a disproportionate impact.

Thus, although there are significant elements of pure resource transfer in the Bill and Melinda Gates Foundation's strategy of creating incentives for pharmaceutical companies by promising to buy their products, the foundation tries to maximize its leverage by encouraging others with deeper pockets to take on the bulk of the long-term purchasing.

The DATA example also highlights that leverage is a somewhat fuzzy concept, particularly when it comes to clearly demonstrating causality and attributing credit. There were many steps and many partners between the original $1 million of seed capital and the G-8 debt relief agreement—and, besides, exactly what impact has that decision had, anyway? As Bono commented, in textbook new philanthropy lingo, after the 2007 G-8 failed to follow through to his satisfaction on the 2005 commitments, "Do they think we can't read or count? We are looking for accountable language and accountable numbers; we didn't get them today."

But it will be no surprise if questions about the legitimacy of all philanthropy become a serious constraint on the role it can play, particularly if the superrich more actively engage in advocacy to shape the political agenda. The abuse heaped on George Soros, arguably the world's most visible, as he describes himself, "political philanthropist," who has been denounced by everyone from Vladimir Putin to Bill O'Reilly and Slavoj Zizek, may be the shape of things to come. To say so is not to add to nor agree with this criticism. Indeed, Soros is one of the most effective philanthropists around, a risk taker with a well-honed understanding of leverage. Nonetheless, if philanthropists are to fully play the useful role that they might, there may be a need for a new "social contract" between the superrich and society at large. If so, the content of such a contract should be debated sooner rather than later, and philanthropists would do well to take the lead in initiating it.

Corporations as Development Actors

The final group of new players are large multinational companies, which increasingly are getting involved in development and poverty issues. They are doing so in several guises, including through corporate philanthropy, corporate social responsibility, global supply chain management, and "bottom of the pyramid" strategies to sell to poorer customers. Strikingly, many corporate bosses are more exposed to the world and its problems than are many politicians—not least the passport-less hordes in Congress. Through their companies, they also command significant resources in developing countries.

Of these, the latter two are most likely to deliver a sustained impact, because they are core to the firm's profit-generation strategy. As Bono said when he launched (PRODUCT)^{RED} to raise funds for the Global Fund to Fight AIDS, Tuberculosis, and Malaria, to get companies to invest real dollars, they need to think they can make money by doing so.

Attempting to persuade firms to be altruistic may prove less fruitful—because good works tend to get cut when business conditions deteriorate—than encouraging them to pursue enlightened self-interest in their core profit-making activities. However, the flip side of this is that firms are likely to focus their efforts fairly narrowly on those activities that they think will yield them long-term benefit and will not make much capital available to noncore causes.

Strikingly, Bono's (RED) brand is not the only example of an attempt by a philanthropist to harness the capital and scaling power of private firms to a social cause. Indeed, many of the new philanthropists are focused on how to achieve their social mission through for-profit or, at least, self-sustaining business models. Pierre Omidyar, the founder of eBay, found a traditional foundation too limiting, and folded his foundation into a new organization, Omidyar Networks, which invests in both nonprofit and for-profit organizations that it believes will advance its social mission. Likewise, Google.org was originally supposed to be a traditional corporate foundation, but instead is a division of Google.com—rather than a legally separate, tax-advantaged organization—and is free to back both for-profits and nonprofits.

Clearly, profitable enterprises can more readily raise growth capital to advance their social cause than loss-making ones. However, it remains to be seen how many profitable social business models can be developed. Omidyar believes that microfinance is ripe to achieve a much greater scale by attracting profit-seeking capital, and that other social causes may be able to follow in microfinance's footsteps. However, it is not yet clear what those causes are, or even if microfinance can live up to Omidyar's profit expectations.

Staying Relevant

So, given the different strengths and weaknesses of both the new and old players, what should be the division of labor in development and poverty eradication—and who will still be relevant in 2020 and beyond? History suggests that philanthropic activity and innovative social enterprise happen in bursts, and end with government taking over the best and scaling it up. Perhaps this will happen again, although it is hard to find a government anywhere that is coping with its existing obligations, let alone wanting to extend itself further. This is true of national governments and even more fundamentally of the pillars of the multilateral system, such as the UN and World Bank, neither of which will prove easy to improve in a way that would reverse the recent surge by the new players.

The likeliest outcome is a continuation, and probably deepening, of the trend for flexible, ad hoc partnerships, issue by issue, between different players—coalitions of the willing, as it were, or flexible geometry or, as the Google staff might put it, networked or open source global governance. Davos and the board of the Global Fund to Fight AIDS, Tuberculosis, and Malaria may be the model for the future multilateral governance system.

That may well be the most effective way forward, as well as the most feasible—given the resistance of multilateral institutions to serious reform. The new players offer the possibility of improving the aid infrastructure's flexibility and responsiveness. Indeed, the greatest danger may be that donor harmonization and the push for alignment around government plans (the Paris Declaration) will push in the opposite direction: toward a more centralized, monolithic aid system.

Ultimately, much will depend on which analysis of the challenges posed by poverty and development prevails. Broadly speaking, there are two main schools of thought. One is that not enough has been spent on the right things needed to boost development and ease poverty. The most vocal proponent of this view is Sachs, who recently argued that if the fifty richest people in the world each give away 5 percent of their fortunes to fight poverty, it would exceed the impact of the 2005 G-8.

The second school, often associated with William Easterly, argues that money is not the primary problem, government is. Too much of the money passing through government coffers in developing countries, including aid dollars, ends up in their leaders' offshore bank accounts. Too often, laws and regulation discourage the entrepreneurship that through creating wealth and jobs offers much the best route out of poverty.

Which is why, although in 2020 the Bill and Melinda Gates Foundation will certainly have had an immense impact on poverty reduction, the most effective new players will be those that generate better governance in developing countries. Although DATA started to focus on this, currently leading the way is Mo Ibrahim, an African cellphone entrepreneur, who has launched a prize for leadership in Africa. Though it is too small to directly incentivize corrupt leaders to mend their ways, it is intended to inspire a broad debate within Africa about what constitutes good governance. If so, its leverage, and impact, could make Ibrahim the most effective new player of them all. That would certainly be something worth making a song and dance about.

3

The New Reality of Aid

HOMI KHARAS

WITH GREAT FANFARE, the leaders of the Group of Eight (G-8) countries reaffirmed at Heiligendamm in June 2007 that they would meet their commitments to increase aid by $50 billion by 2010, with half going to Africa. When this pledge was first announced at Gleneagles in 2005, it was hailed as a breakthrough by aid advocates. Bono gushed that "I would not say this is the end of extreme poverty, but it is the beginning of the end." Now, two years later, with the same commitments on the table, the tone is different. Bono has accused the rich countries of "obfuscation" with the figures, while his companion-in-arms, Bob Geldof, has used even stronger language, calling the G-8 work "a total farce." So who is right, the politicians or the celebrities? Are rich countries serious in their determination to help Africa and to provide "as close as possible" universal access to treatment for HIV/AIDS, malaria, tuberculosis, and polio, as well as education? What is the new reality of aid?

No one doubts the ability of the rich world to provide the required resources. With the total gross domestic product of the Organization for Economic Cooperation and Development (OECD) now topping $33 trillion, and continuing to grow at a real annual rate of about 3 percent, the aid pledges amount to little more than 0.33 percent of rich countries' incomes—1 cent for every $3. Some countries have taken concrete steps to identify the source of funds for development. Both the United Kingdom and France have introduced new innovative financing mechanisms—the International Finance

The author thanks Joshua Hermias for excellent research assistance.

Facility sponsored by the United Kingdom's Department for International Development, and the Solidarity tax on airline tickets issued in France. For its part, the United States has called for a doubling of the commitment amounts under the President's Emergency Plan for AIDS Relief over the next five years. In each case, public opinion appears to be solidly behind the new proposals.

So why are these efforts being called a "total farce"? Partly, it is because some aid, like debt relief and technical cooperation, is inflated in value and impact. Partly, it is because the detailed planning required to use the funds effectively is lacking. The Millennium Challenge Corporation, the newest U.S. agency set up to promote international development in 2002, has signed compacts with developing countries totaling nearly $3 billion, but it had only disbursed $69 million by March 2007.[1] Partly, it is because official development assistance has been linked with corruption and scandal in developing countries, undermining confidence in the effectiveness with which the funds are used. Partly, it is because the needs of the poor seem to be increasing at a faster pace than the increase in funding: postconflict reconstruction, disaster relief, climate change, and the spread of HIV/AIDS are all putting additional burdens on official development assistance, leaving less money for bread-and-butter programs. And progress on issues important for development that go beyond aid—like trade, energy efficiency, and food security—has been uneven, leaving a sense of frustration that a serious, coherent attack on poverty has yet to begin.

Against this backdrop, the nature of development assistance is changing rapidly. On the one hand, new official funding is being channeled more and more through specialized agencies, dedicated to particular targets, like HIV/AIDS or malaria, instead of through traditional agencies, like the International Development Association of the World Bank, which provide support for broad country development programs. On the other hand, a raft of new players has emerged, bypassing traditional channels. One group of new players are the governments of middle-income countries that wish to share their own successful experiences more widely but that could repeat many of the mistakes of the past, like tying aid and paying inadequate attention to maintenance financing. Another group is the private aid sector, comprised of foundations, private philanthropists, religious organizations, and other nongovernmental organizations (NGOs) and nonprofits. Between them, these new groups are growing rapidly and changing the aid landscape in dramatic ways.

The sheer number of aid players, both public and private, has exploded.[2] There are significant benefits to this dynamism: more resources, more innovative solutions, more direct action. But there are also costs. The number of development projects has grown while the average size of a project has declined, burdening weak administrative structures in recipient countries. There is overlap and waste in the many studies needed for each donor. Accountability and sustainability are threatened. Mechanisms for information sharing, coordination, planning, and scaling up are breaking down. The key issues facing development aid are those that arise from this fragmentation and the accompanying volatility of aid disbursements.

Playing with Numbers: What Traditional Donors Really Contribute to Development

There are twenty-two "traditional" donors that report their official development assistance, or official aid, to the OECD's Development Assistance Committee (DAC).[3] The numbers these donors report are meant to capture transfers of resources to poor and middle-income countries for the explicit purpose of economic development and welfare. Official development assistance from traditional donors to poor countries topped $100 billion in each of the last two years, a record high. For perspective, in 1974 official aid stood at $41.3 billion, implying a real annual growth rate of 3.1 percent.[4] In 2001, just before the Monterrey pledge, the figure was $63.8 billion.

On the face of it, these numbers show a remarkable increase in development assistance. But what lies behind the numbers is less encouraging. This is because aid is not just a matter of giving money. Official aid figures include cash, commodities, and services, and it is not easy to value these latter two categories appropriately.[5] For example, the administrative overheads of donor bureaucracies, and their domestic campaigns to raise awareness and funding, are counted as "aid." Debt forgiveness—often on loans never expected to be repaid—is called "aid." In reality, such debt relief is a transfer from one branch of a donor government, the treasury, to another branch, the official export credit agency. Emergency assistance and food aid are included, though these items address short-term suffering rather than long-term development. And a considerable amount of "aid" includes technical assistance, which delivers expert advice, but not funds, to carry out projects. Total aid figures must subtract these items to get a true picture of what is available to finance development projects and programs on the ground.

Looked at through this lens, the trend in official aid, touted by the G-8 countries at Heiligendamm as evidence of their commitment, looks much less promising. Debt forgiveness for Nigeria and Iraq amounted to $19 billion in 2005. This money was not being repaid in the first place and is artificially inflated by compounding in penalty interest rates for the years over which the debt has been in default, and so forgiving it has done little to increase the amounts available for real development problems like schooling, clinics, and infrastructure in the short term. Its real value lies more in normalizing relationships and opening the way for further assistance than in the face value of "relief" that is offered. Additional amounts of $8 billion were allocated for major natural disasters and emergency assistance in 2005, including the tsunami affecting Indonesia, Sri Lanka, Thailand, and India. And the reconstruction effort in Iraq and Afghanistan has boosted aid numbers by $6.4 billion, but this incorporates the high cost of providing security for these operations. Meanwhile, the most rapidly growing component of aid, technical assistance, amounted to $29 billion in 2005.

As figure 3-1 shows, what was left over for real development in 2005 was only $38 billion. Or, in other words, only 37 percent of the total aid headline number was what can be called country programmable aid (CPA)—funds that are available to finance real programs and projects on the ground in developing countries. What has been happening is that this percentage has steadily shrunk over time, from 59 percent in 1975 to the current level of 37 percent. As a result, even though CPA increased between 1995 and 2005, it is now at a level only slightly higher than in 1985 because last decade's growth followed a decade of decline. And if the special assistance for Iraq and Afghanistan is excluded, CPA for other countries was lower in 2005 than in 1985.

But Surely Africa Is Getting More?

This same story is replayed on the ground in Africa. The rhetoric is one of progress: The G-8 has an Africa Action Plan, with special representatives to keep a focus on the poorest continent. But so far, Sub-Saharan Africa has hardly seen any funding increase at all. Astonishingly, estimates suggest that only $12.1 billion of the overall official development assistance takes the form of funds that Sub-Saharan African countries can use to invest in social and infrastructure development programs—one cent for every $27 in rich country income. This is almost the same as the amount received by these countries twenty-two years ago in 1985 ($11.6 billion). In proportion to Africa's needs, its population, its number of poor people, or rich country income, CPA to Africa has been falling with no signs of concrete plans to raise this in an effective fashion. Small wonder that patience with official aid is running thin.

Figure 3-1. Official Development Assistance by Sector and Destination (billions of 2005 dollars)

1995: $63 billion

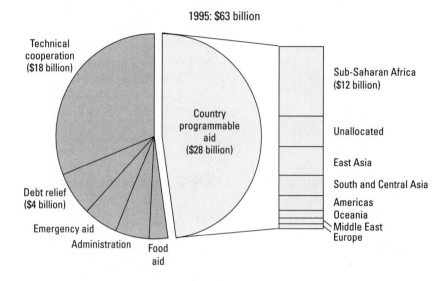

2005: $107 billion

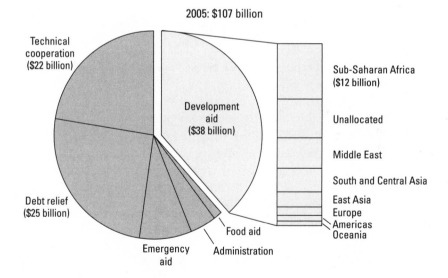

Sources: Development Assistance Committee of Organization for Economic Cooperation and Development; author's calculations.

The Crumbling Pie

When aid advocates in civil society campaign to increase resources for development, they do so with a decent understanding of who gives what, to whom, and in what form. That is an aspect of accountability that is unfortunately absent once the aid arrives in poor countries. From that point on, it is increasingly difficult to trace the flow of funds down to the final beneficiary. It is possible that some funds are siphoned off into the bank accounts of corrupt officials. And every foreign aid project faces a slew of administrative costs; numerous reports, donor missions and committees, and dedicated project management units eat up resources. Case studies suggest that some ministries spend no less than half of their full-time hours accommodating these administrative needs.

One way of estimating the size of these leakages is to measure the difference between the resources a country's treasury disburses for a program and the actual services delivered on the "front line." One study, based on surveys in Ghana, Tanzania, and Rwanda, concludes that "approximately half of the overall amount allocated to clinics and hospitals did not actually reach them."[6] In some cases in that study, the numbers are even higher. Similar figures appear in other studies. The U.S. Government Accountability Office, in its recent analysis of the Millennium Challenge Corporation, was able to identify the allocation of 59 percent of in-country disbursements in the nine compact countries that are currently operational.[7] Of this, 32 percent was for direct project-related expenses, and 27 percent was for administrative, audit, fiscal, and procurement expenses.[8]

As a rough approximation, it is not unreasonable to guess that roughly half the money spent on official development aid actually reaches the poor people it targets. So the $38 billion disbursed in new development aid in 2005 was closer to $19 billion in effective terms. Or put another way, the poor in Sub-Saharan African countries could be getting just $6 billion a year in real assistance. These figures do not compare well with the $107 billion spotlighted by donor governments.

Filling the Gap: The Emergence of New Players

The gap between poor countries' pressing development needs and official development aid has created financial and institutional space for new aid givers. As might be expected, the new players do not yet have standardized methods of reporting their activities; nor are their activities harmonized. But scattered evidence for their contributions to development does exist. When pieced together, these data suggest that amounts are significant and rising. Estimates of aid from new players equaled or exceeded official development aid from traditional donors in 2005.

The new players can be classified into two groups:

—New bilateral donors from the South. Providing assistance to poor countries is no longer the sole province of rich countries. Transition economies and middle-income countries now give to poor countries. At last count, twenty-nine such countries have established or are building aid programs. The new bilaterals include small donors like Thailand, Brazil, and some of the new members of the European Union; medium-sized donors like South Korea and Turkey; and large donors like China, India, and Saudi Arabia, which have annual aid programs of $1 billion or more (table 3-1).

—Private organizations, which include a vast array of actors—tens of thousands of philanthropic foundations, tens of thousands of NGOs, and hundreds of thousands of religious groups and community-based organizations. These organizations mediate resources directly from rich individuals in rich countries to development activities in poor countries. Tables 3-2 and 3-3 list some of the largest international NGOs and largest U.S. foundations giving money to developing countries.

The New Bilaterals

Development assistance has traditionally been the preserve of rich countries—a moral responsibility of the well off to help those less fortunate.[9] But bilateral aid has also been closely linked with political objectives, and several academic studies have shown a close correlation between the amounts countries receive in aid and foreign policy considerations, as proxied by votes in the UN General Assembly, for example.[10] Given that aid motives are both altruistic and self-interested, it is not surprising that a growing number of middle-income and newly rich countries have established development aid programs. At last count, at least twenty-nine non-DAC countries are reported to be giving significant amounts of development assistance on an annual basis (table 3-1).

Our best guess is that the new bilaterals contributed about $8 billion in development aid in 2005.[11] Unlike traditional donors, the new bilaterals give little in the form of debt relief (because they have small outstanding liabilities), and little in the form of technical cooperation (because the domestic consulting industry is small). Correspondingly, a greater fraction of their aid is in the form of projects and programs. One of the largest new donors,

Table 3-1. The New Bilaterals: 2005 Official Aid (millions of 2005 dollars)

Non-DAC OECD countries	
South Korea	752
Turkey	601
Poland	205
Czech Republic	135
Hungary	100
Slovak Republic	56
Iceland	27
Mexico	N.A.
Arab countires	
Saudi Arabia	1,000
Kuwait	547
United Arab Emirates	141
Other donors	
China	2,000
India	1,000
Taiwan	483
Israel	31
Venezuela	N.A.
Chile	N.A.
Brazil	N.A.
South Africa	N.A.
Russia	N.A.
Malaysia	N.A.
Thailand	N.A.
New EU members	
Bulgaria	N.A.
Cyprus	N.A.
Estonia	N.A.
Latvia	N.A.
Romania	N.A.
Slovenia	N.A.
Malta	N.A.

Sources: OECD's DAC, China Exim Bank, and author's calculations.

Note: N.A. = not available. The author assessed combined bilateral aid for those countries marked N.A. at $1 billion, based on general estimates and anecdotal evidence.

China, provides its assistance in the form of turnkey projects, providing planning, finance, labor power, and training to completely implement projects. China has built on its own strong history of infrastructure project management to focus its aid, and it prides itself on short project preparation and implementation periods compared with traditional donors.[12] Other bilaterals also look to share their own development experiences. South Korea places an emphasis on export-led projects, human resources, and rural development, and its ability to pool human resources along with capital is a core comparative advantage.

Table 3-2. Basic Data for Selected Large International Nongovernmental Organizations

Organization	2006 expenditures (dollars)	Focus areas[a]
World Vision International	2,103,700,000	Children, humanitarian
Save the Children International	863,094,631[b]	Humanitarian
Care USA	645,000,000	Multi-sector programs
Catholic Relief Services	597,037,000	HIV/AIDS, humanitarian
Plan International	587,185,000	Health, education, water/sanitation
Oxfam GB	406,272,000	Humanitarian
ActionAid	204,067,080[c]	Humanitarian
Catholic Agency for Overseas Development	94,885,120	Humanitarian
Heifer International	77,465,797	N.A.
Oxfam USA	52,804,000	Humanitarian, small enterprise

Sources: Annual reports of the organizations.
a. More than 20 percent of program expenditures.
b. Revenue.
c. Fiscal year 2005.
N.A. = not available.

Table 3-3. The Ten Largest U.S. Foundations

Foundation	2004 disbursements to international causes (dollars)	Grants	Focus Areas
Bill and Melinda Gates Foundation	1,233,160,002	134	Health, technology
Ford Foundation	258,502,043	1328	Democracy, poverty, community development, education, peace
Gordon and Betty Moore Foundation	83,184,068	79	Conservation
John D. and Catherine T. MacArthur Foundation	73,138,000	223	Sustainable development, human rights, peace, health
Rockefeller Foundation	72,306,649	329	Poverty
William and Flora Hewlett Foundation	56,595,034	165	Education, population, environment
W. K. Kellogg Foundation	56,315,269	122	Poverty
Freeman Foundation	53,456,718	223	Exchange and education
Carnegie Corporation of New York	42,415,000	113	Peace, education
Starr Foundation	41,392,820	101	Healthcare, democracy
David and Lucile Packard Foundation	39,544,027	143	Health, environment
Andrew W. Mellon Foundation	37,741,100	109	Environment, education
Charles Stewart Mott Foundation	25,356,798	211	Civil society, environment, poverty
Lincy Foundation	25,037,847	25	Armenian charities
Harry and Jeanette Weinberg Foundation	22,936,500	44	Poverty
Total	1,970,465,603	2817	

Source: International Grantmaking Update (2006).

Table 3-4. U.S. Private International Giving, 2005 (billions of dollars)

Type of organization	Total giving
Foundations	2.2
Corporations	5.1
Private voluntary organizations and international nongovernmental organizations	16.2
Higher education	4.6
Religious organizations	5.4
Total	33.5

Source: *Index of Global Philanthropy*, 2007.

Rapid growth is anticipated in funds from the new bilaterals. China has announced grand plans for the next three years: $10 billion for developing countries, with an incremental $5 billion for the Association of Southeast Asian Nations, $3 billion for the Pacific islands, and $3 billion for Africa plus another $2 billion in preferential credits.[13] South Korea is aiming to provide $1 billion a year by 2010. And though their contribution will not be large in absolute terms, new member states of the European Union (Czech Republic, Hungary, Poland, and Slovakia) have promised 0.33 percent of their gross national income in aid by 2015.

Private Charities, Foundations, and Other NGOs

Private sector financial flows have transformed the development landscape. Already, private flows like foreign direct investment, private portfolio capital, private bank credits, bond issuances, and remittances are much larger than official flows to developing countries. Is the same happening with international aid? The scope and scale of private nonprofits are expanding rapidly. Though statistics about global numbers of NGOs are notoriously incomplete, it is currently estimated that there are several hundred NGOs operating internationally.[14]

The United States is by far the largest source of private aid giving.[15] U.S. giving is comprised of foundations, corporate donations, private voluntary organizations and NGOs, educational scholarships, and religious organizations (table 3-4). Estimates for the United States suggest a fourfold increase in international giving in the 1990s, and, after a dip in 2002 following the stock market crash, U.S. international giving has grown healthily again.[16] In the 2000s, U.S. foundation giving to international causes has outpaced all other sectors. More remarkable is that this growth is being seen at all levels; at the top, giving from huge philanthropies like the Bill and Melinda Gates Foundation is growing, but small foundations' giving is growing even faster (a 35 percent growth in giving between 2002 and 2004).[17] In the United States, some 65 percent of households with annual incomes of less than $100,000 make charitable gifts.[18] Over the next decade, this trend will likely continue—a considerable share will be buttressed by Warren Buffett's promise of adding $31 billion in to the mix. Record stock market valuations are fueling healthy growth in private giving.

Private giving to developing countries was estimated at $33.5 billion for the United States alone in 2005. In arriving at this figure, best estimates were used to eliminate the double counting that can arise from the simple summing of all private aid agencies. For example, if the Soros Foundation gives money to the Open Society Institute, then counting both Soros and institute contributions would lead to an overestimate of what ultimate beneficiaries really receive. The Soros contribution must be netted out; its value will show up in the Open Society Institute contribution. In addition, NGOs have been generous in mobilizing funds for emergency operations. To compare their contributions with CPA from official agencies, these activities must be deducted. In the United States, the best estimate for humanitarian aid and relief works is 36 percent of the total,[19] much more than is the case for official aid. This implies that $21.4 billion in private giving from the United States goes to development projects and programs.

Cross-country estimates suggest that U.S. philanthropic giving is about 49 to 58 percent of the global total.[20] So, if U.S. private international giving, excluding humanitarian aid and relief, is about $21.4 billion a year, then global international private giving might be about $37 to $44 billion. Not all this is available for development projects. In the United States, there are estimates that administrative overhead and fund-raising amount to 11 percent of NGO expenditures.[21] Applying this percentage to all private aid organizations gives an estimate for private giving in the range of $33 to $39 billion a year. This can be compared with official aid from DAC countries of $61 billion, and $6.7 billion from new bilaterals. Unfortunately, private giving in the form of technical assistance cannot be independently estimated to arrive at a figure comparable to the $38 billion for official DAC CPA. The private sector does spend considerable amounts on advocacy efforts to change rich country policies, and these funds clearly do not go to developing countries for direct poverty alleviation. But there are also case studies showing that contractors to private NGOs charge a third of what equivalent experts get paid by official agencies to work in developing countries. That would suggest that the amount spent by the private nonprofit sector on technical assistance is comparatively low. When one factors in the $6 billion in bilateral funds

Table 3-5. Comparing Official and Private Aid, 2005 (billions of dollars)

	Official aid		Private aid	
Type of aid	DAC members	New bilaterals	DAC members	Only United States
Total	**104.1**[a]	**8**[b]	**58–68**[c]	**33.5**[d]
Less emergency and food aid	(9.6)	(0.5)[e]	(21–24)	(12.1)[f]
Subtotal	94.5	7.5	37–44	21.4
Less debt relief and interest	(29.4)	(0.4)[g]	0	0.0
Subtotal	65.1	7.1	37–44	21.4
Less adminstrative costs	(4.3)[h]	(0.4)[i]	(4–5)	(2.4)[j]
Subtotal	60.8	6.7	33–39	19
Less technical cooperation	(22.4)	(1.4)[k]	N.A.	N.A.
Subtotal	38.4	5.3		
Country programmable aid	**38.4**	**5.3**	N.A.	N.A.

Sources: Author's calculations and: [a]Totals and deductions from OECD DAC. [b]Official and unofficial estimates, see table 3-1. [c]Extrapolated from U.S. figures. Lower bound assumes U.S. private aid represents 58 percent of total (OECD DAC). Upper bound assumes U.S. private aid represents 49 percent of total; L. Salmon, Comparative Nonprofit Sector Project, Johns Hopkins University (www.jhu.edu/~cnp/research/compdata.html [March 2007]). [d]Index of Global Philanthropy, 2007. [e]Based on 2002-5 average of Czech Republic, South Korea, and Turkey, from OECD DAC. [f]International relief NGOs accounted for 36 percent of international nonprofit sector revnues. J. Kerlin and S. Thanasombat, The International Charitable Nonprofit Subsector, Urban Institute Policy Brief 2 (Washington: Urban Institute, 2006). [g]Based on 2002-5 average of Czech Repulic and South Korea, OECD DAC. [h]Includes costs for raising awareness. [i]Based on 2002-5 average of Czech Republic, South Korea, and Turkey, from OECD DAC. [j]A total of 11 percent of international nonprofits' expenditures oriented to administration and fundraising. Kerlin and Thanasombat (2006). [k]Average 2002–5, Czech Republic, South Korea, and Turkey, from OECD DAC.

N.A. = not available. DAC = Development Assistance Committee. OECD = Organization for Economic Cooperation and Development.

that are channeled through private NGOs, in addition to the funds noted in table 3-4, the private aid sector may be as large as the official sector in real terms. Table 3-5 and figure 3-2 show comparable figures for official aid and the private nonprofit sector by component.

The destination of private aid is difficult to assess, but general trends suggest a focus on Africa and Asia. Figure 3-3 displays the geographic focus of three subsamples of private aid donors. Among prominent international NGOs and U.S. foundations, Africa and Asia are clear areas of intense activity. But United States–based NGOs give Latin America nearly twice the attention of Africa, suggesting a propensity to send aid to projects closer to home in geographic and cultural terms.

A Look into the Future

OECD countries have promised to disburse $130 billion in total aid by 2010. A total of $50 billion has been promised to Sub-Saharan Africa alone.

Figure 3-2. Official versus Private Aid, Development Assistance Committee Members, 2005

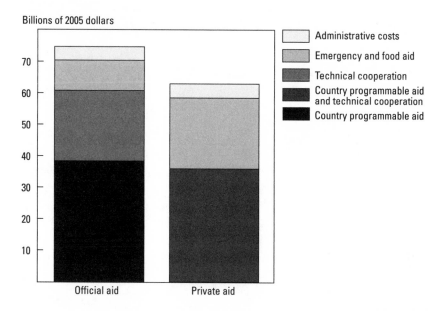

Billions of 2005 dollars

Legend:
- Administrative costs
- Emergency and food aid
- Technical cooperation
- Country programmable aid and technical cooperation
- Country programmable aid

Categories: Official aid, Private aid

Sources: Development Assistance Committee of Organization for Economic Cooperation and Development, *Index of Global Philanthropy* (2007); author's calculations.

Will donors meet this promise? The low levels of CPA from official donors suggest that it has proven to be easier to mobilize funds for things like technical assistance, debt relief, food aid, and emergencies than for real development projects. In 2005, debt relief accounted for nearly one-quarter ($25.4 billion) in total official aid, including the Paris Club's extraordinary debt cancellation for Iraq and Nigeria. By providing funds in this fashion, donors bypass the need to have well-designed and well-implemented development projects.

Looking forward, it is unlikely (and undesirable) that aid increases can continue to be expanded through special purpose flows. All thirty countries that have participated in the Heavily Indebted Poor Countries Initiative will have realized their debt relief packages by 2009. New bilateral disbursements of debt relief are not expected to exceed $4 billion in 2010.[22]

In recent years, donors have increasingly transferred resources through "vertical" funds, meaning agencies that concentrate on narrow sectoral goals, such as health, education, and the environment. The most significant of

Figure 3-3. Geographical Focus of Private Sector Samples
(percentage of expenditures, by region)

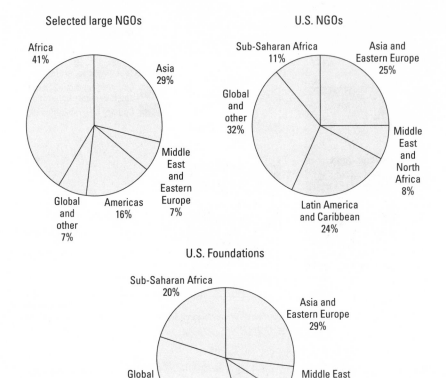

Selected large NGOs

Africa 41%
Asia 29%
Middle East and Eastern Europe 7%
Americas 16%
Global and other 7%

U.S. NGOs

Sub-Saharan Africa 11%
Asia and Eastern Europe 25%
Global and other 32%
Middle East and North Africa 8%
Latin America and Caribbean 24%

U.S. Foundations

Sub-Saharan Africa 20%
Asia and Eastern Europe 29%
Global and other 34%
Middle East and North Africa 7%
Latin America and Caribbean 12%

Sources: NGOs' annual reports; J. Kerlin and S. Thanasombat, *The International Charitable Nonprofit Subsector*, Urban Institute Policy Brief 2 (Washington: Urban Institute, 2006); International Grantmaking Update (2006).

these is the Global Fund to Fight AIDS, Tuberculosis, and Malaria (GFATM), established in 2002 and already disbursing almost $1 billion a year, with plans to increase disbursements to $4 to $6 billion a year in three to five years' time. The GFATM's success comes from simple programs that can be taken to scale in countries and achieve tangible results, such as numbers of people protected by mosquito nets, numbers on antiretroviral medicines, and ex post audits by private firms to assure financial probity. Other specialized funds, like the Global Environment Facility and the Montreal Protocol, have also increased in size. From negligible levels, these new funds have grown and now account for 7 percent of total multilateral aid, or $1.8 billion in 2005. Though vertical funds can be expected to grow rapidly, they cannot absorb the amounts of new aid that should be disbursed by 2010. They may also result in some misallocation of resources at the country level if they expand too rapidly. One now infamous example is in the health sector in Rwanda. There, $48 million a year is available for HIV/AIDS, which affects 3 percent of the population, thanks to significant GFATM funding, while only $1 million is available for maternal and child health programs.[23]

Traditionally, multilateral agencies, such as the World Bank's International Development Association (IDA), other regional development banks, and the UN system, have played a dominant role in aid disbursements. In 1995, these agencies accounted for almost two-thirds of all multilateral net disbursements. But they have been growing slowly in absolute terms and shrinking in relative terms, and they now account for just half of multilateral aid.

Part of the reason for IDA's slow growth is that poor countries often have poor policy frameworks in place, and IDA's country-based allocation system rewards countries with good policies. This means that policy and institutional improvements have to precede major increases in aid allocation. And though many African countries have indeed been moving toward meeting their commitments to the G-8, of better accountability and strengthening democracy,[24] the ones that are deemed to be best placed for major increases in aid are smaller countries: Burkina Faso, Ghana, Madagascar, Mozambique, Rwanda, and Tanzania.[25]

It is important for IDA and other channels to expand significantly if G-8 pledges are to be met, but the brief overview above suggests that this expansion will be hard to achieve. Aid, excluding debt relief, will have to increase from $81 billion in 2005 to $126 billion in 2010, because debt relief itself might fall from $25.4 billion in 2005 to $4 billion in 2010. There are no realistic plans as to how this incremental $45 billion would be channeled to developing countries.[26] In fact, the aid architecture is so convoluted that it is hard to see how donors will allocate their resources in the most effective way.

The messiness in the aid architecture is illustrated in figure 3-4, which shows how aid flows between major players. The initial source of funds is taxpayers in rich countries, who both donate to the private sector ($63 billion) and pay taxes to fund development aid programs ($105 billion). These dollars are then channeled to poor individuals in low-income countries along several routes. Bilateral aid agencies channel their funds through multilaterals,

Figure 3-4. Development Assistance, 2005 (billions of dollars)

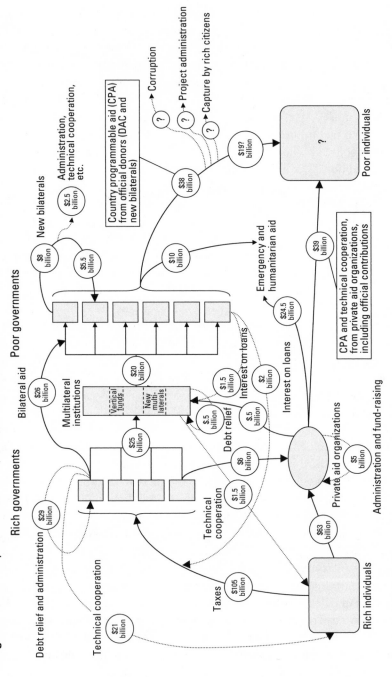

Source: Author's calculations.

Table 3-6. Development Assistance Committee Bilaterals, Official Development Funding, 2005 (billions of dollars)

Source of funds	Amount	Use of funds	Amount
Taxes	104.7	Bilateral development programs	17.8
Interest on past loans	2	Technical assistance	21
		Emergency and food aid	8
		Adminstration and overheads	4.3
		Debt relief	25
		Contributions to multilaterals	24.6
		Contributions to nongovernmental organizations	6
Total	106.7	Total	100.7

Sources: Author's calculations and Organization for Economic Cooperation and Development Development Assistance Committee.

through support to developing country government programs, or through NGO development programs. Table 3-6 illustrates the sources and uses of funds of the DAC bilaterals in 2005. They provided a total of $107 billion in net flows, funded with taxpayer contributions ($105 billion) and interest reflows from previous loans to countries ($2 billion). Of this $107 billion, only $17.8 billion is disbursed through bilateral development programs. The rest goes in technical assistance ($21 billion), emergency food aid and humanitarian assistance ($8 billion), administration and overheads ($4.3 billion), debt relief ($25 billion), contributions to multilaterals ($24.6 billion), and contributions to NGO programs ($6 billion).

Figure 3-4 shows all the flows between major groups in the same way. What is clear is that the amounts that are actually received by poor people for development purposes is a small fraction of what gets financed initially.

Implications for Official Agencies and Private Nonprofits

The new reality of aid is one of enormous fragmentation and volatility. Fragmentation arises because of the multiplicity of groups now involved in the delivery of aid, especially given new private aid players, new bilaterals, and the declining importance of the large multilaterals. As aid amounts increase, it common for recipients to see high volatility in their year-to-year aid disbursements. Large swings in disbursements translate into large swings in a recipient's domestic expenditures—especially recurrent spending, which is difficult to adjust.[27]

The costs of fragmentation and volatility are well known. Fragmentation implies multiple donor requests for studies, individual meetings with country officials,[28] the establishment of separate project management units, multiple procurement practices for the same products, an inability to identify and propagate best practices, and allocative distortions between what gets funded and country development priorities. Volatility implies conservative attitudes by finance ministries and international macroeconomic watchdogs, such as the International Monetary Fund, whose support is a prerequisite by many donors for continued aid, which generates a catch-22 situation.[29] Volatility in recurrent cost financing is especially expensive in terms of development impact.

In such an environment, private aid players cannot rely on shaping donor programs. Donors will have to support recipients' government-led programs, using budget support, sector-wide operations, or recurrent cost financing.

Private nonprofits can best play a catalytic role by providing innovative solutions to major service delivery problems, especially in underserved areas. But this function will require a shift in focus from charitable work to systemic change.

What are the implications for private NGOs? There are six. First, they should focus on project implementation. Many have already started to decentralize their activities to the field,[30] and to develop partnerships with local NGOs. Those with strong field presence and proven programs can expect to receive more funding from official donors and other private foundations. Second, the nature of advocacy needs to change. It is no longer sufficient to encourage rich country governments, or multilaterals, to change their aid practices; that would put these agencies at odds with each other and with countries and contribute to ever greater fragmentation. Instead, advocacy has to turn to country programs and policies, a far more dangerous effort for many NGOs. Third, resources are unlikely to be the critical constraint. Program effectiveness, at scale, will instead be the key. The challenge from the new bilaterals is on precisely this front. They claim that they can implement better programs more effectively based on their own experiences with development, and so should not be subject to the same rules for "tying," for example, to which traditional donors adhere. But, fourth, program effectiveness cannot be assessed at the individual project level alone. With multiple donors, a broad approach to evaluation is required, as the Rwanda case makes clear. Fifth, as NGOs expand, they must do more to evaluate their operations and to engage early on with potential champions that can scale up successful interventions. There are too many "success stories" with little follow-up on scale. This fragmentation reduces effectiveness. Sixth and finally, information, coordination, and planning are becoming harder yet are more important for development effectiveness. Private aid givers need to provide better statistical data on their activities to governments, so as to permit others to identify key gaps and overlaps.[31] That is the minimum level of accountability they owe to the countries where they operate.

Notes

1. According to the Government Accountability Office, the Millennium Challenge Corporation is lagging behind initial plans in the signing of compacts with countries, and is behind in disbursements given their own schedule. The initial planned disbursements from the first 9 signed compacts was supposed to have been $257.6 million by March 2007; that is, the actual disbursement rate is only 26 percent of the corporation's own plan. See D. Gootnick, "Compacts and Challenges in Africa," Government Accountability Office, Testimony Report 07-1049T, June 2007.

2. Estimates suggest that there are 233 multilateral development agencies; 51 bilateral donor countries (most with multiple official agencies); several hundred international NGOs; and tens of thousands of national NGOs, not including community-based organizations, which could number in the millions.

3. These donors are Australia, Austria, Belgium, Canada, Denmark, Finland, France, Germany, Greece, Ireland, Italy, Japan, Luxembourg, the Netherlands, New Zealand, Norway, Portugal, Spain, Sweden, Switzerland, the United Kingdom, and the United States.

4. All numbers are expressed in constant 2005 U.S. dollars; that is, they are adjusted for inflation. The actual numbers for 2005 and 2006 are $107 billion and $104 billion, respectively.

5. The value of noncash transfers is easily inflated to give the appearance of higher aid levels. Debt forgiveness includes penalty payments and "notional" interest that can be exorbitant, especially when accumulated over years of nonrepayment. Food and certain pharmaceuticals, which might be purchased at a fraction of the cost in a recipient's economy, are bought, shipped and recorded at donor country prices. Finally, technical assistance reflects rich country salaries (sometimes topped up by hardship allowances) rather than recipient country benefits. Some studies suggest that private contractors for official aid agencies have compensation levels up to three times as large as equivalently qualified NGO personnel. See *The Index of Global Philanthropy* (Washington: Hudson Institute, 2007).

6. M. Lindelow, I. Kushnarova, and K. Kaiser, "Measuring Corruption in the Health Sector," in *Global Corruption Report* (Berlin: Transparency International, 2007), 29–37.

7. The remaining 41 percent of funds have still not been classified by use.

8. Government Accountability Office, "Analysis of Millennium Challenge Corporation (MCC) Compact Disbursements through March 2007," letter to congressional committees, May 14, 2007.

9. President George W. Bush, "The United States International Development Agenda," statement at press conference, Ronald Reagan Building and International Trade Center, Washington, May 31, 2007.

10. See I. Kuziemko, and E. Werker, "How Much Is a Seat on the Security Council Worth?" *Journal of Political Economy* 114, no. 5 (2005): 905–30; and E. R. Wittkopf, "Foreign Aid and U.N. Votes," *American Political Science Review*, 67 (1973): 868–88.

11. Based on a sample of new bilaterals reporting to the DAC, about 19 percent of aid goes for emergency relief and administrative costs. If this is extrapolated to all new bilaterals, the total CPA would amount to $6.5 billion in 2005.

12. The disadvantage of this approach is that it typically comes as "tied aid" without the benefits of international competitive bidding.

13. China announced intentions to provide up to $20 billion in infrastructure and trade financing for Africa over the next three years at the African Development Bank annual meetings in Shanghai in May 2007.

14. This does not include community-based organizations, which number in the hundreds of thousands, according to the *Duke University Non-Governmental Organizations Research Guide* (http://library.duke.edu/research/subject/guides/ngo_guide/ [February 2008]).

15. Total giving in the United States, both domestic and international, was estimated at $295 billion in 2006, according to *Giving USA Annual Report,* Indiana University, 2006.

16. Foundation Center, *International Grantmaking Update* (Washington: Foundation Center, 2007).

17. Ibid.

18. Richard Jolly, chairman, Giving USA Foundation. For comparison, Warren Buffett's headline-grabbing gift totaled $1.9 billion in 2006.

19. J. Kerlin and S. Thanasombat, *The International Charitable Nonprofit Subsector,* Urban Institute Policy Brief 2 (Washington: Urban Institute, 2006).

20. L. Salmon, Comparative Nonprofit Sector Project, Johns Hopkins University (www.jhu.edu/~cnp/research/compdata.html [March 2007]). This includes both domestic and international giving and shows that the United States accounts for 49 percent of private giving from all DAC countries combined. The DAC itself reports on private giving, but in a very partial way. The DAC reports U.S. private giving as $8.6 billion in 2005, compared to total reported private giving of $14.7 billion, implying that the United States is 58.5 percent of the global total.

21. Kerlin and Thanasombat, *International Charitable Nonprofit Subsector.*

22. The $4 billion includes reimbursement to IDA and the African Development Bank for the Multilateral Debt Relief Initiative. Eight other countries fall under the Heavily Indebted Poor Countries Initiative's financial criteria for debt relief but are not expected to qualify for relief under "decision-point" rules. In another study, *The DATA Report* (2007), there is an assumption of zero debt relief by 2010.

23. World Health Organization/World Bank, "Rapporteur's Report: Follow-on Meeting to the Post-High-Level Forum on the Health MDGs," Tunis, June 12–13, 2006.

24. To quote from the Chair's Summary of the Gleneagles Summit (8 July, 2005): "The African leaders set out their personal commitment, reaffirmed strongly at this week's African Union summit, to drive forward plans to reduce poverty and promote economic growth; deepen transparency and good governance; strengthen democratic institutions and processes; show zero tolerance for corruption; remove all obstacles to intra-African trade; and bring about lasting peace and security across the continent."

25. The good news is that more African countries now meet basic standards of good performance or have credible Poverty Reduction Strategies in place to improve in key areas.

26. The DAC projects that as extraordinary debt relief subsides (like that granted to Iraq and Nigeria), total official development assistance levels will decline in 2006 and 2007; total assistance is not expected to exceed $100 billion again until 2008. This trend requires development aid to increase by $26 billion ($30 billion, less our projections of debt relief efforts in 2010 of $4 billion) in two years.

27. In health, which is one sector that exhibits the greatest degree of fragmentation and volatility, one study estimates that health aid is twice as volatile as budget resources. Lane, Christopher and Amanda Glassman, "Smooth and Predictable Aid for Health: The Role of Innovative Financing," unpublished paper, Brookings Institution, 2007.

28. One study finds that half of all the time of some ministries in developing countries is spent in meetings with donors and satisfying their reporting requirements.

29. The IMF will only certify programs with definite amounts of aid forthcoming, whereas future aid is predicated on an IMF certified program.

30. For example, ActionAid has decentralized its headquarters from London to South Africa.

31. Some countries have adopted a Development Gateway platform to build an appropriate database; see www.amp.developmentgateway.org.

4

Angelina, Mia, and Bono: Celebrities and International Development

DARRELL M. WEST

I T IS THE Age of Celebrity in the United States. Glamorous movie stars run for elective office and win. Former politicians play fictional characters on television shows. Rock stars and actresses raise money for a variety of humanitarian causes. Musicians, athletes, and artists speak out on issues of hunger, stem cell research, international development, and foreign policy.

Although the contemporary era is not the first time celebrities have spoken out on questions of public policy, a number of factors in the current period have given celebrities a far greater voice in civic affairs. The culture has changed in ways that glorify fame and fortune.[1] The news industry has become highly competitive. Media reporters need good copy, and few sources provide better copy than actors, athletes, and entertainers. Voters are cynical and do not trust conventional politicians or experts. The fact that political advocacy has become very expensive places a premium on those such as celebrities who can attract attention and raise money.[2]

In this chapter, I look at the history of celebrity activism; how contemporary activism by Angelina Jolie, Mia Farrow, and Bono falls within a long history of celebrity action by Marlon Brando, Jackson Browne, and Bob Geldof; what factors have contributed to this phenomenon of celebrity activism; what the age of celebrity reveals about our time period; and what risks and benefits arise from celebrities' involvement in international development. In important respects, I argue, the contemporary period has undergone crucial changes that have encouraged celebrity activism. Celebrities have done an excellent job highlighting public and media attention, and raising money for specific causes. But there are risks to civic discourse dominated by celebrities. The media fascination with famous spokespersons drains attention from experts with detailed knowledge, and risks the skewing of civic discourse toward solutions that may not represent effective long-term remedies for complex policy problems.

The Emergence of Celebrity Politics

Celebrity politics is not a new phenomenon. Throughout American history, celebrated writers and nonpoliticos have spoken out on issues of the day. Mark Twain's political satire and quips twitted many a prominent public figure. Ernest Hemingway was involved in a number of foreign and domestic controversies of his era, such as the Spanish Civil War. Charles Lindbergh gained fame as the first pilot to fly solo nonstop across the Atlantic, and then used his newfound prominence to lead America's isolationist movement in the 1930s and 1940s.

In the 1960s and 1970s, a number of singers and actors became active in civic affairs. The folksinger Arlo Guthrie did political benefits to back Chilean freedom fighters. The folksinger Phil Ochs organized a tribute to Chilean president Salvador Allende, who was assassinated during a military coup. The French actress Brigitte Bardot fought against the exploitation of baby seals.

The actor Marlon Brando raised money in 1966 for the United Nations International Children's Education Fund for famine relief. And following the 1968 assassination of Martin Luther King Jr., Brando pledged 12 percent of his earnings to the Southern Christian Leadership Conference in support of civil rights.

In 1971, the Beatles member George Harrison coorganized the Concert for Bangladesh to raise money for starving refugees. He persuaded Bob Dylan, Ringo Starr, Billy Preston, and others to play at Madison Square Garden, and their joint concert raised $240,000 for the United Nations Children's Fund for Relief to Refugee Children of Bangladesh. The singer Harry Chapin led efforts to alleviate world hunger. From 1973 to 1981, he raised half a million dollars a year to fight hunger. His lobbying on behalf of this cause led in 1978 to the establishment of the Presidential Commission on Domestic and International Hunger and Malnutrition.

Throughout the Vietnam War, a number of celebrities spoke out against U.S. administration policies. In 1968, the actor Robert Vaughn worked in the "Dump LBJ" movement, and celebrities such as Paul Newman, Tony

Randall, Myrna Loy, and Leonard Nimoy labored on behalf of the presidential candidate Eugene McCarthy. Jane Fonda became the darling of antiwar activists (and the object of scorn from many veterans) when she condemned American foreign policy during a visit to Hanoi. In 1972, the actor Warren Beatty organized celebrities for the Democratic presidential candidate George McGovern, while John Wayne and Sammy Davis Jr. supported the Republican candidate Richard Nixon.

In the 1980s, a series of "No Nukes" concerts organized by Musicians United for Safe Energy raised awareness about the danger of nuclear energy. Following that effort, Jackson Browne helped to build the nuclear freeze movement designed to stop the arms race. In the summer of 1982, he, along with Linda Ronstadt and James Taylor, played benefit concerts in New York City to raise money for a nuclear freeze. Ronald Reagan's so-called secret war against Nicaragua led Browne to become a strong critic of Reagan's policies. He played concerts, donated money, wrote songs, and gave media interviews protesting Reagan's efforts to undermine the Nicaraguan government.

Meanwhile, the singer Stevie Wonder lent his voice to the battle against apartheid in South Africa and in favor of a Martin Luther King Jr. national holiday in the United States. In the mid-1980s, the Irish rocker Bob Geldof conceived of Live Aid concerts to raise money for starving people in Ethiopia. After seeing a BBC film documenting the starvation and famine in Ethiopia, he organized two giant 1985 concerts called Live Aid. The international television broadcast event reached more than a billion people and raised more than $140 million for the people of Ethiopia. For his efforts, he became the first rock star nominated for the Nobel Peace Prize and was invited to address the European Parliament, meet with British prime minister Margaret Thatcher and Mother Teresa, and speak to the U.S. Congress.

Seeing the success of this effort, Willie Nelson organized a Farm Aid concert for American farmers. Joining with Neil Young, Bob Dylan, and John Cougar Mellencamp, the group raised money and consciousness about the plight of the rural poor. Mellencamp recorded songs about farmers on his *Scarecrow* and *Lonesome Jubilee* albums and testified in support of the Family Farm Act of 1987. The rock singer Bruce Springsteen headlined an Amnesty International Human Rights Now tour along with the singers Sting, Tracy Chapman, and Peter Gabriel. This worldwide effort called attention to the problem of political prisoners in a variety of countries.

More recently, the actor Michael J. Fox has given speeches and worked for candidates who support stem cell research. Hoping to find a cure for Parkinson's disease, Fox featured prominently in Democratic efforts to regain control of the U.S. Congress. The actress Mia Farrow has campaigned to raise awareness about mass genocides. The actress Angelina Jolie has worked extensively on issues of international development, world hunger, and child adoption. Appearing at a press conference at the Washington headquarters of Global Action for Children, an adoption agency, Jolie said, "This is a happy day because it is not often enough that these children are represented in this town."[3]

The U2 singer Bono cofounded DATA (Debt, AIDS, Trade, Africa, now merged with the ONE Campaign) to fight poverty and has toured Africa with administration officials in an effort to encourage debt relief for poor countries. The film *Ocean's Thirteen* stars George Clooney, Brad Pitt, and Matt Damon used their Cannes Film Festival release to publicize the Darfur genocide. The human rights activist John Prendergast argued that "celebrities have been crucial in building awareness on a wide range of things that would otherwise be just a distant concern. Clooney is smarter than any politician I've dealt with on this issue. Angelina Jolie is as clued in on the policy issues as any politician."[4]

The Iraq War has drawn a number of artists into celebrity activism. Among those speaking out against the war have been the actor Sean Penn, the singer Linda Ronstadt, the actor Martin Sheen, and the comedian Al Franken. Musicians such as Ozzy Osbourne and Merle Haggard penned virulent antiwar songs designed to move public opinion against the war. Haggard even went so far as writing a song saying it was time for a woman president: "This country needs to be honest, changes need to be large. Something like a big switch of gender. Let's put a woman in charge." But the country singer Toby Keith remained strongly within the Republican camp. Defending the war with patriotic melodies such as "Courtesy of the Red, White and Blue" and "American Soldier," Keith and the duo Brooks and Dunn became popular performers at Republican rallies.

The Rise of Celebrity Activists

Although celebrity activism is not new, several trends over the past few decades have given celebrities new prominence in debates on public policy. Changes in the structure and operation of the media have contributed to a celebrity culture that provides actors, musicians, and athletes with a platform from which to speak out.[5] The line between politics and entertainment has blurred to the point where actors such as Arnold Schwarzenegger have become politicians and politicians such as former senator Fred Thompson star in prominent television shows and then go on to run for the presidency.

Hardball executive producer Phil Griffin was cognizant of this trend toward celebrity activism when he booked the actress Goldie Hawn for the show after she spoke out at a press conference demanding that Congress vote on a China trade bill. Asked why he invited her to do the show, Griffin replied that "the China trade deal ain't exactly a big winner on these talk shows, or anywhere, for that matter, so I said, 'Let's get her on.'"[6] It was a way to draw attention to a technical subject that normally did not elicit much public or press interest.

The Washington bureau chief for the Fox News Channel, Kim Hume, views the growing trend of celebrity activists appearing on television to lobby for particular causes as mutually advantageous to celebrities and the news media. "We probably have three or four celebrities appear on Capitol Hill a week," Hume said. "Granted, I'm sure there are celebrities who have real passion about particular issues and they really do want to make a difference. But most of it is a collusion between the way they wish the public would see them and the way the public relations people use them in order to get attention for their causes."[7]

With the rise of new technologies such as cable television, talk radio, Web logs, and the Internet, the news business has become very competitive and more likely to focus on famous personalities. Tabloid shows such as *Access Hollywood* attract millions of viewers, glorify celebrities, and provide a "behind-the-scenes" look at the entertainment industry. Reporters stake out "star" parties and report on who is in attendance. The old "establishment" press that kept rumors of President John F. Kennedy's marital infidelities out of the newspapers has been replaced by a news media that specializes in reporting on the private lives of politicians and Hollywood stars.

Celebrity activism becomes a way for actors and musicians to stay in the news even when they have no new movie or CD to promote.[8] In today's rapidly changing world, celebrities feel pressure to keep their names in the news because it is a long time between movies or concert tours. Promoting a charitable or political cause allows celebrities to remain in the public eye and garners appearances on talk and entertainment shows. Though celebrities generally prefer noncontroversial causes such as fund-raising for children living in poverty or breast cancer research, increasingly, entertainment figures are taking stances on controversial subjects, such as the Iraq War, and are making formal endorsements in election campaigns.

Changes in public opinion have given celebrities stronger credibility to speak out on political matters. From the standpoint of political activists, celebrities are a way to reach voters jaded by political cynicism. In the 1950s, data indicated that two-thirds of Americans trusted the government in Washington to do what is right.[9] Presidents had high moral authority, and citizens had confidence in the ethics and morality of their leaders. However, following the scandals related to Vietnam, Watergate, economic stagflation, Iran-Contra, and President Bill Clinton's sexual dalliance with Monica Lewinsky and subsequent impeachment, the public became far less trusting. They are no longer confident about political leaders and are less likely to trust their statements. When asked whether they trust the government in Washington to do what is right, two-thirds of Americans currently express mistrust. Citizens feel that politicians are in it for themselves and that they serve special interests. An electorate that trusts politicians to tell the truth has been replaced by a public that is highly skeptical about rhetoric and intentions.

In this situation, it is difficult for politicians to raise money and build public support because they simply do not have the credibility necessary for political persuasion. Therefore, they need to associate with people who have greater public credibility. These are generally individuals from outside the political realm. Nonpoliticians are considered more trustworthy and less partisan by the electorate, and they have high credibility with the general public. Nongovernmental organizations employ celebrities as proxies for individual donors. This keeps these entities accountable and allows political advocates to reach citizens turned off by the political process and unhappy with conventional politicians.

As long as they keep themselves reasonably clean and scandal free, celebrities are seen as white knights, not tainted by past partisan scandals or political dealings. Citizens trust them to shake up the political establishment and bring new ideas to public policymaking. Their fame attracts press coverage and campaign contributors. Journalists crowd their press conferences and strain to hear what they have to say about foreign and domestic policy. Even though they lack detailed knowledge on these issues, celebrities have a platform that allows them to command attention in civic discourse.

The growing cost of political advocacy in the United States has contributed to the emergence of celebrity politics. Politicians and activists need large amounts of money to promote their causes. This need for cash forces politicians and issue advocates into alliances with athletes, actors, and artists who headline fund-raising events. To guarantee a large turnout at a fund-raising party, it has become common to feature comedians, singers, and other celebrities who can attract a large crowd.

In the 2004 presidential election campaign, for example, Bruce Springsteen gave a series of concerts to raise money to defeat President George W.

Bush, and other Hollywood celebrities such as the actors Sean Penn and
Mike Farrell and the singer Linda Ronstadt spoke out against the Iraq War.
Meanwhile, with their strong support in "red" states, Republicans relied on
country singers like Garth Brooks who lent their names to the cause of elect-
ing Republicans across the country.

There is concern about celebrities' images getting tangled up in political
controversies. Dating back to unhappiness over Jane Fonda's opposition to
the Vietnam War and the Dixie Chicks' negative comments about President
Bush concerning the Iraq War, celebrities have worried that too much political involvement could damage their careers. However, the large number of
entertainers taking active political positions suggests that there is safety in
numbers. As long as many celebrities are politically active, there is far less
danger that any one of them will suffer a debilitating backlash from his or her
political activities. The activism of some encourages activism by other
celebrities.

Celebrity culture is not something that is being inflicted on an unwilling
public. Rather, it is a development that people watch and willingly participate in. Tabloid newspapers have a large circulation: The *National Enquirer*
sells about 2.3 million copies every week, and *Star* magazine has a circulation
of 1.7 million. Television shows devoted to gossip about the famous do well.
An average of 3.5 million viewers watches the syndicated television show
Inside Edition, and the E! Entertainment network attracts several million
viewers to its shows about Hollywood figures.[10] Celebrities dominate the list
of personalities that people would like to meet. A national survey of teenagers
found they would like to meet musicians most, followed by athletes and
actors—politicians are well down the list.

Not only are people fascinated with famous individuals and their personal
lives; they want to be on television themselves. Indeed, their quest for fame is
so strong that they are willing to eat rats or betray loved ones to achieve star-
dom. Note the popularity of "reality" television shows. The final episode of the
first season of *Survivor* earned ratings that were second only to the Super Bowl.

The popularity of this genre led pollsters to ask a national sample what
they would be willing to allow a reality show to film them doing. The most
popular results were 31 percent for being in their pajamas, 29 percent for
kissing, 26 percent for crying, 25 percent for having an argument with someone, 16 percent for being drunk, 10 percent for eating a rat or insect, 8 percent for being naked, and 5 percent for having sex.[11] This "democratization"
of fame, first described by Leo Braudy many years ago, allows people of ordinary talent to become "temporary" celebrities.[12]

It is clear that the celebrity cult of personality resonates with many Americans. Viewers love to hear tidbits about celebrity lives, even what these individuals think about political issues of the day. America is a voyeuristic society that values news and information about prominent people as well as ordinary people who have fleeting moments of fame.

The Risks and Benefits of Celebrity Politics

America's celebrity politics makes for an entertaining show. It is fascinating to see a former wrestler such as Jesse Ventura win the governorship of a major state like Minnesota or Arnold Schwarzenegger capture the California gubernatorial election. Barack Obama's rock star appeal and Hillary Clinton's campaign for president attract great interest, as do the campaigns of various "third-generation" Kennedys around the country.[13] But there is more at stake than merely entertainment in the rise of celebrity culture, particularly in the political arena.

At one level, this celebrity regime is beneficial to our culture and political system. Celebrities bring new ideas to the process. Unlike conventional politicians, celebrities do not have to serve a long apprenticeship before they run for major offices. In a world where entangling alliances are the rule, these individuals are as close to free agents as one can find. This freedom allows them to challenge the conventional wisdom, adopt unpopular stances, and expand the range of ideas represented in our national dialogue. Because they are not conventional politicians and are not limited to mainstream coalitions based on the left or right, they have greater potential to innovate than career politicians. This is one of the reasons why most celebrities who run for public office end up winning. Voters see them as white knights who can shake up a stagnant political system that ignores important issues.

Celebrities have a demonstrated ability to raise money and attract media attention. In some cases, it is clear that they have shaped public opinion, altered the political agenda, and influenced public policymaking. Michael J. Fox has raised awareness of the potential of stem cell research to help those who suffer from debilitating diseases. Bono helped convince leaders at the 2005 Group of Eight meeting to forgive a portion of Africa's International Monetary Fund and World Bank debts. And in the past couple of years, a number of Hollywood actors and actresses have focused public attention on Darfur and other tragic genocides around the world.

Within the United States, national surveys document that more than 10 percent of Americans get information about politics from late-night entertainment shows such as *The Tonight Show* or *Letterman*. And for those under the age of thirty years old, that figure rises to nearly half.[14] As the network news emphasizes entertainment features and lifestyle stories at the expense of hard news, more and more Americans are turning to entertainment shows such as *The Daily Show* with Jon Stewart for political commentary. This gives celebrities great power to alter citizens' awareness of issues neglected by the mainstream press.

But in other respects, a system based on celebrityhood raises problems. Our fascination with celebrities raises the risk that there will be more superficiality and less substance in our political process. Celebrity activists range from the superknowledgeable Bono and Michael J. Fox to the media-crazed Paris Hilton. The latter's calls for prison reform following her release from confinement arose more from public relation needs than serious reflection on the issue. Advocacy organizations have to be careful not to blur their brand with that of the specific celebrity.

The wide variation in celebrity knowledge and dedication contributes to the circus atmosphere in American politics. Increasingly, politics has become a matter of public performance. Advocates get judged more by their ability to deliver crisp sound bites than by their substantive knowledge. With journalists interested in celebrity quotes and good copy, experts with detailed knowledge about public policy are less likely to get taken seriously. It is easier to go to the famous and get their opinions than to seek out less prominent people who may actually know more.

In addition, there is the risk that well-intentioned celebrities will push ill-conceived solutions. The nonprofit activist Franklin Cudjoe put it most bluntly when he criticized celebrity activists: "They use rock star economics, and it's just plain wrong. They ignore history; they peddle the completely misguided belief that poverty, famine, and corruption can be solved with foreign aid, debt relief, and other policies that have already failed Africa."[15]

A lack of knowledge is a particular problem in the area of international development because it is not clear that popular solutions such as country-specific sanctions or debt relief actually solve the intended problems. For example, calls for economic sanctions against nations that violate human rights or engage in repressive behavior assume that sanctions actually work. However, a 1997 article by Robert Pape titled "Why Economic Sanctions Still Do Not Work" suggests that unless there are broad international agreements and strong enforcement mechanisms, sanctions do not stop undesirable behavior.[16] He looked at forty examples of "claimed successes" but found that only five of the forty cases were successful at achieving their aims. In about half the examples, it took military force to produce the desired out-come; in other cases, the target nation refused to make meaningful conces-sions. Countries simply find routes around the sanctions unless the world is clearly united in punishing the offending nation.

In the same vein, proposals to alleviate poverty through debt relief must be combined with measures to reduce corruption and improve public sector capacity. It is easy for one nation to forgive debt and another country to rush in with new loans. Yet without effective political reform, putting more for-eign aid into corrupt countries is not going to improve the plight of average people. Rather, it just becomes a way to enrich the ruling class of that coun-try and line the Swiss bank accounts of corrupt leaders.

It would be interesting, for example, to evaluate what happened to the $140 million raised by Bob Geldof for the people of Ethiopia in 1985. Although there has not been any systematic assessment of the impact of that cash infusion, twenty years later Ethiopia continues to fall at the bottom of virtually every indicator of social and economic well-being. According to 2007 estimates, life expectancy in Ethiopia is forty-nine years, 39 percent of its population lives below the poverty line, and 4.4 percent of its citizens suf-fer from HIV/AIDS.[17] Simply dumping millions of dollars into poor societies does not necessarily improve the plight of ordinary folks.

To be effective at solving problems, the American political system depends on careful deliberation, participation, and engagement. But what we have now is a system where star power is weighted more heavily than traditional political skills, such as bargaining, compromise, and experience. Conven-tional politicians are being replaced by famous, media-savvy fund-raisers. The quality of civic deliberation is becoming trivialized. The gossip quotient has increased, and politics has become a twenty-four-hour entertainment spectacle.

With attention spans for important stories dropping precipitously, the sys-tem rewards celebrity politicians with famous names. Unless these individu-als provide citizens with proper information, it short-circuits our system of governance. Reporters have become much more likely to focus on human features than detailed policy substance. According to William Winter, who was one of America's first television news broadcasters, modern news broad-casts are "increasingly shallow and trivial."[18] Competition in American poli-tics centers on who can reduce complex messages down to understandable, nine-second (or, more recently, five-second) sound bites.[19]

Without good-quality information, voters cannot make informed choices about their futures. American politics never has placed a strong emphasis on substance. In comparison with other Western democracies, fewer people vote at election time, and many appear not to be very informed about their decisions. As celebrity politics takes root, there is the long-term danger that citizens will become even less knowledgeable about policy choices, and they may become content to watch and be entertained. But elections are a key device by which representative democracy takes place. Citizens must feel engaged in the process, must be able to think about their options, and must feel that they have a stake in important decisions. As politics becomes mere entertainment, the danger is that society loses its ability to solve pressing social problems.

Notes

1. Leo Braudy, *The Frenzy of Renown: Fame and Its History* (New York: Vintage, 1986).

2. David Canon, *Actors, Athletes, and Astronauts* (University of Chicago Press, 1990).

3. Quoted in "Jolie Stars for Orphans," *Daily Telegraph,* April 28, 2007.

4. Quoted by Dan Glaister, "Sudan: Not on Our Watch," *The Guardian,* May 19, 2007.

5. Ronald Brownstein, *The Power and the Glitter: The Hollywood-Washington Connection* (New York: Pantheon, 1990).

6. Quoted by Darrell M. West and John Orman, *Celebrity Politics* (Englewood Cliffs, N.J.: Prentice-Hall, 2003).

7. Quoted in ibid, p. 62.

8. Larry Sabato, Mark Stempel, and Robert Lichter, *Peep Show: Media and Politics in an Age of Scandal* (Lanham, Md.: Rowman & Littlefield, 2000).

9. Paul Abramson, *Political Attitudes in America* (San Francisco: Freeman, 1983).

10. *Ulrich's International Periodicals Directory* (New York: R. R. Bowker, 2000).

11. CNN/*Time* Poll conducted June 14–15, 2000; reported at www.pollingreport.com.

12. See Braudy, *Frenzy of Renown.*

13. Darrell M. West, *Patrick Kennedy: The Rise to Power* (Englewood Cliffs, N.J.: Prentice-Hall, 2000).

14. Paul Brownfield, "Iowa, New Hampshire . . . 'Tonight Show'?" *Los Angeles Times,* February 11, 2000.

15. Quoted by Shelley Page, "Star Power, A Cause Célèbre," *Ottawa Citizen,* August 13, 2006.

16. Robert Pape, "Why Economic Sanctions Still Do Not Work," *International Security* 22, no. 2 (Autumn 1997): 90–136.

17. U.S. Central Intelligence Agency, *The World Factbook* (Washington: U.S. Government Printing Office, 2007).

18. Quoted by Ron Miller, "TV News: Increasingly Shallow, Trivial," *Bridgeport Post,* May 17, 1990.

19. Kiku Adatto, *Picture Perfect: The Art and Artifice of Public Image Making* (New York: Basic Books, 1993).

5

Is There a Constituency for Global Poverty? Jubilee 2000 and the Future of Development Advocacy

JOSHUA BUSBY

IN SEPTEMBER 2000, the Irish rock star Bono met with North Carolina's Senator Jesse Helms and urged the conservative head of the Senate Foreign Relations Committee to support developing country debt relief on behalf of Jubilee 2000, a London-based transnational campaign that sought to eliminate the debts of the world's poorest countries in time for the new millennium. Helms was known for equating foreign aid with throwing money down "ratholes." Bono claimed that Helms wept when they spoke: "I talked to him about the biblical origin of the idea of Jubilee Year. . . . He was genuinely moved by the story of the continent of Africa, and he said to me, 'America needs to do more.' I think he felt it as a burden on a spiritual level."[1] Of his meeting with Bono, Helms said, "I was deeply impressed with him. He has depth that I didn't expect. He is led by the Lord to do something about the starving people in Africa."[2] After their meeting, Helms embraced debt relief and, later, funding to combat HIV/AIDS in the developing world. How can we explain this change?

This chapter answers that question through a case study of the Jubilee 2000 campaign—the campaign to write off the external debt of the world's poorest countries. Debt negotiations are normally discussed in a rarefied world of central bankers and Treasury officials, multilateral bureaucrats, and private financiers, nearly all of whom are committed to minimizing moral

This chapter is based on a longer essay titled "Bono Made Jesse Helms Cry: Jubilee 2000, Debt Relief, and Moral Action in International Politics," which appeared in the June 2007 issue of *International Studies Quarterly*.

hazard and are thus skeptical of writing off external debts. Nonetheless, two economists called the campaign "by far the most successful industrial-country movement aimed at combating world poverty for many years, perhaps in all recorded history."[3] It earned the endorsement of leaders of diverse ideological and professional orientations—the pope, Bono, Jeffrey Sachs, and Pat Robertson. The campaign also received the support of strong political allies in the U.K. and U.S. governments, making it harder for other creditors—such as Japan, France, and Germany—to oppose debt relief.

The success of the Jubilee 2000 campaign raises interesting issues about what it did right and whether its success can be replicated. Some other advocacy efforts, notably the campaign for global HIV/AIDS funding, have been successful in recent years. However, even putatively successful campaigns have not succeeded everywhere. For example, the campaign for the International Criminal Court was able to get a court but the United States is still not part of it. Similarly, the Kyoto Protocol came into force but the United States remains opposed. Other campaigns, to date, have been even less successful, such as the Save Darfur Coalition, the Make Trade Fair campaign, and efforts to curb the trade in small arms.

Two key questions emerge from this: Why are some campaigns more successful than others? And why do some campaigns succeed in some places and not others?

Background on the Campaign

Organized around the coming of the twenty-first century, Jubilee 2000 was an international campaign that aimed to relieve the world's poorest countries of their "unpayable" external debts. The reference to "Jubilee" comes from the biblical notion in the Book of Leviticus of a time to relieve the debts of the poor. In the early 1990s, Martin Dent, a professor at Keele University in the United Kingdom, came up with the idea for a "Jubilee year" end-of-the-millennium campaign, inspired by his knowledge of the Bible and ethical commitment to the developing world.[4] Dent's advocacy began with his students but soon attracted Christian Aid, the World Development Movement, and other U.K. charities. Jubilee 2000 was formally launched in April 1996. The movement blossomed, galvanizing millions worldwide to participate in letter-writing efforts and protests before the official campaign closed at the end of 2000. In policy terms, Jubilee 2000's efforts moved donors to more than double the amount of debt relief on offer; by May 2006, nineteen states already qualified to have $23.4 billion of their debts written off through the

Debt Relief Initiative for Heavily Indebted Poor Countries (HIPC).[5] In 2005, a successor campaign was able to induce rich creditors to commit to write off 100 percent of the debts the poorest countries owed to the World Bank, the International Monetary Fund, and the African Development Bank. Moreover, the liberal-religious conservative coalition that came together on debt relief presaged advocacy efforts that would play an important role in the George W. Bush administration's $15 billion financial commitment in 2003 to fight HIV/AIDS.

In October 1996, after years of rolling over poor countries' debts and providing modest debt reduction, several developed countries, the World Bank, and the IMF decided upon a joint approach with the HIPC initiative. HIPC incrementally increased bilateral debt reduction and broke new ground with respect to multilateral debt by creating a Trust Fund to pay for debt relief from institutions such as the IMF and the World Bank.[6] Countries deemed eligible for debt relief reached a "decision point," and if they followed sound macroeconomic policies for several years while enjoying reduced debt payments in the interim, they would reach a "completion point" and be eligible for an actual reduction of debt stock.

Before the Group of Eight (G-8) summit in Germany in mid-1999, the United Kingdom, the United States, and Canada led efforts to enhance HIPC.[7] In late 1998, Germany's newly elected prime minister, Gerhard Schröder, signaled a softening in his nation's long-standing reluctance to participate. Pressure mounted on Italy, France, and Japan to be more supportive. In March 1999, President Bill Clinton announced a plan that established the contours for what would come out of the G-8 meeting in Cologne, including front-loaded relief, increasing bilateral debt relief to 90 percent, and additional multilateral financing.[8] The plan also linked debt relief to Poverty Reduction Strategy Papers, which were designed to guarantee country ownership and that the savings would be invested in education, health, and other worthy expenditures. In June 1999, with 30,000 protesters ringing the Cologne summit, the G-7 countries announced the expansion of HIPC, promising about $27 billion in new debt reduction in net present value terms, on top of the debt relief for which the HIPC countries were eligible under traditional mechanisms.[9]

The Cologne G-8 summit partly involved bargaining by creditors on how much each would contribute to the HIPC Trust Fund and how much bilateral debt relief they would support. The U.S. contribution was $920 million spread out over three years, of which $600 million was to be dedicated to the Trust Fund. However, this was contingent upon Congress appropriating the funds and authorizing the sale or revaluation of IMF gold.[10] The $600 million was roughly equivalent to the European Union's pledged contribution and three times that of Japan. In September 1999, President Clinton announced that the United States would write off 100 percent of bilateral debts, followed soon by the other main creditors. U.S. funding remained in doubt until October 2000, when Congress finally appropriated $435 million for the United States' initial commitments to the HIPC Trust Fund and bilateral relief. Other G-7 creditors that had been waiting to see if the United States would come through gradually made good on their contributions.

Elements of Success of the Jubilee 2000 Campaign

Five elements contributed to the success of the Jubilee 2000 campaign: the nature of the issue, the message, the messengers, an excellent inside strategy, and a differentiated international strategy.

The Nature of the Issue

Despite lingering concerns about moral hazard among technocrats in finance ministries and international institutions, there were no strong domestic constituencies opposed to debt relief. Other international issues, by contrast, have strong, politically connected, and intransigent interest groups on the other side, such as the fossil fuel industry (climate change), the military (the International Criminal Court), farm lobbies (agricultural subsidies), and the National Rifle Association (NRA) (small arms). For those issues, there are concentrated costs that those sectors perceive will affect their interests. Debt relief, by contrast, involved modest, diffuse costs spread out across taxpayers.[11] In the U.S. context, a small number of influential legislators opposed debt relief, particularly on the Republican side, a vestige of the anti-foreign aid contingency within the party. However, the Jubilee 2000 campaign was able to blunt their influence by reaching out to a number of them individually.

The Message

Advocates are more likely to be successful when their goals are perceived to fit with the deeply held values of policymakers and the public.[12] Though the Jubilee 2000 campaign employed tailored messages for different groups, the campaign's name embodied its dominant message. Jubilee 2000, with its explicit connection to religious traditions and the coming of the new millennium, represented a "rebranding" of the debt campaigns that had been around for a number of years, according to Jamie Drummond, Jubilee 2000's former

Figure 5-1. Spike in Newspaper Coverage of Debt Relief, 1993–2000

Number of articles

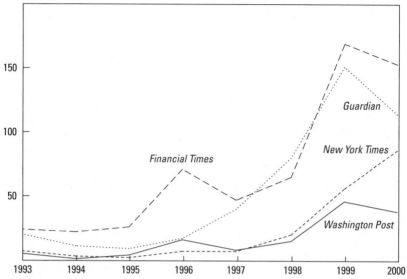

Source: Author's calculations.

global strategist.[13] Before 1994, campaigners had tried without much success to draw attention to the debt issue along with the structural adjustment programs administered by the IMF and World Bank. Unlike earlier efforts, the message of the Jubilee 2000 campaign struck a chord, and debt relief received unprecedented media coverage during the life of the campaign (figure 5-1).[14]

The expiration date of the millennium gave the campaign a sense of urgency and attached it to an already-significant event, but perhaps its faith-based appeal was more important. When we look at the religiosity of most G-7 countries, there is a fount of religious belief that served the campaign well, even in more secular countries like the United Kingdom. At the G-8 meetings in Birmingham and Cologne, the majority of protesters were from church groups and church-linked charities. Similarly, faith groups were the main campaign supporters in the United States, where local clergy encouraged members to contact their legislators.

Debts were also rhetorically linked to cuts in education and health care and, in turn, death, malnourishment, and poverty, particularly among children. This helped recast the issue from fear of corruption and moral hazard to one of morality and justice. As Sebastian Mallaby argued: "Late last year, during the endgame of the budget fight, the Republican line was that aid would drain money from Social Security; it was a choice of 'Ghana vs. Grandma,' they exclaimed, ridiculously. But you don't hear that so much now."[15]

The Messengers

The religious symbolism, coupled with the timing of the new millennium, was such that the Jubilee 2000 campaign was able to attract a wide swath of support from North and South, left and right. Whereas there was a tendency for radical elements to bash capitalism, as in the 1999 World Trade Organization protests in Seattle, Jubilee 2000 garnered influential supporters from the entire ideological spectrum as well as ordinary citizens—what Drummond called "establishment taxpayers."[16] When these politically influential citizens reached out to their legislators, they often found them amenable to their perspective on the issue.

An Excellent Inside Strategy

In March 1999, President Clinton's plan for an enhanced HIPC initiative was announced in the run-up to the Cologne summit. Campaigners quickly realized that Clinton's support would not be enough to secure American support for debt relief. There were other policy gatekeepers who had power over appropriations. Bono's guiding questions for lobbying became, "Who can stop this from happening?" and "Who's the Elvis here?"[17] Advocates began to cultivate ties with Republican committee chairs. After the president's announcement, Bono came to the United States and formed links with the administration, including Larry Summers, and with members of Congress. Bono, through Eunice Shriver, was introduced to her son Bobby and then her son-in-law, Arnold Schwarzenegger, who counseled him to link up with Republicans such as Representative John Kasich, chair of the House Budget Committee. Kasich in turn brokered meetings for Bono with other leading Republicans, including Orrin Hatch, Dennis Hastert, and Dick Armey.[18]

At the same time, U.S. campaigners like Tom Hart, then director of government relations for the Episcopal Church, had formed a lobbying group. They approached Representative Jim Leach, a moderate Iowa Republican who was chair of the House Banking and Financial Services Committee. Leach agreed to introduce a debt relief bill, HR 1095, on March 11, 1999. By approaching a Republican committee chair, the campaigners made what proved to be an excellent tactical move to broaden their base of support. Campaigners from groups like Bread for the World encouraged members of

Congress to cosponsor the bill. One success was Spencer Bachus, an Alabama Republican known for being a "conservative's conservative," who became one of the bill's strongest supporters.[19] As chair of the House Banking Subcommittee on Domestic and International Monetary Policy, he could have blocked consideration of the bill entirely.

Three prominent actors—Summers, Kasich, and Leach—were all persuaded that debt relief was the right thing to do based on technocratic ideas. Though the Treasury had concerns that debt relief would cut poor countries off from capital markets, Summers (who succeeded Robert Rubin as secretary of the Treasury in June 1999) ultimately recognized that because these debts were not going to be paid anyway, it was sound financial practice to write them off.[20] Like Summers, Kasich found this appealing. According to Scott Hatch, a former Republican leadership staff member and confidante of Kasich, the congressman responded because he thought debt relief was a viable way to free up resources for poor countries to spend on education and health care.[21] According to Jamie McCormick, former staff to the House Banking Committee, Leach was motivated by a similar dynamic.[22]

The religious case for debt relief also had direct appeal to important individual lawmakers and created some measure of political mobilization that pressured skeptics. Aside from activists and leaders like Pat Robertson, prominent congressional Republicans—Bachus and Helms in particular—found the religious message compelling.[23] Asked about his position, Bachus said, "This bill is a gift of life. Jubilee 2000 is a celebration of the 2000th birthday of Christ. . . . What more appropriate time to give to these poor in celebration of the birth of Jesus, who gave us life?"[24] Hart suggested that legislators like Bachus were amenable to the message of Jubilee because it came from people with deep roots in local institutions.[25] Like Bachus, Helms was moved by his faith.

How did these gatekeepers then exercise influence over their peers? Hatch argued that Kasich's influence was less based on his role as a committee chair and more informal—that he was able to use "political muscle" and "personal credibility" with his Republican colleagues as a fiscal hawk and solid conservative to get debt relief through the House.[26] Like Kasich, Helms's influence on this question was more informal. A former Helms aide, Mark Lagon, said that the "striking thing" about Helms's support for debt relief was that "it left people with the idea 'Oh well, if Helms thinks this is okay, it must be the right thing to do.' It was certainly hard to be outflanked on the right." In Lagon's view, Helms's support could potentially sway up to twenty-five of the most conservative and purest free-marketeers in the Senate.[27]

Gatekeepers who remained opposed to debt relief—Alabama congressman Sonny Callahan and Texas senator Phil Gramm—appear to have been moved by political pressure, lobbying, and shaming. In the weeks before the October 2000 vote, Robertson asked Texas viewers of the *700 Club* to "let Senator Gramm know that this is a good initiative."[28] Another pressure tactic was the threat of a presidential veto of the budget. For opponents, the specter of a veto forced them to ask: Did they want to be known for denying education spending just to prevent spending on debt relief?[29] Callahan, chair of a House Appropriations subcommittee, argued that given the ubiquity of veto threats, he "never paid much attention to that." He did not object to debt relief but worried that without "contingencies" states would return to their bad behavior. He acknowledged the role of lobbying pressure: "All I did was make a little fuss over it and I incurred the wrath of the church community worldwide." Realizing that the appropriations bill's supporters had the votes to amend it on the floor, Callahan let it go forward.[30] As he admitted, "The debt relief issue is now a speeding train. We've got the pope and every missionary in the world involved in this thing, and they persuaded just about everyone here that this is the noble thing to do."[31] So, whereas moral reasons motivated many supporters, opponents found themselves subject to the piety of their peers.

A Differentiated International Strategy

The Jubilee 2000 religious message was not a winner everywhere. It lacked local cultural foundations in Japan, and the costs of debt relief, though a small share of gross domestic product (GDP), were much larger than for other G-7 countries (table 5-1). However, reframing the issue as a test of Japan's international contribution proved compelling.

Although the Japanese public was generally supportive of foreign aid, the government, and particularly the Finance Ministry—the dominant gatekeeper—found debt relief inimical. Where did these views come from? In the 1980s, the United States feared the Japanese would overtake it as a global leader and pressured the Japanese to share the leadership burden. Given constitutional restrictions on playing a military role, the Japanese sought to satisfy these concerns by becoming the biggest provider of foreign assistance, building on their experience in East Asia. By the late 1990s, the international political environment had changed, with persistent poverty, particularly in Sub-Saharan Africa, motivating debt forgiveness. Given their own experience in East Asia, the Japanese were very uneasy about debt relief. They worried that debt relief would damage the "credit culture" and cut developing countries

Table 5-1. Group of Seven Debt Holdings, ca. 1998–99

Indicator	Canada	France	Germany	Italy	Japan	United Kingdom	United States
Bilateral claims of 40 countries (millions of dollars)	711	13,033	6,586	4,311	11,200	3,092	6,210
As percentage of GDP	0.1	0.9	0.3	0.4	0.3	0.2	0.08
As percentage of Group of Seven claims	1.57	28.9	14.6	9.5	24.8	6.8	13.8

Source: U.S. General Accounting Office, *Debt Relief Initiative for Poor Countries Faces Challenges,* GAO/NSIAD-00-161 (Washington: Government Printing Office, 2000) (www.gao.gov/new.items/ns00161.pdf [February 2008]).

Note: Japanese and French costs were about $8 billion each as neither did much provisioning for bad debts. U.S. costs were about $3.7 billion due to provisioning for bad loans. Costs for HIPC have risen with the inclusion of new debtors and topping up to account for commodity price shocks.

off from access to capital markets. They believed that their official development assistance loans had been indispensable tools in their foreign assistance programs in Asia.[32]

Japan signed on to the enhanced debt relief program at Cologne, but it remained unenthusiastic about complete bilateral relief. In the run-up to the Okinawa G-8 meetings in July 2000, Japan announced that it would accept 100 percent bilateral relief. Why did Japan change its policies? The argument was recast by activists and other creditor governments as something Japan could do to be a solid contributor to the international community. Takehiko Nakao, director of the Coordination Division in the Ministry of Finance's International Bureau, provided an authoritative account. Japan, Nakao said, appreciated that other G-7 countries supported debt relief. If all G-7 countries support an initiative, Japan tends to support it. Nakao said that Japan puts a lot of importance on G-7 summits, the UN General Assembly, and the Organization for Economic Cooperation and Development. Though the United States–Japan bilateral security relationship is strong, Japan is not a member of NATO. Given its limited ability to participate in military operations, Japan pursued other means in order to be recognized as a good member and contributor to the international community. To that end, Japan assumed a big responsibility by contributing to the IMF and the World Bank as well as through bilateral official development assistance.[33] Thus, Japan supported debt relief because its leaders want to be perceived as good international citizens.

Counterintuitive Lessons

In thinking about the significance of the Jubilee 2000 campaign for other advocacy efforts, it is useful to consider three counterintuitive lessons. *The first lesson: In most countries, there is likely never going to be a large coalition for*

global poverty alleviation. Few if any elections will ever be lost over development issues; the concerns of poor foreigners just do not loom large enough.
That said, campaigners can make some development issues sufficiently popular that politicians will want to be seen as supportive and avoid being seen as
anti-poor.[34] The G-8 protests aside, Jubilee 2000 was only able to bring modest pressure to bear in different national contexts. In the United States, for
example, the national rally campaigners organized in April 2000 was
attended by 6,000 people, hardly comparable to the hundreds of thousands
that participate in marches for and against hot-button issues like abortion.
Though celebrity participation enhanced the visibility of the campaign,
Bono himself acknowledged that "in the U.S., Jubilee 2000 had been a lot
slower to catch on. We were running out of time to grow the grassroots. I
had to go straight to the decision-makers."[35] Political pressure was not over-
whelming. Former Treasury secretary Larry Summers made a similar observa-
tion, "We could have not done it, and it wouldn't have been a political disaster."[36] The campaign had success in part because of the message, but also
because campaigners reached out to "the grasstops," leaders of key groups
from around the country who were able to reach and persuade legislators
who trusted them.

Since the Jubilee 2000 campaign, there has been a visible effort to bring in
the mass public for a variety of development causes, including the ONE
Campaign to Make Poverty History, the Make Trade Fair campaign, the
(PRODUCT)[RED] brand, and *American Idol's* fund-raising for Africa. These
efforts have gotten a lot of publicity, but it is unclear how deep public
engagement and support are for development. The American public, for
example, has long had a reputation for overestimating how much foreign aid
the federal government provides. Support for development assistance is qualified; citizens in advanced industrial countries are much more likely to support aid to democracies.[37] They are particularly supportive of aid for humanitarian relief, health, and education, which complicates efforts to provide
more open-ended budgetary assistance rather than project support.[38]

Between January and November 2006, the highly visible ONE Campaign
succeeded in mobilizing 500,000 people to take some form of action to support the campaign. Is this a lot? MoveOn.org, another new Internet-age
advocacy organization, regularly trumpets hundreds of thousands mobilized
for discrete issues on a monthly basis.[39]

Although Bono once likened the ideal influence of groups like DATA
(Debt, AIDS, Trade, Africa, now merged with the ONE Campaign) to an
NRA for the poor," global HIV/AIDS is not an issue over which many voters

are willing to turf out politicians. Advocacy groups are able to exercise influence more through their ability to praise behavior they like (which DATA was especially known for) and shame politicians for failure to keep promises. As Tom Hart said, "Our design is not to elect and defeat" politicians. Rather, DATA is about having political weight and being "taken seriously."[40] Advocates for HIV/AIDS appropriations, for example, had a limited role influencing the executive branch through pressure; their efforts to collect votes in the U.S. Congress in the appropriations process were more influential. In fact, they have relied as much on an inside strategy of good information, contacts, and credibility as they have on a mass strategy of brute political power.

The second lesson: Celebrities compensate for weak mass movements, but their previous success depended in part on personality, strategy, and low expectations. Celebrities compensate for movement weakness by drawing attention to the cause, but when they get in the room to talk with decisionmakers, they have to be well briefed. Bono succeeded in part because of his personality, but also because of initially low expectations that he would know anything about the issue. He has raised the bar for competence, both in the strategic sense about how to appeal to policymakers and also in substantive knowledge. Movements that bank on celebrities may fail because they overrely on personality.

The third lesson: The nature of the issue and the relative vulnerability of targets are perhaps more important than the structure of the advocacy movement itself. Analysts of campaigns often focus on the structure of the network and the amount of resources they possess. The Jubilee 2000 campaign is often cited for its pioneering use of the Internet, its strategic use of celebrity, and its diffuse network structure that facilitated local flexibility. Certainly, the strategic use of the Internet to mobilize supporters has increased in sophistication and scale in the past seven years.[41] However, too little emphasis is paid to the strategic context for advocacy, both the nature of the issues ("How difficult would it be for states to comply?") and the vulnerability of the targets ("Which states and institutions are most and least vulnerable to advocacy?"). For example, in the U.S. context, treaties are almost impossible to get through the Senate with the two-thirds majority required for advice and consent. By contrast, in the United Kingdom and Canada, a strong parliamentary majority means that if the prime minister or the chancellor of the exchequer is on board, advocates do not need to spend a lot of energy on parliament. Activists also have to evaluate how powerful their opponents are. If they are so powerful that their opposition can never be challenged with a rival coalition, activists need to court them, either by seeking to split them or by moderating their demands.

Dangers for the Future

There are two dangers for future development advocacy efforts. *First, do not get tied to any single political party.* There is a risk that the development cause will get too identified with one particular party or political figure. For example, when Republicans controlled both the executive and the legislative branches in the United States, advocates smartly sought to develop relationships with powerful politicians of that party. However, when the Democrats took over Congress in 2006, Democratic lawmakers had the sense that some advocates had been overly fulsome in their praise for President Bush's support for HIV/AIDS funding. Democrats almost cut planned increases in HIV/AIDS funding because it was becoming a partisan issue. By the same token, the commitment to development in the United Kingdom is identified quite strongly with the Labour Party and Gordon Brown in particular. Should he lose in a general election to the Conservative Party, advocates for development might lose influence.

The analogue to this is what has happened to environmental issues and climate change, in particular in the United States. Democrats and Republicans are so polarized that opinion polls show that members of Congress have very different views about the science of climate change based on their politics.[42] It is in the development advocacy community's interests to continually seek a balanced basis of political support rather than allow its cause to be seen as yet another partisan issue.

The second danger: Be careful about overreliance on celebrity interlocutors. Celebrities bring media attention to issues that may otherwise remain in obscurity. That coverage may drive public involvement, fund-raising, and make politicians feel a generalized sense of needing to do something. However, that interest can be fleeting, and politicians without a genuine interest in the issue may then merely engage in "competitive promise making" in an effort to placate advocacy campaigns. Too often, those promises are not matched by actions.[43] When celebrities become the de facto interlocutors between citizens and advocates as well as between the campaign and decisionmakers, the highly stylized messages intended to mobilize the public may also translate into oversimplified messages about what policies are needed.

Instead of a complex message about additional resources and new ways of delivering foreign assistance, all policymakers may hear is "More foreign aid, please." No matter how you dress up that policy (as a moral obligation, as a national security imperative), that prescription on its own is likely to be a nonstarter. Almost no one actually believes that all Africa needs, for example, is more money. Some advocacy groups may feel that this is an unfair carica-ture; most are as concerned about the quality of aid as they are about the quantity. However, too much attention in recent years has been dedicated to quantity, such as whether or not countries are meeting the commitment to spend 0.7 percent of gross national product on foreign assistance.

A New Development Agenda

Development advocates need to think about whether just getting more money for aid and for HIV/AIDS should be their main focus. Donors have embarked upon a multi-billion-dollar open-ended commitment to antiretroviral therapy for HIV/AIDS sufferers. Unless countries both come to prevent new HIV infections and build broader health systems, the experiment could run aground if local capacity remains lacking and if donor money ever runs dry. There is a recognition that project-based development is broken, and donors have not had great success improving governance in weak and failing states. The Millennium Challenge Account from the United States has been an experiment in this direction, but it has not been sufficiently funded, despite strong advocacy by groups like DATA. The U.S. and other governments do not have adequate tools for institution building. The main U.S. development agency, the U.S. Agency for International Development, is underfunded, is perceived in some quarters as ineffective, and increasingly has had its mandate taken away by other institutions.

Advocates need to consider tough questions about the appropriate institu-tions and instruments for future development assistance:

—Should the Global Fund to Fight AIDS, Tuberculosis, and Malaria be a model for other kinds of targeted programs creating a rival set of alternative issue-specific funds?

—What should advocates seek to do about the World Bank?

—How should advocates deal with China as a rising donor to and in-vestor in poor countries?

—What is the future of public sector support for development policy in a world of remittances, philanthropy, and private finance?

—How can foreigners help the development process in weak and failing states?

—Does the United States need a department for international develop-ment, a Cabinet-level development agency?

Although much effort is directed to the G-8 meetings, the 2008 U.S. elec-tions could prove pivotal for the future of global development assistance.

Under George W. Bush, deficit concerns disappeared. Will his successor have such fortune and be able and willing to expand support for global HIV/AIDS efforts and champion new models of development assistance? The 2008 U.S. elections provide advocates an opening to educate candidates about the challenges of development beyond money. Even if the electorate for development issues is small, advocates can, through their skilled use of the media and their "grasstops" contacts, create demand on both sides of the aisle to appear prodevelopment. They should seize that opportunity.

Notes

1. Quoted by Susan Dominus, "Questions for Bono; Relief Pitcher," *New York Times,* October 8, 2000.

2. Quoted by John Wagner, "In Helms, Bono Finds the Ally He's Looking For," *Raleigh News and Observer,* September 21, 2000.

3. Nancy Birdsall and John Williamson, *Delivering on Debt Relief* (Washington: Center for Global Development, 2002), 1.

4. Martin Dent and Bill Peters, *The Crisis of Poverty and Debt in the Third World* (Aldershot, U.K.: Ashgate, 1999).

5. World Bank, *HIPC Initiative: Status of Implementation,* 2006 (http://siteresources. worldbank.org/INTDEBTDEPT/ProgressReports/20894658/032106.pdf [April 2008]).

6. Forty-one countries were initially listed as HIPCs, thirty-four in Africa, four in Latin America, three in Asia, and one in the Middle East. World Bank, *HIPC Map,* undated (http://web.archive.org/web/20030217010431/http://www.worldbank.org/ hipc/about/map/map.html [April 2008]). Eligibility is based on threshold indicators beyond which a country's external debt is deemed "unsustainable": the net present value (NPV) of its debt to export ratio, the NPV debt-to revenue, and the ratios of exports to GDP and revenue to GDP. Debt relief is conditional upon good policymaking, both macroeconomic and poverty reduction.

7. The G-8 consists of the seven largest advanced industrialized countries—Canada, France, Germany, Italy, Japan, the United Kingdom, and the United States—plus Russia, which was invited to participate in the annual gathering in 1997. The original group of seven (G-7) were the major creditors targeted by advocates for debt relief. Though a creditor in its own right, Russia's economic troubles at the time made it a petitioner of aid rather than a provider of relief. Hence, I refer to the G-8 summits and the G-7 creditors.

8. Bill Clinton, *Remarks by the President to Conference on U.S.-Africa Partnership for the 21st Century* (Washington: White House, 1999) (www.state.gov/www/regions/africa/ 990316_clinton.html [April 2008]).

9. The expansion of HIPC in 1999 also lowered the threshold of what were deemed sustainable debt targets including: a debt-to-export ratio of 150 percent, down from 200 to 250 percent; a debt-to-revenue ratio of 250 percent, down from 280 percent; and a lowering of the export-to-GDP and revenue-to-GDP thresholds to 30 percent and 15 percent. World Bank, *Outcome of the 1999 Review,* 1999 (http://siteresources.worldbank.org/ INTDEBTDEPT/PolicyPapers/20252909/1999-Outcome-Review-1.pdf [April 2008]).

10. Thomas Hart, personal communication, January 2001.

11. Looking just at bilateral debts held by the G-7 advanced industrialized countries, in no case did the nominal values of these debts exceed 1 percent of GDP. Early estimates of complying with the Kyoto Protocol suggested recurrent costs of nearly 1 percent of GDP per year.

12. There is a rich literature in political science about the importance of "cultural match." Contact the author for citations.

13. Jamie Drummond, personal communication, January 2001.

14. These data are based on a LexisNexis key word search of "debt relief" in the *Financial Times,* the *New York Times,* the *Washington Post,* and the *Guardian.* Articles were assessed for their relevance.

15. Sebastian Mallaby, "Why So Stingy on Foreign Aid?" *Washington Post,* June 27, 2000.

16. Drummond, personal communication.

17. Bono and Michka Assayas, *Bono: In Conversation with Michka Assayas* (New York: Riverhead Books, 2005), 91.

18. Jonathan Peterson, "The Rock Star, the Pope, and the World's Poor," *Los Angeles Times,* January 7, 2001.

19. Michael Grunwald, "GOP's Bachus Makes Debt Relief His Mission," *Washington Post,* October 9, 1999.

20. Lawrence Summers, personal communication, December 9, 2004.

21. Scott Hatch, personal communication, April 6, 2005.

22. Jamie McCormick, personal communication, February 10, 2005.

23. On the broader mobilization of religious conservatives on international issues, see Allen D. Hertzke, *Freeing God's Children: The Unlikely Alliance for Global Human Rights* (Lanham, Md.: Rowman & Littlefield, 2004).

24. Quoted by Mike McManus, "Jubilee 2000: Debt Relief for the Poor," *Birmingham News,* October 17, 1999.

25. Hart, personal communication.

26. Hatch, personal communication.

27. Mark Lagon, personal communication, June 15, 2005.

28. Dennis Hoover, *What Would Moses Do? Debt Relief in the Jubilee Year,* 2001 (www.trincoll.edu/depts/csrpl/RINVol4No1/jubilee_2000.htm [April 2008]).

29. Summers, personal communication.

30. Sonny Callahan, personal communication, January 27, 2005.

31. Joseph Kahn, "Leaders in Congress Agree to Debt Relief for Poor Nations," *New York Times,* October 18, 2000.

32. Former official of the Japanese Ministry of Foreign Affairs, personal communication, July 22, 2004.

33. Takehiko Nakao, personal communication, August 22, 2004. See also David Halloran Lumsdaine, *Moral Vision in International Politics: The Foreign Aid Regime, 1949–1989* (Princeton University Press, 1993) on reputational concerns in Japanese foreign assistance.

34. Of the G-7 countries, only in the United Kingdom might there be a truly sizable constituency for development. Though major charities like CARE are based in the United States, there are few development advocacy organizations, Oxfam USA and Bread for the

World being the most prominent. Newer groups include Bono's DATA (Debt Aid Trade Africa). Contact the author for comparative data.

35. Bono and Assayas, *Bono*, 89.

36. Summers, personal communication.

37. In 2006, more than 85 percent of Americans and Europeans favored aid to poor democracies but fewer than 50 percent supported aid to poor nondemocracies. German Marshall Fund, *Perspectives on Trade and Poverty* (Washington, 2006) (www.gmfus.org/trade/research/survey.cfm [April 2008]).

38. A 2006 Zogby Poll for InterAction found 87 percent U.S. support for humanitarian relief. Mohammad Akhter, "Results from a Nationwide Poll on International Assistance, InterAction, 2006" (www.interaction.org/library/detail.php?id=4931 [April 2008]). A 2004 poll for the Chicago Council on Foreign Relations found more than 75 percent support for global AIDS funding and women's education. Chicago Council on Foreign Relations, *Global Views 2004* (Chicago, 2004) (www.thechicagocouncil.org/past_pos.php [April 2008]).

39. In June 2005, MoveOn delivered 360,000 petitions on the Downing Street memo; in May 2005, 580,000 signed petitions opposing attempts to rein in the Senate filibuster; and, in December 2006, 400,000 members signed petitions to get out of Iraq. See www.moveon.org/success_stories.html (April 2008). In 2006, MoveOn claimed that its members had made 7 million calls on behalf of the various issues it championed over the year. See http://pol.moveon.org/2006report (April 2008).

40. Tom Hart, personal communication, November 13, 2006.

41. Vinay Bhagat, "Online Advocacy: How the Internet Is Transforming the Way Nonprofits Reach, Motivate, and Retain Supporters," in *Nonprofit Internet Strategies: Best Practices for Marketing, Communications, and Fundraising Success,* ed. T. Hart, J. M. Greenfield, and M. Johnston (New York: John Wiley & Sons 2005), 119–34.

42. A 2007 National Journal poll of congressional insiders found that 95 percent of Democrats thought that climate change had been proven to be human made beyond a reasonable doubt, compared with only 13 percent of Republicans. Richard E. Cohen and Peter Bell, "Congressional Insiders Poll," *National Journal,* 2007 (http://syndication.nationaljournal.com/images/203Insiderspoll_NJlogo.pdf [April 2008]).

43. The G-8 commitment at Gleneagles in 2005 to double aid to poor countries by 2010 is a good example.

6

Nigeria's Fight for Debt Relief: Tracing the Path

Ngozi Okonjo-Iweala

O N JUNE 29, 2005, Nigeria and the Paris Club reached a historic agreement on an $18 billion (or 60 percent) write-off of Nigeria's Paris Club debt. The write-off was implemented from October 2005 to March 2006, bringing to a close Nigeria's long quest for a Paris Club debt agreement. This chapter traces the background, issues, and elements that led to this success, including the implicit and explicit roles played by various parties, such as civil society. What were the ingredients for success, and how can the lessons learned be applied to other countries or other similar campaigns?

The story of Nigeria's quest for debt relief is also, in a sense, the story of a personal journey into the uncertain waters of Paris Club debt negotiation. The reason is that shortly after I was sworn in as Nigeria's finance minister on July 17, 2003, I received a letter from President Olusegun Obasanjo with terms of reference instructing that one of the items I had to deliver during my tenure was Paris Club debt relief for Nigeria. The president had made obtaining Paris Club debt relief both a personal and national priority, and his instructions placed me squarely at the center of this daunting challenge. I knew that meeting the challenge would require drawing on many resources, including the hard work of the excellent economic team that President Obasanjo had assembled and that I led.

Background

Nigeria took its first loan from the Paris Club of creditor countries in 1964 for a sum of $13.1 million. This loan, taken from the Italian government, was for the construction of the Niger dam. From then until 1970, Nigeria borrowed moderately, despite the fact that it experienced a devastating civil war from 1967 to 1970. In 1970, at the end of the war, Nigeria's external debt was less than $1 billion.

The situation changed dramatically during the oil boom years of 1971–81, which were a boon to Nigeria. Despite the high oil revenues, the country's leaders borrowed unsustainably to finance postwar reconstruction and other state projects and infrastructure, perhaps convinced by those hawking loans of the country's strong creditworthiness. By 1985, Nigeria had accumulated an external debt of $19 billion. A great deal of this money was from export credit agencies of Paris Club members and commercial banks for projects ranging from road construction to the development of manufacturing and agriculture, as well as the building of health clinics and water projects. Unfortunately, many of these projects were either not implemented at all (the money disappeared) or were poorly implemented with very poor results, leading to a situation of high external indebtedness with less than commensurate results.[1]

Given the prevailing high interest rates of the 1980s, debt service climbed to $4 billion per annum, or 33 percent of exports of goods and services in 1985, as against the recommended international norm of 25 percent. With the economy growing at a low 1 percent per annum and the oil price crash that began in 1982, Nigeria entered an era when it was unable to service its loans. To ease the situation, the country sought rescheduling of its obligations, and successive Paris Club reschedulings took place in 1986, 1989, 1991, and 2000. However, relief was only temporary and arrears began to mount, including interest and penalties on interest. Nigeria sought substantive relief based on new Paris Club initiatives, such as the Naples terms—designed to provide low-income qualifying countries with up to two-thirds flow or stock relief. However, this was denied. This refusal was in contrast to the agreement reached with the London Club of commercial creditors to consolidate and treat private debt arrears and obligations under the Brady Plan in 1991. Under this plan, Nigeria obtained 60 percent debt relief on 62 percent of its $5.8 billion London Club obligations by executing a buyback at 40 cents on the dollar. The remaining $2.04 billion was collateralized with U.S. zero coupon bonds maturing in 2002.

By the mid-1990s, under the Sani Abacha regime, relationships with the Paris Club hit a low point and Nigeria no longer serviced its Paris Club debt. In 1998, a transition military regime came into power, and an attempt was

Figure 6-1. Paris Club External Debt Outstanding by Creditor Category, as of December 31, 2004

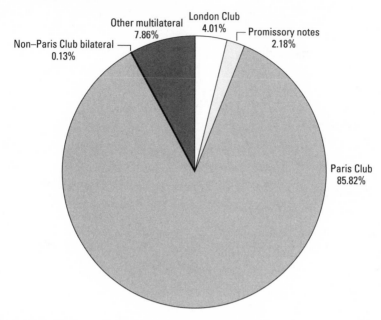

Source: Paris Club data.

made to revive relations with the Paris Club by making a goodwill payment to the club of $1.5 billion. However, it was only in 1999 under the democratically elected regime of President Obasanjo that the debt issue once more took center stage as the president campaigned for debt relief. By December 31, 2004, when external debts were being reconciled for the negotiations, Nigeria's external debt stood at $ 35.994 billion, of which Paris Club debt was 86 percent or $ 30.9 billion. Figure 6-1 shows Paris Club debt outstanding by creditor category prior to debt relief, and figure 6-2 displays the debt stock by creditor.

Total debt service stood at approximately $3 billion a year, made up of about $2.3 billion to the Paris Club, with the balance of $0.7 billion being payments for debt servicing to other multilateral and commercial creditors. In reality, however, only $1 billion in Paris Club debt service was being implemented under a tacit agreement with the club. Had Nigeria undertaken the full Paris Club annual debt service, it would have left the federal

Figure 6-2. Paris Club Debt Stock by Creditor, as of December 31, 2004

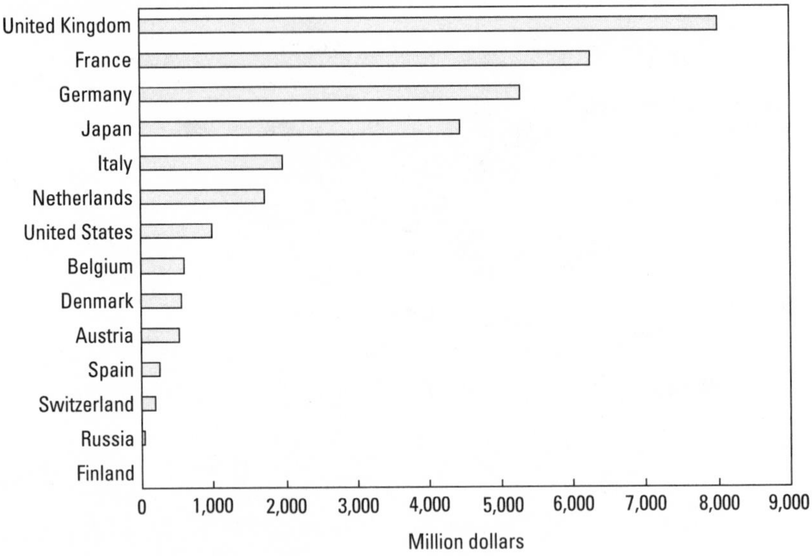

Source: Paris Club data.

government with little or no budget for capital expenditures, so some accommodation was reached with the club on a temporary basis. This arrangement was nevertheless like a band aid as payment arrears continued to accumulate. It was imperative that a fundamental and sustainable solution be found to Nigeria's debt problem. To do this, we had to craft a strategy—one that would deliver on the Paris Club core criteria for debt relief while at the same time mobilizing key constituencies and individuals in Paris Club creditor countries to support Nigeria's cause. Let me now turn first to the subject of the core criteria.

Navigating Paris Club Debt Relief: Fundamental Elements

For Nigeria to be considered for Paris Club debt relief, it had to meet some fundamental criteria of the club, most of which it was not well positioned to meet in 2003. At the time, the country was experiencing considerable macroeconomic instability and weak growth in the run-up to 2003, as evidenced in the economic indicators given in table 6-1.

Paris Club debt relief of the sort Nigeria desired—that is, involving a substantial debt write-off—would require a number of preconditions:

Table 6-1. Nigeria's Economic Indicators, 1992–2002
(annual percentage change)

Indicator	1992	1993	1994	1995	1996	1997	1998	1999	2000	2001	2002
Total gross domestic product	2.43	0.58	–1.61	2.29	6.2	2.77	0.23	1.49	5.64	3.31	1.42
Oil gross domestic product	2.27	1.24	0.12	2.17	4.48	1.47	–5.39	–4.13	11.54	1.42	–11.63
Non-oil gross domestic product	2.52	0.21	–2.58	2.35	7.17	3.51	3.4	4.39	2.84	4.28	7.96
Consumer Price Index (year-on-year inflation)	48.8	61.3	76.8	51.6	14.3	10.2	11.9	0.2	14.5	16.5	12.2

Source: Federal Government of Nigeria, unpublished data.

—implementation of economic reforms under a formal IMF program;

—eligibility of the country for International Development Association (IDA)–only borrowing status at the World Bank—that is borrowing from the soft loan arm of the Bank reserved for the poorer countries;

—regularization of debt service or establishment of a good debt service record; and

—meeting the threshold of the International Monetary Fund–World Bank debt sustainability analysis (DSA) that would indicate that the country's debt was not sustainable in the long term and could ultimately severely undermine growth.

For each of the criteria above, Nigeria faced a challenge for differing reasons, as outlined below, and each of the challenges had to be met with a solution.

Implementation of a Formal IMF-Supervised Economic Reform Program

The implementation of a formal IMF-supervised economic reform program was a major hurdle. During the structural adjustment years of the mid-1980s to early 1990s, Nigerians had developed strong negative feelings about IMF- and World Bank–led adjustment programs and had, in fact, in what was tantamount to an informal national referendum, indicated that they wanted no truck with IMF programs. Even if a program were to exist, they did not want to draw on IMF resources.

How, then, could the president or the new economic team convince Nigerians to get into a formal IMF economic reform program? We decided that we could not, especially because there was already a suspicion that people like myself who came from these institutions would try to force the country into such a program. Instead, what we came up with was the idea of crafting our

Table 6-2. Nigeria's Economic Indicators, 2002–06
(annual percentage change)

Indicator	2002	2003	2004	2005	2006
Real GDP (at 1990 factor cost)	1.42	10.9	6.1	6.2	5.7
Oil GDP	−11.63	26.5	3.5	2.6	−4.5
Non-oil GDP	7.96	4.4	7.4	8.2	8.9
Inflation rate (year-on-year)	12.2	21.80	10.00	11.60	8.5
External reserves (billion dollars)	7.7	7.5	17.0	28.3	43.8

Source: Federal Government of Nigeria, unpublished data.

own economic reform program as strong or stronger than what the IMF would have put in place and implementing this, and then inviting the IMF to monitor our progress in the hope and expectation that such an approach would be acceptable to the Paris Club. Thus, we developed the National Economic Empowerment and Development Program (NEEDS), which sought to stabilize the macroeconomy, fight corruption, and bring transparency to government business, strengthen fiscal policy, and improve the management of the budget, privatize inefficient state assets and liberalize key sectors, and implement public service reform as well as financial sector restructuring. The program was comprehensive and touched on all the key areas where Nigeria had serious economic problems. The program was result oriented with a matrix developed that set targets and results, including responsibilities and accountabilities for such results.

For the first time, we had a reform program that was owned and crafted by Nigerians for themselves and the IMF was formally invited to monitor its implementation, which it accepted. This approach was uncharted territory for the IMF, but there was no reason why it should not accept to work with a country determined to do the right thing. The IMF and World Bank teams responsible for Nigeria at the time were good listeners, smart, confident, and excellent partners, and they recommended to their management that they form a partnership with us in the way requested. Menachem Katz, IMF mission leader for Nigeria, was instrumental in persuading senior managers at the IMF, such as Anne Krueger, the first deputy managing director to support Nigeria's proposed new approach to working with the IMF. We were lucky that they were willing to listen and support us. Despite the opposition of vested interests, Nigerians by and large accepted the reform program and we successfully implemented it for more than fifteen months before approaching the Group of Eight (G-8) and the Paris Club to request consideration for debt relief (table 6-2).

Ultimately, the Paris Club insisted that this approach was too informal and could set "dangerous" precedents for other countries wishing to negotiate with it in the future. It insisted that some way be found to capture Nigeria's program under a more formal IMF instrument. By sheer coincidence, at the fall and spring 2004–5 meetings of the IMF and World Bank, an ongoing debate centered on creating a new IMF instrument for countries that wanted IMF oversight of their programs but did not need access to IMF resources. Nigeria's situation fit this bill exactly, and we lobbied IMF senior management, developing country finance ministers of the Group of Twenty-Four, and developed country treasuries to support the creation of the new instrument with Nigeria as the first pilot country to test it. The creation of the instrument ultimately got support. It was called the Policy Support Instrument (PSI), and Nigeria became the first country whose homegrown program was encapsulated in a PSI and taken to the IMF Board for approval in September 2005, thus paving the way for final Paris Club negotiations and implementation of the debt relief agreements.

Eligibility for IDA-Only Status at the World Bank

At the 2004 World Economic Forum in Davos, Nancy Birdsall, president of the Center for Global Development (CGD)—a Washington-based think tank and a former colleague of mine at the World Bank—asked me why Nigeria was not eligible for the Heavily Indebted Poor Countries (HIPC) initiative and why Nigeria was not classified as a country eligible to borrow only from the soft loan arm of the Bank (IDA), given that it had all the income characteristics and human development indicators of IDA-only countries. Nigeria was classified by the World Bank as being eligible to borrow both from IDA and the International Bank for Reconstruction and Development (IBRD)—the regular window of the Bank, meaning that it was considered more creditworthy than these IDA-only countries. This automatically made it difficult, if not impossible, for the Paris Club to consider Nigeria for any substantial debt relief that initiatives, such as the Naples terms, accorded highly indebted low-income countries. Yet, Nigeria had, for twelve years, not been allowed by the Bank to access any IBRD lending in practice. So a contradictory situation emerged in which Nigeria, because of its access to oil revenues, was classified as entitled to access nonconcessional IBRD borrowing in theory, but in practice, because of its actual low creditworthiness situation, had been restricted from any IBRD borrowing for more than a decade. Nancy and I discussed the lack of fairness of this situation and the accompanying lack of a level playing field for all countries.

As a result, CGD undertook to do a policy paper on the issue to be disseminated to the World Bank and other audiences likely to have some influence on the Paris Club process. At the same time, I formally approached the

Bank to correct this anomaly and make Nigeria IDA only. The World Bank president, James Wolfensohn, and managing director, Shengman Zhang, were sympathetic, but we had to overcome the objections of those in the Bank's finance complex who felt Nigeria was undeserving, and in any event, might request a large slice of IDA funds if made IDA only. This would, in their thinking, undercut the access of other smaller countries to IDA. I promised that if made IDA only, Nigeria would not request access to a larger share of IDA resources than what was already programmed. We were only interested in this for the purposes of meeting the Paris Club requirement of IDA-only status for Naples terms or other deep discount debt relief. With the strong support of the Bank's Nigeria country director, Hafez Ghanem, and his team, a case was made and approved within the Bank for IDA-only status for Nigeria based on improved economic performance, a strong fight against corruption, and poor social indicators.

Regularizing Debt Service

Beginning in the mid-1980s, Nigeria's ability to service its Paris Club debt deteriorated. When the debt service payment due in 1985 was $4 billion, Nigeria was only able to pay $1.5 billion. The four Paris Club reschedulings did not solve the problem as the country quickly fell behind again in the context of the low commodity price of its main export—oil—and its need for basic expenditures during this period. Nigeria did faithfully service its remaining London Club debt as well as its multilateral obligations given the good treatment it had received at the hands of London Club creditors and the seniority of multilateral debt service. Its Paris Club debt service arrears, penalties, and interest accumulated, giving Nigeria a poor track record with the club. Compounding this was the lack of a real dialogue between the parties in the 1990s.

Regular dialogue was restored starting in 2000, when I was first invited by President Obasanjo to help sort out Nigeria's tangled debt situation, and I created the Debt Management Office (DMO), which cleared up the debt. This provided the basis for an informal agreement with the club to pay about $1 billion of the $2.3 billion that was due annually at that time. The service of Paris Club debt fell mainly on Nigeria's federal government budget ($13 billion in 2004), and the full debt service payment of $2.3 billion for the Paris Club plus another $0.7 billion for the London Club and multilaterals ($3 billion in all) would have amounted to about five times the Nigerian education budget, and over ten times the federal health budget. Politically, this was extremely difficult to defend, hence the need to negotiate for a realistic $1 billion of annual debt service for the Paris Club. The trick was then to

Table 6-3. Debt Sustainability Indicators for Nigeria

Indicator	World Bank-IMF debt sustainability framework benchmark	2004 Nigeria, actual	2015 projected baseline	2015 projected (with oil price shock)[a]
Net present value (NPV) of debt as percent of GDP	30	48.8	21.9	70
NPV of debt as percent of exports	100	90.4	46.1	211
NPV of debt as percent of revenue, excluding grants	200	114.5	58.9	N.A.
Debt service as percent of exports	15	7.5	3.9	N.A.
Debt service as percent of revenue	20	12.9	6.4	N.A.

Sources: IMF and Word Bank (2004) and World Bank (2005).

a. Assumes a permanent reduction in oil prices of $16 per barrel equivalent to 2 standard deviations of Brent oil prices for the period 1976–2004.

N.A. = not available.

maintain this informal agreement to establish good faith and create a reasonable track record. With one breach in the 2002 election year, Nigeria was able to keep to this informal, unwritten agreement, thereby restoring a level of regularization to its debt service record.

Dealing with Debt Sustainability Analysis and Thresholds

A crucial part of the Paris Club's decisionmaking process as to whether to grant countries debt relief and the measure of relief to be granted is based on IMF and World Bank analyses that establish whether a country's debt is sustainable. Debt sustainability analyses assess whether the country can comfortably service its Paris Club debt given its level and pattern of growth, export levels and potential (which measures ability to earn foreign exchange), revenue and expenditure levels, and projections into the future of all these. The two institutions establish certain debt ratios based on these DSAs that serve as benchmarks against which a country's debt sustainability situation can be measured and projected into the future. Examples are the ratio of debt to gross domestic product, the ratio of debt service to exports, and the ratio of debt service to revenues. Table 6-3 provides the indicative norms for these ratios.

If a country falls within these norms, then it can service its debts and the debt burden is deemed to be sustainable. Outside these benchmarks, the degree of unsustainability is examined for decisions as to whether the country's debt should just be rescheduled to give it breathing room until its finances are more robust and it can resume regular debt service or a deeper type of debt relief or write-off should be considered. Over time, developing countries have protested that these ratios fail to take into account many factors that capture their real situations. For example, most developing countries often have domestic debt that has to be serviced as well, and the typical DSA does not take this into account, often making ratios look more optimistic than should be the case. There have been attempts by the World Bank and the IMF to refine their methodologies based on these criticisms, and the DSA has improved, but issues still remain, as we argued in Nigeria's case.

Nigeria was seeking debt relief at the end of 2004, when the prices of its main export commodity oil were increasing. Oil prices rose from an average $28.9 per barrel in 2003 to an average $37.8 in 2004 and $53.4 in 2005. Many analysts projected continued increases in oil prices, and Paris Club members were in no mood to entertain debt relief for a so-called oil-rich country whose commodity price was robust. The standard DSA showed that Nigeria's debt could be sustainable given such prices. But we knew that for Nigeria the standard analysis could not capture the country's true situation and we had to get these elements on the table. There was the issue of the extreme volatility of oil prices, which had bedeviled the country's debt service and indeed its development for so long. Just as the price of oil could keep rising, it could also fall dramatically, as was the situation in the mid-1980s when it fell to about $14 per barrel. If this happened, Nigeria's situation could quickly become unsustainable. Any DSA for Nigeria would have to factor in a downside as well as an upside. In addition, Nigeria had a substantial domestic debt burden of about $10 billion with annual debt service at $1.4 billion at the time, and it had contingent pension and other liabilities that also needed to be taken·into account.

Most important, however, was the issue of how Nigeria could meet the development targets set by the international community as crucial for poverty reduction and improved human development—the Millennium Development Goals (MDGs)—while still sustainably servicing its Paris Club debt. Nigeria, like most African countries, was off target for meeting the MDGs and would need substantial investments in education, health, and basic infrastructure such as water, rural roads, and electricity to make substantial leaps toward meeting them by 2015. The push by the international community to get developing countries to work toward meeting the MDGs, on the one hand, while at the same time insisting on debt service, on the other, seemed contradictory and hypocritical. On a given day, we would meet with people from the aid departments of our creditor countries of the Paris Club and they would speak about the need to invest effectively to meet the MDGs. Yet, on the same day, people from the Treasuries of these countries would also demand that we meet the debt payments. It was clear that the two sides were not talking to each other or they would have realized that we would not be able to do both.

We decided that this crucial factor of investment for the MDGs had somehow to be factored into the thinking on the Debt Sustainability Analysis. This very notion of a DSA with MDGs factored in was scary to Treasuries of Nigeria's creditor countries, and we were warned that this approach would not be accepted by the Paris Club because it could be precedent setting for other countries. We nevertheless went ahead and asked the World Bank to work with us to do an analysis of what Nigeria's DSA would look like if needed investments for the MDGs were factored in. Our reasoning was simple. Nigeria was one of the lowest aid recipients in the developing world, at $2 per capita per year, compared with $28 per capita for Sub-Saharan Africa. In fact, with Nigeria's level of annual debt service of $1.7 billion, it was sending out more money to the developed world than it received, with a net transfer per capita per year of $11. If Nigeria was to make MDG investments, it would have to come from its own resources, and it would simply not be able to do so if it continued with the high Paris Club debt service. Alternatively, Nigeria would have to borrow afresh to invest, which would not be a sustainable situation.

The World Bank study asked the question "Can Nigeria meet the Millennium Development Goals by 2015 . . . while simultaneously lowering indebtedness?" Using the Bank-Fund Low Income Countries DSA template, which showed under standard assumptions that Nigeria would have no external or fiscal sustainability problem, the study showed that if oil price volatility were introduced by dropping the average oil price by $8 (equivalent to a decline of one standard deviation of Brent oil prices over the period 1976–2004), Nigeria's external and fiscal sustainability would immediately derail. Next, the study tackled the issue of increased MDGs spending while maintaining debt service under an optimistic high growth, high oil price and good policies scenario. The findings showed that Nigeria would encounter a sizable insolvency problem, with a fiscal gap emerging by 2012 and growing fast thereafter. The net present value (NPV) of this gap would amount to $50 billion, implying that even if all of Nigeria's Paris and non–Paris Club debt of $36 billion at the end of 2004 were to be written off, Nigeria would still face a fiscal NPV gap of $14 billion. The results further showed that under less optimistic scenarios of falling oil prices, the fiscal gap would appear much earlier in 2008 and the gap would climb much higher than $50 billion.[2]

Despite the resistance, the study found its way to both members of the G-8 and the Paris Club. We were able to use it to demonstrate that Nigeria would

need Paris Club debt relief if it were expected to make any appreciable
progress toward meeting the MDGs.

Additional Enabling Factors to Debt Relief

Finding solutions to the formal Paris Club requirements was a necessary but
not sufficient condition for debt relief. Other factors contributed, such as the
role played by civil society, academics, and think tanks in the debt relief and
poverty reduction debate, as well as the lobbying of Paris Club officials of
various levels. In addition, the Nigerian Legislature played an important role,
while other personal contacts in major Paris Club country treasuries were
also often helpful.

The Role of Civil Society, Academics, and Think Tanks

Civil society played an important role in Nigeria's debt relief in both direct
and indirect ways. The most powerful role, in my opinion, was indirect as
they prepared the political ground for greater receptivity to Nigeria's request
for relief. The Jubilee 2000 debt relief movement had been an important factor in softening the ground. The movement helped to bring about the HIPC
initiative that led to the cancellation of poor countries' bilateral and eventu-
ally multilateral debt to the tune of $41.9 billion (NPV values) to date for
thirty countries—most of them in Sub-Saharan Africa. Nigeria had all the
characteristics of a HIPC country and was in fact initially listed as one and
then removed. Jeffrey Sachs had argued in 2003, "Nigeria needs debt cancellation. Its status is comparable to the rest of the HIPC countries and it was
once on the list and deserves to be on the list now." Successful debt relief for
the HIPCs was in some sense helpful to Nigeria's case.

The interlinked Make Poverty History campaign was similarly helpful in
getting politicians' attention focused on the issues hindering developing
countries, from making progress on poverty reduction to tackling unsustainable debt burdens and also addressing the inequity and injustice of the global
equation in this regard. Both high-profile campaigners such as Bono and Bob
Geldof, and the rank and file of Jubilee 2000 and Make Poverty History
campaigners, exerted pressure that made a difference.

On the direct side of the issue, we realized sometime at the end of 2004 in
the middle of our campaign that getting more direct support and a partnership with both domestic and international civil society would be helpful to
Nigeria's quest. We found a perfect partner externally in the person of the
former Jubilee 2000 lead campaigner, Ann Pettifor. She worked with us to

make the Nigerian story compelling for the international nongovernmental organization (NGO) community so they could get beyond Nigeria's unfavorable image abroad and understand the real issues behind the country's quest for debt relief. A website was developed with facts and figures. Pettifor truly believed that Nigeria was often misunderstood and was a really deserving country. Her efforts were fruitful in engaging NGOs in Europe and the United Kingdom in bringing Nigeria to the notice of their politicians. Pettifor also helped link Nigerian NGOs interested in the debt relief campaign to their counterparts abroad. The media in Nigeria and abroad were also called upon to understand the story so that they could report as accurately as possible with the correct facts and figures.

It is important to mention that a whole array of academics, staff members of think tanks, and individual practitioners believed in Nigeria's quest for debt relief and contributed in many ways—providing forums for the economic team to address important audiences or individuals and undertaking supportive analysis. One think tank stands out in having made a difference. The Center for Global Development's Nancy Birdsall and Todd Moss took an early interest in Nigeria's case and contributed to the IDA analysis referred to above. They also proposed the key idea that helped to break the impasse on our debt relief quest when it arose; Birdsall and Moss suggested that Nigeria include a buyback option of a portion of the debt as part of the debt relief package so that creditor countries would be assuaged by a sweetener. The CGD was not only instrumental in terms of its intellectual contribution to finding solutions that helped make debt relief happen but also played an important advocacy role in treasury and development circles where it mattered. Another influential publication that helped create an atmosphere conducive to debt relief was U.K. prime minister Tony Blair's Commission for Africa report, which made a compelling case for debt relief and the need to provide additional financing for Sub-Saharan African countries. The whole push by the United Kingdom, 2005 chair of the G-8, for the year of Africa before the Gleneagles summit was very helpful. The important part played by civil society in Nigeria's successful quest for debt relief underscores how useful it can sometimes be to develop constructive partnerships between governments and civil society organizations to forge a path on difficult issues.

Other Factors

Debt is at once an economic but also a supremely political issue, and so is debt relief. In the past, creditor countries of the Paris Club have granted debt relief because it was politically useful, even though the countries still had to meet Paris Club technical criteria. Poland was granted debt relief following the unraveling of the former Soviet Union because it was important to support a country trying to democratize and establish a market-based economy. Yugoslavia, Côte d'Ivoire, and Egypt all at some stage received debt relief because of strong political will to support them. There is always, therefore, a political element to the debt relief quest.

Nigeria did a lot of lobbying supported by hard facts to make the political case for debt relief in addition to the economic one. President Obasanjo lobbied presidents of the G-8 and of other creditor countries. He had made debt relief a cardinal measure of his administration's success, so the lobbying went on for six years during his tenure until the relief was granted. The president's central argument was that Nigeria was now a young democracy emerging after years of authoritarian military rule. Africa's largest democracy needed nurturing and support, and debt relief would be one way of granting the country a "democracy dividend." I lobbied at the level of the finance ministers while trying to make sure that the technical work they would ultimately look at and rely on for decisions was done to a high standard to help justify the case for debt relief. A couple of anecdotes illustrate how agile one had to be to get the right kind of attention for Nigeria's campaign.

One anecdote involves an official visit to the White House in early 2005, to which I accompanied President Obasanjo. A key objective was to gain President George W. Bush's support for debt relief so that a message could in turn go to the U.S. Treasury to be more supportive of our request. Whereas we had garnered sympathy from the State Department, the National Security Agency, and other parts of the U.S. government, we were having a bit of a difficult time still with Treasury, just as we were with other treasury departments of Paris Club members.

During the meeting, at which Secretary of State Colin Powell, National Security Adviser Condoleezza Rice, Jendayi Frazier, Cindy Corville, and others were present, President Obasanjo explained our desire for debt relief and presented the tremendous change Nigeria was undergoing in implementing difficult economic reforms. President Bush responded jokingly that Nigeria was an oil-rich country and that oil prices were high. Nigeria should be lending money to the United States, not asking for debt relief. It seemed that our request was about to be brushed aside. I was terrified that we were about to miss a unique opportunity, and I totally broke protocol by jumping in and asking my president's permission to explain further to President Bush. He gave his permission, and I knew I had a few seconds only to make my points.

I made two points: (1) Though oil prices were high, Nigeria was still a poor, large country with a population of 140 million. As such, the net amount earned, for example in 2004 of $25 billion, amounted only to 50 cents per Nigerian per day. (2) Nigeria's economy would need to depend largely on private sector investment for growth. Yet such investment would be severely limited if we did not invest in infrastructure. We would need upward of $7 billion a year for the next five years for this purpose. That is why we would need debt relief to free up resources for this. These two points seemed to catch President Bush's attention and interest, and he turned around and said we should send him a letter outlining the points I had just made. At that point, I knew we had made some kind of breakthrough and that we would get his support.

As I made the round of Group of Seven finance ministers to argue the case for debt relief, I noted that there was one minister I had not managed to see. It was the then Italian finance minister, Domenico Siniscalco. Each time I tried, I was told he was too busy to receive me. Finally, at the Davos World Economic Forum in 2005, I heard he was participating and was in fact in a session close to where I was. I resolved to waylay him in the corridor and make my case. As he exited from his session surrounded by aides, I darted in between them, grabbed his jacket, and introduced myself and my mission. He promptly agreed to a meeting, and over tea I was able to brief him on the Nigerian situation and get his support.

Another anecdote concerns my first meeting with then–U.K. chancellor of the exchequer Gordon Brown in Dubai at the World Bank–IMF annual meetings in 2003. I was given just five minutes by his staff. I decided I would not do the expected thing just yet—that is, ask his support for Nigeria's quest for debt relief. I was sure that this would make his eyes glaze over. Instead I used the five minutes to brief him on Nigeria's ambitious economic reform program and on progress, noting that only if we implemented this success-fully for a year would I ask for his support. This approach, I believe, helped spark his interest in supporting Nigeria. Overall, my strategy for persuasion focused on our important economic reforms rather than pleading for debt relief. This strategy worked.

One very important factor that helped our case was the presence of people who knew me and my track record in key positions in treasuries and develop-ment ministries in the G-8 and other creditor capitals. For instance, at the U.K. Treasury, a former colleague of mine at the World Bank, former chief economist Nicholas Stern, had joined the Treasury as one of Gordon Brown's senior officials; in Germany, my former boss, Caio Koch-Weser, was the deputy finance minister; in Japan, another former colleague, Kiyoshi Kodera, was senior deputy director general at the Ministry of Finance; and at the Paris Club secretariat, another former colleague, Emmanuel Moulin, was secretary-general—to name but a few. This situation brought an unprecedented measure of trust that if I said we would deliver on our commitments we would and it helped smooth our path to debt relief.

Finally, the members of the Nigerian legislature were also an important factor through their work to convince members of the legislatures of several of our creditor countries that Nigeria meant business about its reform program and that they would support it by passing appropriate legislation as needed.

The Process

Nigeria had resolved to ask for debt relief under Evian terms. This was the customized case-by-case approach to debt relief agreed to by the G-8 heads of state at Evian, France, at the 2004 G-8 summit. It seemed the best approach for a country that did not fit into the ongoing large-scale debt cancellation initiatives such as the HIPC initiative. Following Evian, our strategy for obtaining debt relief was to ensure that Nigeria fulfilled all or most of the formal requirements for debt relief and set a good track record before making a real push for debt cancellation.

We Nigerians also worked the other enabling factors as we were implementing our reform program. There was no need, I thought, to be sent back repeatedly because one requirement or the other had not been properly implemented. The first task was to implement our economic reform program successfully for a period of time, similar to what the IMF would have demanded if it had been running the program. The IMF typically has a standby program for twelve to eighteen months, and we thus focused on reform implementation with clear measurable results for at least fifteen months before beginning the campaign for debt relief. During this period, the IMF undertook three successful reviews of our program.

On the basis of these assessments, we Nigerians were felt to have a case for approaching the Paris Club. Yet, previously, we had received helpful advice—based on past lessons learned—that it may be best to have a G-8 creditor that would be Nigeria's sponsor during internal creditor debt relief discussions. This creditor could help, first, to convince fellow G-8 members of our case and then further help push it at the Paris Club. Like other developing countries that had gone through this, we chose our largest creditor and ally with strong historical ties to whom we owed $8 billion: the United Kingdom. Prime Minister Blair, Chancellor (now prime minister) Brown, and Secretary for International Development Hillary Benn gave their support. Chancellor Brown, backed up by a treasury and Department for International Development team, presented Nigeria's case to the G-8 finance ministers at various meetings; but it was in the May 29, 2005, meeting before the Gleneagles G-8 summit on June 30 that he was able to convince his colleagues to consider a debt relief package for Nigeria composed of 60 percent debt cancellation and including a buyback component. Chancellor Brown negotiated far into the night on this occasion, calling back from time to time to check in with me, and I in turn checked in with President Obasanjo on the acceptability of the G-8 creditors' position. From an opening offer of less than 50 percent debt relief from creditors and an opening demand for 75 percent debt relief from Nigeria, he was able to convince the G-8 to move to 60 percent.

Once this was agreed to, work began to convince the non–G-8 members of the Paris Club to accept the deal that had been worked out. This was not easy. There was resentment that we had gone first to a subset of creditors while ignoring others. Feelings had to be assuaged, and we made visits at both ministerial and even presidential levels in a couple of cases to all the non–G-8 creditor countries to convince them of the merits of the case. We also had to work hard with the Paris Club secretariat.

Late in 2004, the then-president of the Paris Club, Jean-Pierre Jouyet, had agreed to a rare meeting for me and my team from Nigeria's Debt Management Office with club representatives to present Nigeria's case for reduced debt service and eventual debt relief. At the presentation, I made a case based on the reforms, our human development indicators, and our need to invest to reach the MDGs. The case was compelling and was key to convincing Paris Club members that Nigeria had a case. This made it easier for us to approach non–G-8 members later when it was needed. The deadline we in Nigeria had set was that we should have some indication or agreement from the Paris Club before the heads of state's Gleneagles summit in early July 2005. Tension continued as we tried to get a Paris Club agreement.

Finally, on June 29, 2005, at its last meeting before the Gleneagles summit, the Paris Club announced its agreement in principle to grant Nigeria debt relief. Underlying the general Paris Club statement was an agreement to negotiate a debt relief package on Nigeria's $30 billion debt whose essential elements would consist of (1) payment of $6 billion of arrears owed—a standard Paris Club requirement; (2) Naples terms treatment on the remaining $24 billion of debt, that is, a two-thirds write-off on this portion; and (3) a discounted (at 25 percent) buyback on the remaining $8 billion after reduction under Naples terms. This would yield another $2 billion of debt relief for a total debt relief package of 60 percent, or $18 billion.

Finalization of the debt relief package would be contingent on Nigeria getting its reform program formally approved as a PSI at the IMF board. Nigeria's PSI—again, the first ever test of this instrument—was approved by the IMF Board in October 2005. Negotiations between Nigeria and the Paris Club took place immediately thereafter. At these negotiations, agreement was reached on all elements of the package, including the fine print, and later in the month Nigeria initialed an agreement with the Paris Club. Debt relief was implemented in three stages between October 2005 and March 2006, when Nigeria finally exited the Paris Club.

The country's external debt burden fell from $35 billion to approximately $5 billion. Nigeria's debt relief package was the second largest ever for any country in the Paris Club's fifty-year history, and Nigeria was the first low-income country to be allowed to execute a discounted buyback on a portion of its debt.

Conclusion

Nigeria's journey to Paris Club debt relief is a remarkable one in which many actors and many factors played important roles. The debt relief package finally obtained was not without controversy, because some civil society groups and some members of the Nigerian public felt that the country should not have paid anything at all to the Paris Club members and should have had a 100 percent write-off. For practical purposes, this was an approach that Paris Club members were unwilling to entertain, and in the end the majority of Nigerians accepted the package that was obtained as good for the country under the prevailing circumstances. Civil society organizations, both domestic and foreign, were essential partners in this journey, and they worked both directly and indirectly to facilitate debt relief. The country approached its quest for relief strategically, flexibly, and pragmatically, using a combination of tested and new instruments. At the core of its strategy was its ability to deliver measurable successes on its reform program and couple this with effective technical and political footwork.

Debt relief opened hitherto closed doors for Nigeria on the investment front. The country was able to obtain its first-ever sovereign credit rating from Fitch and Standard & Poor's. Both agencies assigned Nigeria a BB– rating, with a stable outlook. This has facilitated greater foreign direct investment flows into the country; flows into the non-oil sector have increased from about $2 billion before debt relief to just under $4 billion. The beneficial effects of debt relief on the economy have proved sustainable. Debt relief for Nigeria can be seen as one of the most striking and sustained achievements of a remarkable three-year reform effort that turned around the Nigerian economy. For me personally, it was the culmination of three years of extremely hard work that was technically, intellectually, and oftentimes emotionally exhilarating.

Notes

1. See Ngozi Okonjo-Iweala, Charles Soludo, and Mansur Muhtar, *The Debt Trap in Nigeria: Towards a Sustainable Debt Strategy* (Trenton: Africa World Press, 2003).

2. World Bank, "Nigeria's Opportunity of a Generation: Meeting the MDGs, Reducing Indebtedness," report prepared for Africa Region, 2005.

7

Philanthropy and Enterprise: Harnessing the Power of Business and Social Entrepreneurship for Development

J. Gregory Dees

> I have never known much good done by those who affected to trade for the public good. It is an affection, indeed, not very common among merchants, and very few words need be employed in dissuading them from it.
>
> —Adam Smith,
> *An Inquiry into the Nature and Causes of the Wealth of Nations* (1776)

MORE THAN TWO hundred years after Adam Smith penned these words, his wisdom on this matter is being challenged by social entrepreneurs and enterprising philanthropists who are deliberately using business ventures to serve the public good. George Soros candidly describes his own change of heart on this matter: "Where I have modified my stance is with regard to social entrepreneurship. I used to be negative toward it because of my innate aversion to mixing business with philanthropy. Experience has taught me that I was wrong. As a philanthropist, I saw a number of successful social enterprises, and I became engaged in some of them."[1]

The idea of using business in strategic ways to promote social improvements is not new. Many philanthropists have made grants and program-related investments to business enterprises that serve their philanthropic missions, including investments in organizations that take the legal form of a for-profit venture. Without this philanthropic support, microfinance, for instance, would not have grown nearly as quickly and would not be reaching the 100 million or so that it is serving today.

What is new is the openness and enthusiasm with which market-oriented approaches are being embraced as an integral element in creating lasting social change. Established philanthropists are opening to this idea, and new philanthropic organizations are being designed to embrace it. With founding support from the Cisco Systems Foundation, the Rockefeller Foundation, the Kellogg Foundation, and many other foundations and individual philanthropists, the Acumen Fund was established in 2001 to invest in enterprises that deliver "affordable, critical goods and services—like health, water and housing—through innovative market-oriented approaches." The goal was to use enterprise as a tool for solving global poverty. In 2004, Pierre Omidyar, the founder of eBay, and his wife Pam decided to restructure their philanthropic activities, dramatically replacing the Omidyar Foundation with the Omidyar Network, a limited liability company that could make investments in for-profits as well as nonprofits.[2] In 2006, when the founders of Google, a wildly successful Internet search and media company, took steps to formalize their company's "philanthropic" arm, they announced that it would be structured as a for-profit organization, "allowing it to fund start-up companies, form partnerships with venture capitalists and even lobby Congress."[3] These are just a few of the most visible recent examples of enterprising philanthropy.

This trend is a reflection of a wider social entrepreneurship movement that emerged in the final decades of the twentieth century and has been accelerating into the twenty-first.[4] This movement challenges old sector boundaries and encourages innovative approaches, using the tools from any sector that are most likely to be effective.[5] The argument for including enterprising business ventures as part of the tool kit can be boiled down to three premises:

—Business ventures and markets play an important role in creating lasting improvements in social conditions.

—Independent entrepreneurs are particularly well positioned to discover and craft innovative approaches for addressing social problems.

—Philanthropists have an essential role to play in stimulating, supporting, shaping, and even subsidizing beneficial entrepreneurial business activities.

In this chapter, I first outline the logic behind each of these premises, particularly in the context of poverty reduction.[6] I then explore the new challenges facing philanthropists who use enterprise as a tool for achieving their social objectives, and I close with observations about how to move forward with this development strategy.

Business, Markets, and Sustainable Social Change

Social and economic progress are inextricably intertwined. Charity and aid can improve the quality of life and the life chances of the poor by subsidizing interventions to improve education, provide health care, increase access to clean water, reduce conflict, and distribute food. But none of these interventions will alleviate poverty in a sustained way without increased economic participation and empowerment for the poor.[7] Only a vibrant and open local economy will be able to sustain improvements purchased with aid and charity. Charitable relief and aid may be necessary to relieve the symptoms of severe poverty long enough to pursue more sustainable strategies. But without local economic development that engages the poor, charitable interventions cannot provide lasting solutions. They may even be harmful. Muhammad Yunus, the founder of Grameen Bank, pioneer in microfinance, and 2006 Nobel laureate, is particularly critical: "When we want to help the poor, we usually offer them charity. Most often we use charity to avoid recognizing the problem and finding a solution for it. . . . Charity is no solution to poverty. Charity only perpetuates poverty by taking the initiative away from the poor. Charity allows us to live our lives without worrying about those of the poor. It appeases our consciences."[8]

One need not fully embrace Yunus's assessment of charity to recognize the importance of increased economic participation by the poor. Other interventions, such as improvements in schools or creation of health clinics, can increase the capacity of the poor for economic engagement; but alone, they cannot guarantee that engagement. Increased economic opportunities do not automatically follow from educational or health care interventions. Educated and healthy people without access to affordable capital, appropriate technology, open markets, suitable jobs, and specific business know-how will have a hard time putting their improved capacity to use productively.

Martin Fisher, a social entrepreneur whose organization KickStart sells irrigation pumps in Kenya and Tanzania, frames the argument:

> Within less than a generation, poor families in Africa have been thrown from essentially a subsistence lifestyle into a primarily cash-based economy. Ability to earn income is suddenly a paramount skill. Yet approaches to development continue to be based on the assumption that the primary need of people in poor places is something other than a way to make money—better healthcare, education, water, housing, and so forth. This is misguided. . . . The way to address the challenge of persistent poverty is to create sustainable income-earning opportunities for millions of people. Income is development.[9]

Income is essential, but Fisher's logic should also be extended to other forms of life-improving economic participation as well. Increases in income alone are not enough to improve the quality of life for the world's poor. As people increase their earnings, they need access to markets with suitable and affordable goods on which to spend their income and through which to improve the quality of their lives.[10] They need access to savings institutions in order to build financial reserves as a cushion against tough times and as a source of capital to invest in education, housing, or business opportunities. The poor also need access to credit that will allow them to leverage their own resources to improve their quality of life and productive capacity. Anyone who is serious about finding lasting solutions to poverty needs to consider supporting economic participation through four key roles:

—producer: income-generating and productivity-enhancing opportunities;
—consumer: affordable goods that improve the quality of life;
—saver: secure and accessible methods to accumulate financial assets; and
—borrower: capital and credit on reasonable terms.

In most developing countries, there are serious barriers to economic participation by the poor. Markets developing on their own typically have been slow in providing avenues for constructive engagement with the poor. Profit-seeking investors and business executives are drawn to opportunities that they believe will generate higher returns at lower risk than most ventures constructively engaging the poor. This may reflect biases and false assumptions about businesses that aim to improve life for the poor. It may also reflect the reality that many of these enterprises require patient capital with low return expectations, at least in their early stages. The Grameen Bank benefited from a great deal of this kind of capital for well over a decade before it became self-funding. Fisher acknowledges that KickStart's pump business may take many years to reach profitability. Whatever the reason, most investors focused on profit are likely to direct their capital elsewhere. In certain cases, profit-oriented investors see opportunities in businesses that benefit the poor, as they did with Celtel, the highly successful African telecommunications company. However, philanthropists who wish to reduce poverty in a timely fashion cannot afford to wait for mainstream markets to support enterprises that engage the poor in these four constructive ways (box 7-1).

Entrepreneurship, Innovation, and Discovery

In theory, existing large corporations could take on the job of supporting economic engagement by the poor. Why support relatively new, small entrepreneurial efforts? Economies tend to work best when they empower independent entrepreneurs to engage in innovation alongside larger organizations. Entrepreneurs engage in a process of innovation, experimentation, and

BOX 7-1
Social Enterprises Addressing Four Economic Roles

The poor as producers: KickStart's main product is a relatively low-cost, portable, human-powered irrigation pump that it markets to farmers in Kenya and Tanzania. This technology significantly increases crop yields and income. Over 59,000 pumps have been sold, leading to the creation of over 40,000 new businesses, 22,000 new wage jobs, and $40 million in new profits and wages. See www.kickstart.org.

The poor as consumers: Scojo Foundation makes reading glasses available and affordable to the poor through low-cost production, a creative micro-franchise distribution system, and partnerships with some major NGOs. Its franchise system allows Scojo to reach remote areas. Scojo has sold more than 50,000 pairs of glasses in Guatemala, El Salvador, and India, with a goal of selling 1 million pairs by 2110. See www.scojofoundation.org.

The poor as savers: Opportunity International, a pioneer in microfinance, operates through a network of forty-two organizations in twenty-eight developing countries. To make secure savings accounts available, despite problems of illiteracy, Opportunity uses biometric fingerprint readers and "smart cards" to replace signatures. Opportunity banks opened nearly 250,000 accounts in 2006 worth nearly $160 million. See www.opportunity.org.

The poor as borrowers: Kiva matches entrepreneurs in developing countries with individuals who have money to lend through the Internet, working with local partners to screen the entrepreneurs and upload information about their businesses and financial needs. Lenders choose the amount they would like to lend starting at $25. In just over two years, Kiva reportedly brokered over $6 million in loans to some 9,000 entrepreneurs. See www.kiva.org.

adaptation that is much harder to execute in the more constrained, centralized, bureaucratized, and politicized environments often found in larger organizations. According to the economist William Baumol and his colleagues, "Radical breakthroughs tend to be disproportionately developed and brought to market by a *single individual or new firm*."[11] If there is an arena in which societies need breakthrough innovations, it is in poverty reduction.

The social sector needs the same kind of independent innovators to develop effective, high-potential solutions to social problems. To quote Soros again: "Philanthropy, social work, and all forms of official intervention are mired in bureaucracy. Yet there are imaginative, creative people who really care about social conditions. I have come around to thinking that entrepreneurial creativity could achieve what bureaucratic processes cannot."[12]

Entrepreneurs have the flexibility to take risks, learn, and adapt as they go. Many will fail, and many others will significantly modify their original ideas as they learn what works and what does not. They serve as a learning laboratory for society. This is particularly valuable because there is no way to know in advance what will work as a tool for solving a persistent social problem, such as poverty. Entrepreneurs act as "searchers," to use the developmental economist William Easterly's term: "A Searcher admits he doesn't know the answers in advance; he believes that poverty is a complicated tangle of political, social, historical, institutional, and technological factors. A Searcher hopes to find answers to individual problems only by trial and error experimentation."[13] This is much harder to do from within a bureaucratic environment, which tends to favor those Easterly calls "Planners."

Major corporations, government agencies, and large nongovernmental organizations have a role to play in addressing social issues, including poverty, but they are not a substitute for social entrepreneurs. Social entrepreneurs often serve as the catalysts for engaging larger firms. They do this by finding opportunities that would escape the notice of larger firms, demonstrating the profitability of a new product market, and/or providing a valuable complementary service, perhaps as part of what Bill Drayton, founder of Ashoka and pioneer in social entrepreneurship, calls a "hybrid value chain."[14] Major banks are getting involved in microcredit only now that the market is established, and they are typically engaging only at a secondary market level, leaving the loan origination and collection process to a local social enterprise. It is not clear how much large corporations, particularly publicly held companies, would do in the absence of social entrepreneurs. Similarly, social entrepreneurs serve as partners, sometimes as contractors, in helping government agencies and larger nongovernmental organizations serve their development agendas. Leading aid organizations have learned the benefit of tapping into the creativity and flexibility of the entrepreneurs who are closely embedded in the communities the aid is designed to serve.

Philanthropic Value Added

Philanthropists can add value by accelerating market development in ways that improve the lot of the poor, and by directing their capital and resources to the ventures most likely to engage the poor in constructive ways. It is only natural for the profit seekers (both entrepreneurs and capital providers) who are driving market expansion in developing countries to start with what they see to be the low-hanging fruit, offering the highest return relative to the risk involved. Many business enterprises that engage the poor in constructive ways are, rightly or wrongly, seen as costly, risky, and likely to grow slowly. Profitability, if it comes at all, may be a long way out. Philanthropists and social entrepreneurs are in a position to pursue business opportunities that do not appear to have a high profit potential but that constructively engage the poor, because profits are not their primary consideration, not their measure of success. They can take the risks, subsidize higher cost structures, and be more patient than profit-seeking investors and entrepreneurs. It is useful to think of this kind of philanthropic support as falling into three categories, though the boundaries can be blurry.

The first category of philanthropic support is for launching and growing enterprises designed primarily to achieve social impact.[15] Social enterprises have, by definition, a social purpose, and they often need patient, low-return, or no-return capital to pursue that purpose. As Soros notes, "In social entrepreneurship, profit is not a motive, it is a means to an end."[16] Social entrepreneurs are valuable because they have an inherent incentive to find opportunities where others are not even looking and to develop innovative approaches that make the opportunities into viable enterprises, when possible. If Yunus were simply looking for the best profit opportunities in Bangladesh, he would not have focused on microcredit and would not have crafted Grameen's innovative peer-lending model. Because he was determined to reduce poverty in his country, he discovered an opportunity and engaged in a process of innovation that would otherwise have been neglected. Philanthropic capital was crucial during the early development and expansion of the bank. This is true for most business ventures started by social entrepreneurs. Philanthropists are a good source of support for these ventures because they are focused more on social return than financial return. The Ford Foundation's early support for Grameen is a good example. Even with ongoing subsidies, a social enterprise might represent the most cost-effective use of philanthropic funds to reduce poverty and do it in a way that builds capability.

The second category of philanthropic support is for facilitating the movement of social enterprises into mainstream capital markets. Some social enterprises may always need philanthropic subsidy; others may have the potential to become "self sustaining" or generate modest profits, but below what profit-oriented investors would require. However, many have the goal of becoming commercially viable, able to provide market-rate returns and, thus, to tap into mainstream capital markets. Some social entrepreneurs see this as the only way to achieve sufficient scale, given the limits on philanthropic capital. Philanthropists can make enterprise investments to demonstrate the commercial viability of businesses that serve the poor. This is the logic behind the Omidyar-Tufts Microfinance Fund. The fund was created with a $100 million endowment gift from Pierre and Pam Omidyar to Tufts University to invest in microfinance, "demonstrating its potential commercial viability to a wider institutional investor audience."[17] These philanthropic investments are not about providing subsidies, accepting low returns, or taking the long view, in exchange for a "social return." They are about generating market-rate returns in a timely fashion to attract mainstream capital providers.

The third category of philanthropic support is for fostering the development of socially beneficial forms of private enterprise. A business enterprise does not have to be a social-purpose enterprise to improve social conditions. As Adam Smith pointed out, businesses frequently serve the public good without having the specific intention to do so. Philanthropists may wish to support selected private enterprises when these happen to serve the poor or result in other social improvements. By making these investments, philanthropists can help accelerate market development and influence the direction of that development in ways that increase constructive participation by the poor.

In countries without an infrastructure to support entrepreneurship, markets are likely to favor those who have power, connections, and resources. As a result, many talented potential entrepreneurs will lack access to the kind of capital and expertise they need to launch and grow their businesses. Even in the United States, many entrepreneurial businesses have limited access to capital markets. They have to "bootstrap" their ventures, drawing down personal savings, borrowing from family and friends, using personal credit cards, and taking home equity loans.[18] In developing countries, many business entrepreneurs simply do not have access to this kind of "bootstrap" capital. Philanthropists can fill this capital gap by selectively investing in profit-seeking businesses that have a significant potential to increase the economic participation of the poor. These could include businesses owned by members of groups normally excluded from mainstream economic activity (for example, women, or religious, racial, tribal, and ethnic minorities); businesses that locate in economically distressed areas and provide skill-building employment to people in those areas; and businesses that provide needed products and services, such as cell phones,[19] to the poor at affordable prices.

Philanthropists can also support this kind of business development indirectly, helping to foster a more open entrepreneurial economy in economically distressed areas. This could include, for instance, interventions that lower barriers to business formation; improve the legal protections of property rights and enforcement of contracts; and increase access to capital, entrepreneurial education, and technical assistance.[20]

Some would take this point further, arguing that philanthropists should not limit their involvement to ventures that "need" philanthropic funding and cannot raise capital in private markets. Through strategically selected investments in private businesses that have major implications for the poor, philanthropists may enhance the social impact of those businesses. Their involvement may also give enterprises additional credibility as the enterprises negotiate with governments or interest groups. Developing markets may benefit if there is a philanthropic voice among the investors backing major new private enterprises. Companies may benefit from having a mix of investors. For example, Nicholas Sullivan argues that Celtel, the highly successful African telecommunications company, benefited by taking funds from development finance organizations as well as mainstream venture capitalists.[21]

New Challenges of Enterprising Philanthropy

When business and philanthropy are treated as separate realms, practitioners have a relatively clear understanding of how to make decisions. The traditional logic of business investing focuses on financial return and risk. The traditional logic of making grants focuses on achieving an intended social impact. Some observers object to this bifurcation, arguing for a common logic of "blended value" creation.[22] Whether or not the world is ready to embrace a common logic of value creation, philanthropists who support enterprises are faced with making decisions about their investments that blend social and economic considerations. This poses four distinctive challenges.

The first challenge is defining and measuring success. Ultimate success may be measured in sustainable social impact, in this case permanent poverty reduction. Measuring this kind of impact is often difficult to do in a rigorous, reliable, timely, and cost-effective way. Enterprise investments pose an additional complication: To what extent should the financial performance of the enterprise be included in the assessment? Even when profit is simply a means to an end, financial performance is an indicator of the ability of an enterprise to survive and grow in the future, with minimal (or perhaps no) further philanthropic subsidy. This surely has value beyond the direct social impact achieved by the organization during the investment period. When a grant is made to a charity, it is often more of an expenditure than an investment, in the sense that the grant covers a portion of operating costs for the organization to do its work during a given period of time. In the next period, the organization needs a new grant. Donors are essentially paying for service delivery. In the case of enterprise, philanthropic support can help move the organization away from future dependence on any philanthropic subsidies. Philanthropic support that moves an enterprise closer to profitability, even when it takes the form of a grant, should be viewed as an "investment" in that it will yield more social benefits in the future. How should this ability to create a future impact with less (or no) philanthropic support be factored into the "social return" of an enterprise investment? Failing to place a value on the improved capacity and financial condition of the venture underestimates the social impact of an enterprise investment.

The second challenge is setting the terms of engagement. Philanthropists who want to support enterprises also face a more complex array of options for structuring the "deal." An enterprise may have the potential to repay the philanthropist for the financial support, now or later. Financial support can take the form of grants, recoverable grants, loans at various rates and on various terms, loan guarantees, and, in the case of for-profit enterprises, equity. In addition to the form and terms of initial financial support, the deal between a philanthropist and an enterprise can include conditions for follow-on funding, provisions for nonfinancial support (management assistance) or involvement (board membership), and exit strategies. These deals can be as simple as a basic charitable grant or as complex as a private convertible debt transaction. In determining the terms of engagement, philanthropists investing in enterprises will have to grapple with how their support can create the most beneficial impact relative to the resources expended. Does the enterprise need a subsidy? If so, what is the best form (grant, low interest loan, and so on)? How long should one be willing to subsidize this particular social enterprise? Fisher acknowledged that it is likely to take a long time before KickStart is able to achieve sustained profitability, but in the meantime, it is generating tremendous income gains for Kenyan and Tanzanian farmers, far in excess of the subsidy required.[23] Could some enterprises, because of their social impact, justify indefinite financial support? How can you provide such support while still providing appropriate incentives and pressure for better financial results? What conditions, positive or negative, should trigger an "exit" by the philanthropist? How will a positive exit be achieved? Most of these organizations are not likely to go public or be acquired. In summary, how can the whole deal be structured to provide incentives and rewards for an optimal mix of social and financial performance?

It is important to note one significant implication of the possible range of deal structures with regard to determining a "social return on investment." The "investment" element must be calculated to reflect the *net* financial resources used to achieve the impact. Obviously, a $1 million grant has to be treated quite differently from a $1 million loan, even at 0 percent interest and even if the probability of repayment is only 50 percent ex ante. The grant is gone. With the loan, the philanthropist is likely to get back some and perhaps all the capital to use in the future. One way to think about this is to focus on the net costs of the investment (including transaction costs, monitoring costs, costs of in-kind assistance, and the like) relative to the social return generated.

The third challenge is aligning incentives to assure the creation of intended social impact. When philanthropists invest in enterprises, they need to be confident that the incentives inherent in the enterprise are aligned with their intended social impact, or that safeguards are in place should financial rewards ever threaten to pull the organization away from the desired social impact. For most enterprises, managers will face decisions in which they have to make trade-offs between financial returns and social impact. Defining the optimal balance is not easy, because financial success may allow an organization to have greater social impact in the long term. How can a philanthropist develop confidence that a given enterprise is likely to produce the intended social impact? The best assurance is provided when market forces are perfectly aligned with the intended social impact. This is often not the case.

When the natural alignment is not obvious, it is wise for an investing philanthropist to look at other factors that could affect social performance. The deal's structure can certainly make a difference, as mentioned above. However, other mechanisms can also play an important role. For instance, the legal form of an enterprise can have a powerful effect. Options vary widely, with different variations falling into the broad categories of nonprofit, for-profit, cooperative,[24] or some combination. In the United Kingdom, social entrepreneurs can now choose a new legal form, the "community interest company," that allows limited financial returns to equity investors. Legal forms affect governance, possible sources of financing, and financial rewards to those in control of the organization. Perhaps more important than the legal form is who controls the organization, by law and in practice, and what are their values and interests. In the case of for-profit social ventures, it is helpful for control to be kept in the hands of those who care about the social impact or who have a vested interest in achieving it but also understand the role of financial success as a means to that end.[25] Finally, the culture, processes, and staffing strategies of an organization can work to align effort with the intended social impact.

The fourth challenge is scaling the organization and the impact. How can philanthropists be sure that their enterprise investments will lead to significant, widespread impact? One potential drawback of an entrepreneurial approach to social problems is the existence of many small, fragmented efforts with little learning and sharing between them. The innovations embedded in the successful social enterprises may not reach the vast majority of locations and individuals that could benefit from them. This might be fine if all solutions were truly local, but past experience teaches us that many socially beneficial innovations can and should spread to new locations. Consider microfinance, which has reached more than 100 million families in a variety of developing and developed countries. If entrepreneurial business ventures are to put a serious dent in poverty, they need pathways to spread what works to new markets where it is also likely to work.

Geographic expansion typically requires new talent and capital. Both can be problematic. Social enterprises often require hybrid skills that blend business, political, and social savvy. It is essential to expand and develop suitable talent pipelines. Philanthropists who invest in social enterprise have a vested interest in supporting the development of those pipelines. Capital is a problem because investing in the original innovation seems to provide more visceral satisfaction than investing in the expansion, even though greater social returns may come from supporting the expansion. Many social entrepreneurs and philanthropists are attracted by the business enterprise model because they believe that it will reduce the need for outside capital to scale and that commercial success will significantly increase chances of raising capital for scale. For instance, One Roof, Inc, a for-profit social venture that provides essential services to the poor through a network of stores in Mexico and India, grew out of the nonprofit World Corps, whose leading staff members "determined that private capital, rather than philanthropic dollars, was the best means by which to 'scale up.'"[26]

This logic is appealing, but the evidence is far from compelling. Will mainstream capital flow to successful social ventures? Will theses ventures become sufficiently profitable to finance their own expansion? Microfinance spread for more than two decades with significant support from philanthropists, governments, and aid agencies before some of the leading microfinance institutions achieved the ability to fund their own growth. Nearly three decades after the introduction of this innovation, mainstream profit-oriented investment capital is finally starting to flow into the field—but still tentatively. Beyond microfinance, there are not many recent success stories of social enterprises that have scaled up to affect millions of lives. Philanthropic support is likely to be needed for considerable time in the expansion of social enterprises. It would be helpful to fund experiments with new, more cost-effective expansion strategies and structures, such as creative franchise systems; the licensing of programs or technologies; and alliances with corporations, governments, and other social sector organizations. It would also be helpful to support the creation of new funding platforms that are designed to support scaling activities.

Getting the Most Out of These Experiments

The success of microfinance demonstrates that philanthropic support for social and business enterprise activities can play a crucial role in combating poverty, but the potential practitioners of this art do not know much about how to engage in this kind of investing effectively. They do not know its strengths and limits. Standards of practice do not exist. Performance benchmarks and evaluation criteria for social enterprise are often lacking. Those who would engage in this strategy for accelerating development need a better understanding of the conditions under which business ventures can achieve a significant, positive, lasting social impact. Philanthropists and social investors need a better understanding of how they can best contribute to creating that impact. All the parties involved need a better understanding of the institutional structures and supports that would allow social enterprises to thrive. With a deeper understanding, enterprising philanthropy could become a powerful new strategic lever for positive social change, one that blends social objectives with business methods.

What will it take to achieve this deeper understanding? It will require a systematic effort to mine the growing base of experience with this strategy. Current activities create a cluster of experiments testing different ways to bring markets to bear on serious social problems. Some of these experiments will be successful; a significant number will fail or fall far short of expectations. To assure that these experiments are not in vain, independent researchers need to examine them and, through critical analysis, draw out the lessons. As the philosopher Karl Popper put it, "We make progress if, and only if, we are prepared to *learn from our mistakes*: to recognize our errors and to utilize them critically instead of persevering in them dogmatically"[27]—or, I might add, instead of hiding them from view, as is common in the world of philanthropy. Harvesting these lessons requires rigorous research, supported not just financially but also with the active cooperation of philanthropists and social entrepreneurs. Only in this way will the failures become truly "constructive."[28] The result will be the development of knowledge that should make all the interested parties smarter at supporting healthy, sustainable development.

Philanthropists who venture into this arena are pioneers. They have the opportunity to play a key role in shaping the institutions and standards that will guide development strategies in the future, provided they are prepared to participate in an open and mutual learning process.

Notes

1. George Soros, *Open Society: Reforming Global Capitalism* (New York: PublicAffairs, 2000), 162.

2. Private foundations can and do invest in for-profits that serve their missions, but there are restrictions on this kind of activity to prevent self-dealing. A for-profit "philanthropy" avoids that issue.

3. Katie Hafner, "Philanthropy Google's Way: Not the Usual," *New York Times*, September 14, 2006.

4. See J. Gregory Dees and Beth Battle Anderson, "Framing a Theory of Social Entrepreneurship: Building on Two Schools of Practice and Thought," in *Research on Social Entrepreneurship: Understanding and Contributing to an Emerging Field*, ARNOVA Occasional Paper Series, vol. 1, no. 3, ed. Rachel Mosher-Williams (Indianapolis: Association for Research on Nonprofit Organizations and Voluntary Action, 2006); and J. Gregory Dees, "Taking Social Entrepreneurship Seriously," *Society* 44, no. 3 (March–April 2007): 24–31.

5. It is important to note that social entrepreneurship is not simply about enterprise creation. It is also about finding innovative solutions to social problems. Enterprise is only one tool social entrepreneurs might use. For a general introduction to the concept, see David Bornstein, *How to Change the World: Social Entrepreneurs and the Power of New Ideas* (Oxford University Press, 2004).

6. Social enterprise is not simply about poverty reduction. Enterprise can be used to address any area of potential social improvement, including health care, education, the environment, and the arts.

7. See Nicholas Stern, Jean-Jacques Dethier, and F. Halsey Rogers, *Growth and Empowerment: Making Development Happen* (MIT Press, 2005), esp. 225–42.

8. Muhammad Yunus, *Banker to the Poor: Micro-Lending and the Battle against World Poverty* (New York: PublicAffairs, 1999), 237.

9. Martin Fisher, "Income Is Development: KickStart's Pumps Help Kenyan Farmers Transition to a Cash Economy," *Innovations* 1, no. 1 (Winter 2006): 9.

10. This is where efforts to create products for the "base of the pyramid," the world's poorest, can play an important role. See C. K. Prahalad's *The Fortune at the Bottom of the*

Pyramid: Eradicating Poverty through Profits (Upper Saddle River, N.J.: Wharton School Publishing, 2005); and Stuart Hart, *Capitalism at the Crossroads: The Unlimited Business Opportunities in Solving the World's Problems* (Upper Saddle River, N.J.: Wharton School Publishing, 2005).

11. William J. Baumol, Robert E. Litan, and Carl J. Schramm, *Good Capitalism, Bad Capitalism, and the Economics of Growth and Prosperity* (Yale University Press, 2007), 86; emphasis in the original.

12. Soros, *Open Society,* 162.

13. William Easterly, *The White Man's Burden: Why the West's Efforts to Aid the Rest Have Done So Much Ill and So Little Good* (New York: Penguin Press, 2006), 6.

14. See http://ashoka.org/hvc for a brief explanation. The concept is also discussed by Jane Nelson and Beth Jenkins, *Investing in Social Innovation: Harnessing the Potential of Partnership between Corporations and Social Entrepreneurs,* Corporate Social Responsibility Initiative Working Paper 20 (John F. Kennedy School of Government, Harvard University, 2006).

15. Note that not all examples of social entrepreneurship take the form of business enterprises. Also note that the enterprises that philanthropists support are not all social enterprises.

16. Soros, *Open Society,* 162.

17. See the press release at www.tufts.edu/microfinancefund/?pid=8 (October 2007).

18. See Amar V. Bhide, "Bootstrap Finance: The Art of Start Ups," *Harvard Business Review,* November 1992, 109–117; and Amar V. Bhide, *The Origin and Evolution of New Businesses* (Oxford University Press, 2000).

19. See Nicholas P. Sullivan, *Can You Hear Me Now: How Microloans and Cell Phones Are Connecting the World's Poor to the Global Economy* (New York: John Wiley & Sons, 2007).

20. This list draws on the discussion by Baumol, Litan, and Schramm, *Good Capitalism, Bad Capitalism,* 153–63.

21. Sullivan, *Can You Hear Me Now,* 116.

22. Jed Emerson is the primary developer of the blended value concept; see www.blendedvalue.org for background material. Specifically see the World Economic Forum Report, *Blended Value Investing: Capital Opportunities for Social and Environmental Impact,* at www.blendedvalue.org/media/pdf-blendedvalue.pdf (October 2007).

23. Fisher, "Income Is Development," esp. 26–30.

24. In this category, I am including a variety of member-serving structures such as mutuals, credit unions, and collaboratives, as well as cooperatives.

25. For more on this topic, see J. Gregory Dees and Beth Battle Anderson, "For-Profit Social Ventures," in *Social Entrepreneurship,* ed. Marilyn Kourilsky and William Walstad (Dublin: Senate Hall Academic Publishing, 2004), a special issue of the *International Journal of Entrepreneurship Education,* vol. 2.

26. See history page at www.oneroof.com.

27. Karl Popper, *The Poverty of Historicism* (London: Routledge & Kegan Paul, 2002; orig. pub. 1957), 80; emphasis in the original.

28. For a discussion of constructive failure in philanthropy, see Peter Frumkin, "Failure in Philanthropy: Toward a New Appreciation," *Philanthropy Roundtable,* July–August 1998, 7–10.

8

Leveraging Knowledge to End Poverty

ASHOK KHOSLA

O VER THE PAST couple of centuries, the world as a whole has made undeniable, and often quite dramatic, "progress" on many fronts. People in scores of countries have attained unprecedented levels of health, wealth, and knowledge. Diseases that were for millennia the scourges of whole nations have been conquered. Food production has grown to levels inconceivable even a few decades ago. An ever-growing range of products from industry is accessible to an ever growing range of customers. In addition, cheap sources of energy have made possible facilities for travel and communication that enable large numbers of people to live a life of convenience and comfort on a scale never known before.

The spectacular improvements that have occurred in our lives over this period are the direct result of an unprecedented explosion of scientific knowledge. Knowledge is, in fact, now widely recognized to be the primary factor at the root of the revolution in our material well-being.

The Premise

However, this extraordinary progress has not come without cost. The unprecedented creation of wealth has gone hand in hand with an unprecedented expansion of poverty and human deprivation, a loss of societal resilience, and the destruction of the environmental resource base.

A large part of the cause for this global dichotomy—historically unparalleled concentrations of wealth side by side with untold and unacceptable oceans of poverty and misery—lies in the differential access that people have to knowledge. Knowledge based on modern science gives such an advantage to those who already have it, particularly if they are already in a position of dominance, that it totally overpowers those who do not—whether in warfare or in the marketplace. To put this in a clearer perspective, one might simply ask what modern science or technology has done for the 1.3 billion people who still have to walk more than a mile from their homes to get clean drinking water. Traditional knowledge systems that had their own vast and time-tested value, serving humanity quite well for millennia, are now completely impotent in the face of modern science—but will no doubt come back into their own in due course as the limits of the modern scientific method inevitably manifest themselves.

If the global economy is to flourish and the benefits it brings are to reach everyone on the planet, now and in the future, we will have to substantially change the way we choose our technologies; design our institutions, particularly our financial systems; and relate to nature. A sustainable world will need a more socially just, environmentally sound, and economically efficient form of development than the one being widely pursued today.

Sustainable Development

To achieve a sustainable future, the developing world clearly has two priorities that must come before all others. The first is to ensure that all citizens have access to the means of satisfying their basic needs. The second is to evolve practices that bring the environmental resource base, on which their lives and futures integrally depend, back to its full health and potential productivity. To achieve these two primary goals requires action on two fronts. We must

—create *sustainable livelihoods* on a very large scale, particularly for the poor and marginalized; and

—encourage *sustainable lifestyles* among all people, particularly the rich and privileged.

As major components of the overall objective of sustainable development, these two goals are simply another way of stating that every developing country, as indeed any industrial one, must reorient its economy toward production and consumption systems that are sustainable. Furthermore, if the creation of jobs is one of the master keys to achieving this objective, enterprise is the keyhole.

The eradication of poverty and the conservation of nature, however, need jobs and enterprises of a very different kind from the conventional ones of today. This task is complex and will not be easy; to get it done, societies will need widespread access to deep and sophisticated knowledge. Creating this body of knowledge and building the army of practitioners needed to use it for the benefit of all will require considerable financial support and, consequently, a major redirection of current resource flows, which have served mainly to accentuate unsustainable outcomes.

Sustainable Livelihoods

The developing world now has to create sustainable livelihoods on a very large scale. The developing countries need, among them, to create more than 50 million new jobs every year.[1] At the same time, even in the poorest countries, the capacity of agriculture to absorb additional labor is rapidly diminishing.

The creation of livelihoods and jobs should, generally, be the job of the corporate sector. However, the corporate sector is not currently geared to creating jobs or livelihoods in developing economies in the numbers needed. Besides, as decades of experience show, the technology, financial, and marketing imperatives faced by big business operating in a globalizing economy make it unlikely that it will, in a reasonable time frame, be in a position to do so. The compulsions of global competition encourage industrialists to invest in machines rather than people.

Second, and related to this, is the fact that, partly because of the mechanization ordained by the perceived need to be globally competitive, it costs a great deal of investment to create one workplace—a job for one person—in modern industry. Depending on the level of automation, the capital required to create one industrial workplace in an industrial country can be anywhere between $100,000 and $1 million, after allowing for all the upstream and downstream jobs created as a result.[2] Given the lack of infrastructure and basic supporting systems in developing countries, the costs there can also be very high. The requirement of such heavy investments acts as a major barrier to the creation of new enterprises in the formal sector and therefore to jobs.

Third, competitiveness means delivering products demanded by the clients. Today, for economies in the global South, this means either commodities or primary products at subsistence prices, or technology-based products that generate better surpluses when their manufacture is automated or at least mechanized. Naturally, more and more emerging countries are choosing the latter, leading to the further takeover of jobs by machines. For example, during the past fifteen years India's economy has reached new

heights, yet the total number of persons employed in the country's large, formal corporate sector (including the business process outsourcing companies
whose growth is perceived as a threat to Western jobs)—actually declined
from more than 11 million in 1991 to about 10 million in 2006.[3]

The point here is not that globalization is bad per se—or good. Rather, it
is simply that the evidence, at least from India, does suggest that in this
period of rapid economic integration, jobs are not being created at the rate
needed to keep up with the growth of the labor force. Indeed, the indications
are that certain kinds of jobs, including large industry and agriculture, are
being *lost,* and that there continues to be a net addition of several million
unemployed people every year.

In the meantime, the other formal sectors are not in a position to take up
the slack. Despite the many political temptations to the contrary, governments at all levels have begun to cut back gradually on their payrolls. Civil
society, with all its commitment and ambition to bring about a better world,
does not have the resources, the reach, or the skills to create employment on
a large enough scale.

Somebody else, then, will have to take responsibility for creating jobs and
sustainable livelihoods. This is where the small and medium-sized enterprise
sector comes in—market-based, profit-making businesses that are mostly
small and generally local. In most economies, they happen to be the largest
generators of jobs and livelihoods.[4]

Perhaps the most important yet least understood impact of large-scale
livelihood creation is on a nation's demography. Together with programs for
the education of girls and women, sustainable livelihoods are probably the
most effective stimuli for smaller families and lower birthrates. For the longer-
term interests of planetary health, it is in the interest of all, rich and poor, to
accelerate the process by which the demographic transition to low fertility
and, as a result, to low population growth is achieved in poor countries.[5]

Sustainable Lifestyles

Given that the ecological footprint of the world's economies has already
reached 1.2—that is, our use of natural resources now exceeds the Earth's
capacity to produce these resources on a sustainable basis by 20 percent—we
clearly need to do something drastic and immediate.[6] Consumers in the
North now need to bring down their use of materials—according to one
credible estimate, by a factor of ten. As much as half this dematerialization
can be achieved with technologies that are already available, without any

major change of behavior or human aspiration.[7] In industrial countries, the full factor of ten is also probably not difficult to achieve by bringing together a combination of technology innovation to gain much higher resource productivity, the modification of market mechanisms to ensure the full-cost pricing of resources, and some minor changes of behavior regarding such issues as miniaturization, product durability, and sharing of physical assets. Dematerialization beyond a factor of ten will require these kinds of measures plus deeper structural changes in the economy, in industrial production systems, and in consumption behavior and social aspirations.

However, here we are concerned primarily with removing poverty. The biospheric resources consumed by the poor are so pitiably small in quantity that, unquestionably, consumption of materials, energy, water and other resources will have to go up for a while before it can reach levels where a basic minimum standard of living is within the grasp of all. This is the fastest practical means for achieving the quality of life that can lead to the demographic transition needed to stabilize the world's population at the lowest possible level (which, unfortunately, will still be very high).

Improvement in the lives of the poor is essential not only to improve the prospects for planetary survival and for reducing the potential threats to the world's political and economic status quo. It is also necessary for ethical and basic human rights reasons. Take, for example, a simple and ubiquitous appliance, the wood-burning cookstove, which is used in more than 200 million homes worldwide. The cookstove, as presently used, burns biomass fuels (mainly wood and animal dung) with very low levels of efficiency and with extremely high levels of emission (of poisonous gases such as carbon monoxide, sulfur oxides, and particulates).

Recent studies have shown that some 1.5 million women and children die prematurely *every year* because of diseases caused by this source of indoor pollution.[8] In addition, hundreds of millions of women and girls could save several hours a day of walking to collect the biomass fuel they need if the efficiency of the stoves were to be slightly improved; a mission that is surely not as complicated as designing an intercontinental ballistic missile—but has yet to be accomplished.

At the same time, because of the numbers involved—nearly half the world's population—it becomes even more important for the developing world to pursue a path of development that employs the highest possible resource productivity in sectors such as agriculture, industry, and habitat—and particularly in job creation. This entails the use of major innovations in technology and the institutions of governance and markets—all of which require highly sophisticated capacities for analysis, design, and implementation. Such capacities (institutions and experts) are not common or cheap.

Furthermore, lifestyles and livelihoods are inextricably linked. Simplistic theories on how the global corporate sector could create a completely new market for its products by redesigning, recosting, and repackaging them to suit the tastes and expectations of the poor at the bottom of the economy miss the point that people must have the interest and the disposable income to be able to buy these products. In today's economy, purchasing power among the poor comes from income, and income comes largely from taking part in the production process—unless job opportunities are created at the same time as the products, there can be neither buyers nor sellers for long.

Bringing about widespread adoption of sustainable lifestyles requires the concerted efforts of everyone in a position to influence social and behavioral change. Because neither those who run government in most countries (of whatever political party or administrative cadre) nor those in business have shown much inclination to provide such leadership, it must come from the others—namely, civil society, which includes most organizations that are not in the government or private sectors. Although civil society has not, so far, fared much better in delivering the results needed than either government or business, it still offers some hope and could serve as an effective catalyst and the source of new institutional designs for building a better and more equitable world. By providing strong leadership, civil society could, in principle, position itself even to influence the practices of the public and private sectors.

Community Ventures

The new kinds of institutions required are actually local businesses or community-based not-for-profits that can deliver goods and services that people in their communities need for their basic functioning—building materials, energy sources, water systems, clothes, microfinance, livelihoods—but find difficult to access locally or affordably. Such goods and services are not confined to tangibles; communities also need help in building up their knowledge of the world around them and their vocational skills, strengthening their ability to demand and get their entitlements under the law, and being able to take a full and active part in their economy and systems of governance. In the past, many of these services were considered the domain of public agencies or civil society. Often, they have not been delivered as effectively or as widely as needed. The new institutions proposed here are a kind of marriage between the small, local private sector; civil society; and the public sector. We like to call entities of this type "community ventures," organizations that deliver basic-needs products and services through both the for-profit and not-for-profit strategies. Both of the primary objectives for sustainable development—sustainable livelihoods and sustainable lifestyles—are also best met by the same community ventures—small, local, environmentally benign businesses or voluntary organizations that create jobs and generate products and services in the community. Such businesses are usually technology based, employ a small number of workers, and can be highly profitable. In size, they lie roughly between the realm of what is often termed "small or medium enterprises" at the top end and "microenterprises" at the bottom.

A community venture is not likely to be sustainable for long if it does not quickly master the art and science of making a profit. In a market that is widely dispersed, has virtually no infrastructure or regular supply chains, and tries to cater to clients who have virtually no money, this is not easy to do. Moreover, to operate successfully in it, the community venture needs considerable knowledge and skills on a variety of fronts—knowledge that takes time and money to acquire. It needs to carry out market research and develop a business plan. It needs to choose, acquire, and master complex technologies. Once it goes into operation, it needs technical support to keep these technologies in good shape. It requires financing for fixed and working capital. It needs help in creating markets for its products. Such full-spectrum support systems for sustainable enterprises do not exist in the developing world's village economies. To succeed quickly in this marketplace, a community venture therefore requires support systems of many kinds. Fortunately, with recently introduced connectivity and the availability of the Internet, many of the knowledge-based inputs needed to run a successful venture are now more accessible than in earlier times.

Network Enablers

Thus, one of the critical elements in any effective strategy to deploy and nurture community ventures is the setting up of support (or "enabling") organizations that can provide such integrated services and assistance as are needed to make the local ventures profitable (figure 8-1). These supports may be supplied directly from internal resources or through aggregation of inputs available from others. Such a support organization, which might be called a network enabler, has to bring both for-profit and socially oriented motivations together in a seamless synthesis of services designed to help its partner community ventures succeed in the marketplace. Network enablers are a special

Figure 8-1. Network Enablers/Social Enterprises

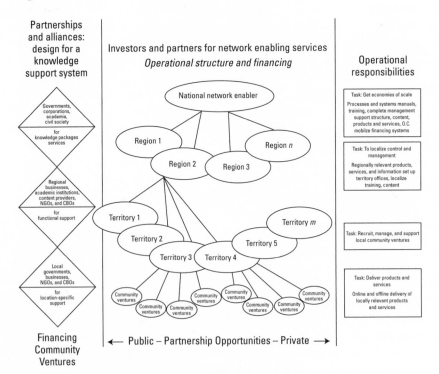

Source: Development Alternatives Group.
NGOs = nongovernmental organizations; CBOs = community-based organizations.

kind of social enterprise, perhaps the most important kind for scaling up the delivery of solutions to development-related problems. For local solutions to work, they need the same things as big business: technology and know-how, training, finance, brand equity, and marketing.

Many of these business supports are available at little or no cost to large urban industries. For network enablers similarly to be able to offer reasonably priced support services to their community venture partners, they themselves usually need financial support to cover the costs of initial investments in research, product design, and building their capacity to deliver the services. This is probably one of the few types of subsidy that can be justified.

Network enablers thus need external resource inputs from public funds or from philanthropic or social investment funding sources for their capital investments. Such funding brings the incremental costs of each unit of product or service down to a level that is affordable to the community venture, and therefore to the buying public. In addition, they need private sector inputs: operational financing, management efficiency, and the ability to deliver results. In the longer run, realistic business analysis shows that even the dispersed rural market can provide commercially viable opportunities for many types of products and services, a fact that might be of interest to some companies with strategic interest in rural markets.

The nature of the rural market (particularly its dispersion and remoteness from major centers of economic activity) also means that we must learn to adopt different time horizons, financing instruments, and profit expectations from those of today. After all, even in the United States, with far higher purchasing power among its consumers, rural infrastructure such as electrification was achieved with financing at 1 to 3 percent, with repayment moratoria of several years and break-even time horizons of twenty to forty years.

By the nature of their work, network enablers and such social enterprises engage themselves in highly complex sets of issues, which need very sophisticated responses. They have to bring cutting-edge understanding of business, economic, technological, and other commercial issues together with considerable sensitivity to the social, cultural, and political environment in which their community venture partners operate. They also need to perform at the highest levels of innovation and implementation—which in turn involves the very best in creativity and management expertise.

By way of example, Development Alternatives, a social enterprise dedicated to sustainable development, has operated several network enablers in the Indian marketplace for some years. Representing the profit-oriented side of the spectrum is the commercial entity Technology and Action for Rural Advancement (TARA) and its Internet franchised network TARAhaat. At the other end of the spectrum is Development Alternatives' small-grant-making facility, the Poorest Areas Civil Society Program (PACS).

TARA manufactures and markets technologies to rural entrepreneurs, who then supply basic needs goods and services to their local clients. These include cost-effective building materials, water and sanitation systems, energy systems, handloom textiles, and other products needed for day-to-day use in the village. It is TARA's responsibility to ensure that the entrepreneurs get whatever support they need—technology, marketing materials, and access to financing to become profitable quickly. TARA operates as a classic network enabler. Its subsidiary, TARAhaat, has a growing network of franchised entrepreneurs who operate local cyberkiosks and supply a wide range of products and services such as vocational training, insurance, and renewable energy devices to village clients.

As a result of TARA's efforts over the past two decades, a wide variety of basic-needs products have been made available in the rural market through local enterprises. For example, close to a 100 million MicroConcrete Roofing tiles have been sold, sufficient to cover more than 200,000 village houses. Some of TARA's technologies, such as machines to make bricks using fly ash, a major waste from coal-fired power plants, have now become mainstream products for the construction sector. One hundred and twenty-six small dams on local rivers have enabled local farmers to cultivate one or two additional crops, covering some 10,000 hectares of land and creating several hundred thousand livelihoods. Overall, the technologies pioneered by Development Alternatives and disseminated by TARA and the networks that they have supported through technology and skill-building support have led to the creation of over 1 million rural livelihoods.

TARAhaat, the rural Internet subsidiary of TARA, has set up nearly 300 franchised cyberkiosks in small towns and villages in Northern India. The franchising model, where it is appropriate, is one of the most effective ways to enable networks with a commercially viable approach to delivering sustainable products and services. With the supports it receives from TARAhaat (which includes technology, training, branding, attractive and affordable products, and management systems), a franchise can become profitable within five to eight months. Once it is profitable, its ability to serve a growing market grows rapidly.

PACS, conversely, services a network of nongovernmental organizations and community-based organizations by providing project grants and wide ranging support services. PACS was funded by the U.K. government's Department for International Development and has been disbursing about $10 million a year for the past six years. Its mode of operation is entirely knowledge based, aimed at building the capacity of local civil society organizations to deliver the highest quality services.

Through the network of 650 nongovernmental organizations and 35,000 community-based organizations it has built up over the past six years, PACS has directly helped more than 1.3 million poor households—comprising more than 6 million people in about 20,000 villages in six states—by building their capacity to demand and get their entitlements from local governments. It has taught more than 30,000 illiterate women how to read and write and is now graduating 5,000 students each month.

The experience gained from these network enablers and their partner ventures in the field is the basis of the analysis in this chapter. In all the cases described above, the growth of the networks and their operations has taken them beyond the "pilot" stage, but a lack of capital for the network enabler function has restricted their ability to become fully mainstreamed.

Resolving the Contradictions in the Rural Market

Servicing the rural markets of the developing world is not easy; if it were, it would have been done on a significant scale by now. The reasons for the intractability of this market lie in four fundamental contradictions that make it difficult or unattractive for conventional types of initiatives.

The first contradiction is financial: The costs of delivering products using conventional methods of delivery are very high, and the purchasing power of the final customers served by local businesses is very low. A good solution to this lies in the network approach, where the community venture is a kind of franchise and the network enabler becomes the franchiser. By selling standardized products, purchasing raw materials or goods in quantity, having access to financing and technical support and building up a brand image, the network can do together what a single business operating in a remote village cannot.

The second contradiction is institutional: The objectives that need to be met to improve lives in a village community are largely driven by social considerations— basic needs, human rights, the participation of women—and are best dealt with by not-for-profit organizations or local businesses. The strategies needed for scaling up are largely commercially oriented. The resolution of these conflicting requirements also lies in a knowledge-based partnership between the network enabler and the community venture. Keeping the different motivations of the organizations separate and setting up systems of interchange based on mutual respect can be a very effective method for delivering socially desirable products and services on a very large scale.

The third contradiction is economic: Apart from low-priced food, the rural economy, and particularly rural industry, produce little of interest to national-level decisionmakers, who mostly live in the city; innovation, financing, and other amenities of concern to the rural venture therefore get little or no attention. By bringing the strength of the whole network, the enabler is able to mobilize national resources, including much-needed knowledge resources, to address the problems faced by rural ventures.

The fourth contradiction is political: Governments, which normally bear primary responsibility for the issues of sustainable development, have short time horizons limited by electoral and constituency considerations. They therefore tend to focus on those issues that bring quick political gains. Network enablers are generally less influenced by the kinds of considerations that encourage governments and businesses to make decisions based on short-term calculations. It is no coincidence that much of the deep societal change witnessed over the past century—universal suffrage, civil and human rights, right to information—has been the result of civil society action amplified into people's movements by network-enabler-type entities.

Integrating the Public and the Private

In evolving the institutional framework to deliver products and services cost-effectively to the rural market in India, which is not atypical of rural markets in any developing country, Development Alternatives and its affiliates such as TARA and PACS have found it necessary to mix the public and the private, something that is contrary to any conventional institutional design theory. The practical breakthrough lies in clearly separating the objectives from the strategies. In addition to commercial viability, the objectives for such an enterprise are primarily social, environmental, and developmental. The strategies and methods used to achieve them, however, are purely business. This means that we need sources of capital that can accept longer time horizons for achieving profitability and possibly lower profits than are sometimes available in the market.

Figure 8-2 shows how the expectations of different types of investors vary. Conventional venture capitalists are primarily interested in very high and very quick returns. Capital for infrastructure usually comes from cash-rich, deep-pocketed investors who are looking for high returns but are willing to wait for them. Regular, commercial investors—including banks and financing agencies—usually want return on equity a little above the bank interest rates, starting after the break-even period, which is usually expected to be around three to five years. "Green" or "socially responsible" investors also expect good returns on their investments but are prepared to accept somewhat longer time horizons and take lower dividends.

There is considerable justification for initially funding network enablers in the form of grants and donations, because the earning capacity in the first establishment phase can only be very small. However, given the potential size and voracious appetite of this market, venture capitalists with a little imagination and a longer view would find all the returns they could wish for by investing in it (figure 8-3). Until such a realization becomes widespread

Figure 8-2. Profitability of Different Types of Investment

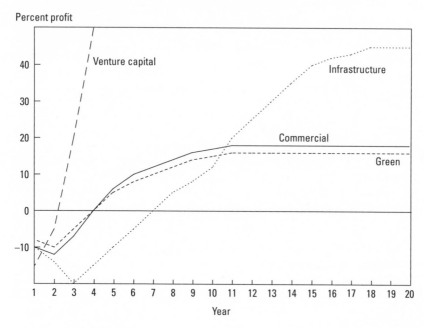

Source: Author's calculations.

Figure 8-3. Trade-offs among Solutions to Poverty

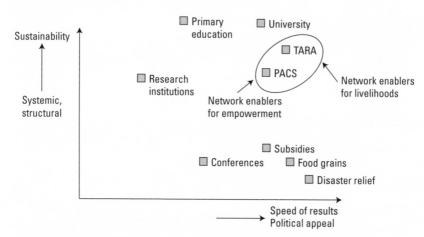

Source: Development Alternatives Group.
TARA = Technology for Action for Rural Advancement; PACS = Poorest Areas Civil Society Program.

among the private sector, the onus will be on the social enterprise sector, the businesslike end of civil society, to carry the war against poverty and environmental destruction forward.

Notes

1. International Labor Organization, *Global Employment Trends 2003* (Geneva: International Labor Organization, 2003).

2. Ashok Khosla, "Social Enterprises for Sustainable Livelihoods," *Development Alternatives* 12, no. 12 (December 2004): 1.

3. For Indian statistical information, see www.indiastat.com.

4. European Association of Craft Small and Medium-Sized Enterprises, "Economic Growth and Job Creation: Unleash the Potential of SMEs," March 2005.

5. For more information, see Ashok Khosla, "More Is Less," *Our Planet* (UN Environment Program) 16, no. 3 (2006): 16–17.

6. World Wildlife Fund, *Living Planet Report 2004* (Geneva: World Wildlife Fund, 2004).

7. Ernst von Weizsaecker, *Factor Four* (London: Earthscan, 1998).

8. World Health Organization, *Fuel for Life: Household Energy and Health* (Geneva: World Health Organization, 2006).

9

Effecting Change through Accountable Channels

JANE NELSON

D URING THE 1970s, 70 percent of resource flows from the United States to developing countries originated from the U.S. government in the form of official development assistance. Today, private capital from American citizens, residents, and companies accounts for more than 80 percent of such flows.[1] These private resources are being channeled to developing countries through a combination of foreign direct investment and portfolio investment, commercial bank loans, remittances, nongovernmental organizations (NGOs), religious groups, universities and colleges, foundations, and corporate philanthropy. Together with new approaches to official development assistance, they are changing the face of America's engagement in international development. Similar fundamental shifts are under way in other countries.

The statistics for the United States and elsewhere mask an even greater shift in the manner in which these resources are being mobilized and deployed for development. They give little sense of the dynamism, diversity, and innovation that is characterizing the emergence of new development players and approaches, ranging from new types of activists and funders, to emerging entrepreneurs and technologies, to new sources and models of official donor assistance. Nor do the statistics capture the alliances that are developing between these new players, or the opportunities and accountability challenges that they are creating, both for themselves and for traditional government-funded development programs.

This chapter briefly outlines some of the characteristics of these emerging players and models, before focusing on their implications for accountability in four core areas:

—Their impact on increasing the accountability of governments, official donor agencies, and large corporations.

—Their response to their own organizational accountability and effectiveness.

—Their role in enhancing the accountability of the increasingly complex, multistakeholder partnerships and networks in which they participate.

—The accountability implications of "new" official donors and investors, in particular the reemergence of China as a major player in Africa.

The chapter concludes by considering emerging areas of consensus and makes recommendations for a more collaborative approach to the governance and operations of development initiatives. It calls for an ethos and practice of "mutual accountability."[2] For new and traditional development players to work more proactively together to build accountability mechanisms that are not only compliance driven but also led by a commitment to shared learning and responsibility, and a focus on building local capacity, assets, and political "voice" for the poor themselves in developing countries.

New Development Players and Models

Over the past two decades, we have witnessed a dramatic growth in the number, diversity, reach and influence of nonstate players in international development. These include civil society organizations, new forms of social enterprise, microfinance institutions, corporate responsibility initiatives, foundations, public-private partnerships, and both physical and virtual networks. Their scale ranges from multi-million-dollar transnational coalitions to millions of low-budget community-based initiatives and individual citizens taking personal action. They are supported by unprecedented communications capacity via the Internet and global media, other enabling technologies, more open societies in many countries, and high levels of private wealth creation and entrepreneurship.

It should be noted at the outset that some of these emerging nonstate players are far from beneficial or accountable in their impact on peace, security, and poverty alleviation. Cross-border crime syndicates, terrorist networks, illicit drugs and arms dealers, child and sex traffickers, money laundering, and trade in conflict commodities and counterfeit products are all examples of nonstate actors that have been equally empowered by new technologies and the process of globalization. Although such activities have a long-standing history, the scale and reach of their impact is unprecedented. As Moisés Naim has commented, "The global nature of these five wars [illegal international trade in drugs, arms, intellectual property, people, and money] was unimaginable just a decade ago. . . . The world's governments are fighting a quantitatively new phenomenon with obsolete tools, inadequate laws, inefficient bureaucratic arrangements, and ineffective strategies."[3]

These illegal or illicit nonstate actors and networks are clearly a major force to be reckoned with, but despite their growing importance they are not addressed in this chapter. The chapter instead focuses on new players, models of engagement, and sources of official donor assistance that are legal and that publicly state their intent to effect positive change through accountable channels.

Lester Salamon, director of the Center for Civil Society Studies at Johns Hopkins University, has argued, "We seem to be in the midst of a 'global associational revolution'—a massive upsurge of organized voluntary private activity, of structured citizen action outside the boundaries of the market and the state, that I am convinced will prove to be as momentous a feature of the late 20th century as the rise of the nation-state was of the late 19th century."[4] Though the role of nation-states and the market will, and should remain central, new actors as well as traditional actors, such as foundations and government development agencies, operating in new ways offer a variety of innovative and potentially important approaches for tackling global poverty. Consider the new development actors listed in box 9-1.

These widely diverse initiatives, organizations, and networks have four key characteristics in common:

—They are all focused on different ways of alleviating poverty.

—They have all been established within the past decade, most of them in the past five years.

—To achieve their objectives, almost all of them are harnessing new types of technologies, ranging from information technology to biotechnology and clean technology to new media, and innovative financial instruments and governance mechanisms.

—They are all mobilizing new players, resources, and approaches for international development. In some cases, they are led or catalyzed by governments and official donors operating in nontraditional ways. In many others, they are being driven by a combination of markets, personal wealth, technological innovation, privately funded research, celebrity status, and civic activism. In almost all cases, they involve new types of cooperation and collective action across the traditional boundaries of public, private, and civil society sectors.

At the risk of oversimplifying an extremely varied and dynamic landscape, figure 9-1 illustrates five categories of emerging development players and models, which are often overlapping and mutually reinforcing:

BOX 9-1
Sample of New Development Actors

Acumen Fund
African Investment Climate Facility
Afrigator
AfriMAP
Alliance for a Green Revolution
     in Africa
American Idol Gives Back
Amyris Biotechnologies

Billion Tree Campaign

Children's Investment Fund
     Foundation
China-Africa Business Council
China Guangcai Program Abroad
Clinton Global Initiative

Digital Diaspora Network

Extractive Industries Transparency
     Initiative

Fair Labor Association

Global Alliance for Vaccines and
     Immunization
Global Fund to Fight AIDS,
     Tuberculosis, and Malaria
Global Reporting Initiative
Google.org
Grameen-Jameel Pan-Arab
     Microfinance Network

Hedge Funds versus Malaria
Helsinki Process
HungerMovement.org

InnoCentive
International Finance Facility for
     Immunization

LifeMakers

Millennium Challenge Compacts
Mohammed Bin Rashid Al Maktoum
     Foundation
Mo Ibrahim Foundation
M-PESA

NineMillion.org

ONE Campaign
Open Budget Initiative

(PRODUCT)RED
Publish What You Pay
Purpose Driven Network

Revenue Watch Institute

Shell Foundation's Excelerate

TED-Global

UN Global Compact

Virgin Unite

—New activists and engagement models
—New private funders and financing models
—New entrepreneurs and business models
—New technologies and dissemination models
—New public funders and official assistance models.

Many of these new players are influenced by and influence each other. They also influence and interact with the operations of more established

Figure 9-1. Forging New Partnerships and Alliances

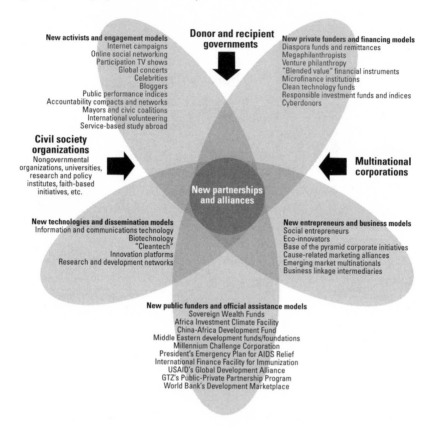

New activists and engagement models
Internet campaigns
Online social networking
Participation TV shows
Global concerts
Celebrities
Bloggers
Public performance indices
Accountability compacts and networks
Mayors and civic coalitions
International volunteering
Service-based study abroad

Donor and recipient governments

New private funders and financing models
Diaspora funds and remittances
Megaphilanthropists
Venture philanthropy
"Blended value" financial instruments
Microfinance institutions
Clean technology funds
Responsible investment funds and indices
Cyberdonors

Civil society organizations
Nongovernmental organizations, universities, research and policy institutes, faith-based initiatives, etc.

Multinational corporations

New partnerships and alliances

New technologies and dissemination models
Information and communications technology
Biotechnology
"Cleantech"
Innovation platforms
Research and development networks

New entrepreneurs and business models
Social entrepreneurs
Eco-innovators
Base of the pyramid corporate initiatives
Cause-related marketing alliances
Emerging market multinationals
Business linkage intermediaries

New public funders and official assistance models
Sovereign Wealth Funds
Africa Investment Climate Facility
China-Africa Development Fund
Middle Eastern development funds/foundations
Millennium Challenge Corporation
President's Emergency Plan for AIDS Relief
International Finance Facility for Immunization
USAID's Global Development Alliance
GTZ's Public-Private Partnership Program
World Bank's Development Marketplace

Source: Author.

NGOs, research institutes, foundations, corporations, and both donor and recipient governments. Indeed, some of the greatest innovation and leverage occurs at the core of figure 9-1, where both new and traditional players are working collaboratively in partnership with each other.

In some cases, these partnerships constitute a new legal entity with its own governance structure and operations. There are now more than twenty global public-private health partnerships, for example, bringing together hundreds of organizations to research, fund, and advocate for improved global health outcomes. Examples include the Global Alliance for Vaccines and Immunization; the Global Fund to Fight AIDS, Tuberculosis, and Malaria; and the Global Alliance for Improved Nutrition. Nonhealth examples include the

Extractive Industries Transparency Initiative, Global Environment Facility, and Global Reporting Initiative.

In other cases, these cross-sector partnerships consist of specific programs, projects, or campaigns between an official donor agency, foundation, or corporation and a variety of new players. GTZ's Public-Private Partnership Initiative and the U.S. Agency for International Development's Global Development Alliance are two bilateral agency examples that are leveraging public donor funds through cofinancing and joint implementation efforts with corporations. UN agency examples include the UN Global Compact, UN Fund for International Partnerships, the NineMillion.org project of the Office of the United Nations High Commissioner for Refugees, the United Nations Environment Program's Billion Tree Campaign, and the United Nations Development Program's Growing Inclusive Markets Initiative, which are all being undertaken with corporate, NGO, and foundation partners.

In many cases, these alliances take the form of more informal, noncontractual global coalitions and networks, with legally and operationally autonomous players cooperating around a common cause or issue, usually enabled by information technology and the media and/or by shared donors and investors. Examples include the Make Poverty History and Publish What You Pay campaigns, the Digital Diaspora Network, HungerMovement.org, and Hedge Funds versus Malaria. The vignettes in the next section illustrate how some of these emerging alliances and networks are working in practice, and the leverage that can be gained from the dynamic linkages between them.

New Networks Leveraging Science, Technology, and Capital to Deliver Pro-Poor Solutions

Terms such as innovation, venture capital, design, and technology have long been associated with the world's most competitive nations and corporations, and with the most successful entrepreneurs, scientists, and universities. They are not commonly linked to the term "poverty" or to the process of developing products and services for the poor. In recent years, a variety of new players and networks have started to experiment with novel ways to apply these more market-oriented, high-technology solutions to alleviating poverty. These include: new marketplaces and innovation platforms; venture philanthropists and venture capitalists; diaspora funds, remittances, and microfinance networks; and social entrepreneurs and eco-innovators. It is useful to briefly describe each.

New marketplaces and innovation platforms. Conveners such as the Clinton Global Initiative, the World Bank's Development Marketplace, the Rockefeller Foundation and InnoCentive's Web-based innovation center, and the annual Technology, Entertainment, and Design (TED) Conference are bringing together some of the world's leading scientists, inventors, social entrepreneurs, corporations, foundations, philanthropists, and venture capitalists to explore new ideas for delivering affordable products and services to the poor and for developing clean technologies. They are also brokering deals and obtaining concrete commitments aimed at turning these ideas into cost-effective and often commercially viable realities. In its first two years, for example, the Clinton Global Initiative mobilized nearly $10 billion through some 500 commitments. The Rockefeller-InnoCentive innovation platform, which was launched in 2007, plans to link more than 100,000 registered scientists from 175 countries with entrepreneurs, companies, and organizations that are developing products and services targeted specifically at the poor.[5]

Venture philanthropists and venture capitalists. Key "investors" in this process are, on the one hand, corporate and private foundations that are taking a more enterprise-based and competence-led approach to philanthropy. On the other hand, they include venture capitalists who are applying their investment acumen and resources to invest in social entrepreneurs with an explicit aim to deliver both market value and social value. It is useful to examine several examples.

On the philanthropy front, for example, Google.org is leveraging the company's core competencies—its talent and capacity in information and communications technology—and providing investments as well as grants. Other corporate foundations, such as Virgin Unite and the Shell Foundation, are adopting similar business-led approaches. Shell's Excelerate program is catalyzing and scaling up small enterprises in Africa and Asia that provide modern energy and affordable infrastructure services to the poor, while Virgin Unite is investing in social enterprises and clean technology.

The Bill and Melinda Gates Foundation and the Rockefeller Foundation are also taking the linkages between philanthropy, investment, innovation, science, and technology to a new level. In 2006, for example, the two foundations launched the $150 million Alliance for a Green Revolution in Africa (known as AGRA), which will support both technology-driven and market-based solutions in an effort to improve the availability, affordability, and variety of seeds and other essential inputs to smallholder farmers. Among AGRA's goals will be to develop networks not only of African scientists and universities but also African entrepreneurs, including some 10,000 African agro-dealers.[6]

At the same time, leading venture capitalists such as Khosla Ventures, Kleiner Perkins Caufield & Byers, and Texas Pacific Group Ventures are investing in clean technology and biotechnology enterprises with the potential to develop leapfrog technologies and affordable solutions to meet global environmental and social challenges. The CleanTech Venture Network, established in 2002, now convenes over 8,000 of these investors and almost 10,000 companies.[7] Private equity and hedge funds, such as the Children's Investment Fund and Hedge Funds versus Malaria, are also mobilizing philanthropic dollars to support evidence-based poverty alleviation initiatives.

Diaspora funds, remittances, and microfinance networks. The growth in cross-border remittances and in microfinance institutions and networks provides two other burgeoning sources of finance that have the potential to seed fund and incubate new technologies and innovative market-driven approaches to serve the poor.

It is estimated that total global remittances from workers to their families reached $318 billion in 2007, up from $170 billion in 2002. Most of this money finds its way to developing countries, about $240 billion, which is more than double the value of official foreign aid.[8] At present, the majority of such remittances move directly between low-income workers and their families to meet basic consumption or small business development needs, rather than innovative, high-technology development solutions. There are some diaspora funds, and knowledge networks beginning to emerge that link the financial resources, skills, and contacts of wealthier migrants back to high-potential projects in their home countries. Examples include ChileGlobal, Ghana Skills Bank, LatIPnet, and the Digital Diaspora Network. Although such networks are in their infancy, they offer a new model worthy of further analysis and support.

A number of increasingly commercial and technologically-enabled microfinance institutions and small enterprise funds are also beginning to scale up to reach larger numbers of people. Whether it is commercial banks such as Citigroup, Barclays, or Deutsche Bank setting up business units or "blended-value" financing mechanisms to deliver such services, small enterprise funds such as GroFin, or innovative intermediary networks such as Grameen–Jameel Pan–Arabic Microfinance Limited, there is great potential for these new funding sources to help small firms and microenterprises move up the value chain.

Social entrepreneurs and eco-innovators. Key "implementers" in this emerging "pro-poor value chain" include for-profit and nonprofit social enterprises, which are incubating new models of research and development, technology dissemination, product development, and service delivery. Although most are still at a pilot stage and the challenge of scaling up remains daunting, they offer interesting models and potential investments for development agencies, financial institutions, corporations, and diaspora funds and remittances. Here are three different approaches among many market-led social enterprises:

—Amyris Biotechnologies, Inc., is a privately held company applying the latest advances in synthetic biology to develop cost-effective, renewable biofuels (funded by leading venture capitalists) and an affordable, accessible antimalaria drug (in partnership with the University of California, Berkeley, and the Institute for OneWorld Health, America's first nonprofit pharmaceutical company, with funding from the Bill and Melinda Gates Foundation).

—The Acumen Fund is a nonprofit venture fund that provides a combination of loans, equity, and occasional grants, plus managerial and technical assistance, to enterprises that deliver affordable health care, housing, and water to low-income consumers. Its start-up "investors" included the Cisco Systems and Rockefeller foundations. Acumen Fund's own investments to date include malaria bed nets in Africa, housing for the poor in Pakistan, and drip irrigation in India.

—M-PESA in Kenya is a commercial business providing money transfers and other financial services through cellphones to low-income people, many without bank accounts. It was created by the global telecommunications corporation Vodafone, working with the local operator Safricom with support from the United Kingdom's Department for International Development. Less than six months after its launch in early 2007, M-PESA had more than 175,000 customers, and some 600 agents operating throughout the country via gas stations, supermarkets, cybercafés, and small retailers, in a country where the formal banking sector reaches less than 20 percent of the population.

New Networks Mobilizing Citizens, Voters, and Consumers to Take Personal Action against Poverty

Two of the greatest challenges in mobilizing the public to either advocate for or contribute resources to tackling global challenges are lack of awareness and complexity of the issues. Speaking at Harvard University's 2007 Commencement, Bill Gates summed up the challenge as follows: "The barrier to change is not too little caring; it is too much complexity. To turn caring into action, we need to see the problem, see a solution, and see the impact. But complexity blocks all three steps. Even with the advent of the Internet and twenty-four-hour news, it is still a complex enterprise to get people to truly see the problems."[9]

Initiatives such as the following are helping people to make sense of this complexity by tapping into the outreach capacity and interactive nature of social networking and new media, and combining this with popular culture, consumer brands, relatively simple messages, and compelling human interest stories. These initiatives are effectively communicating the link between an individual's personal action and results on the ground, often thousands of miles away. In doing so, they are capturing the imagination and support of a new generation of citizens, voters, and consumers. Such efforts do not match and cannot substitute for official development assistance and private sector investment, but they can spur greater public support for development issues, and increase the flow of private resources to support poverty alleviation initiatives:

—*The ONE Campaign* was inspired by the global Make Poverty History initiative and describes itself as "an effort by Americans to rally Americans— one by one—to fight the emergency of global HIV/AIDS and extreme poverty. ONE is students and ministers, punk rockers and NASCAR moms, Americans of all beliefs and every walk of life, united to make poverty history."[10] By the end of 2007, over 2.4 million people had signed up to the campaign. ONE.org provides these participants with direct links to more than fifty NGO partners and faith groups, updates on key development challenges, and guidelines on how to advocate for government action on specific issues and initiatives.

—*The Global Fund to Fight AIDS, Tuberculosis, and Malaria* is one of the initiatives supported by ONE. Itself an innovative new approach to mobilizing public and private resources, the Global Fund had approved grants for more than 450 projects in 136 countries with a total commitment of $6.6 billion by the end of 2007. To date, despite aiming to raise 10 percent of it funds from the private sector, most of the Global Fund's resources have come from governments, with less than 1 percent from business. As of July 2007, however, it had received over $30 million from private sources through another innovative new initiative called (PRODUCT)[RED].[11]

—*(PRODUCT)[RED]* was launched at the 2006 World Economic Forum by Bobby Shriver and Bono. It is a multicompany, cause-related marketing campaign, raising both awareness and funds to support the Global Fund and its projects in Africa. Employing world-class marketing, advertising, and brand management expertise, and both traditional and new media, (RED) is working with iconic consumer brands such as American Express, Converse, Gap, Giorgio Armani, Motorola, and Apple to sell (RED) products that contribute a percentage of sales to the Global Fund. The founders argue that, "(RED) is not a charity or 'campaign.' It is a commercial initiative designed to create awareness and a sustainable flow of funds from the private sector into the Global Fund to fight the AIDS pandemic in Africa."[12] Its targeted approach and its ability to identify specific projects and to communicate their beneficial impact on the lives of specific individuals enhances the value proposition for consumers and beneficiaries even further.

—*American Idol* is heralding in a new era of participation television that engages viewers to act and respond. Though there may be debate on its merits, 63.5 million votes were cast in one night for *Idol*'s 2007 finalists. In 2007, the program also hosted its first *Idol Gives Back* shows, coinciding with the first U.S. Malaria Awareness Day. The effort raised almost $70 million to support United States–based and global initiatives focused on children and on tackling hunger and malaria. As Bono commented in the lead-up to the event, "We'll see worlds collide when Africa appears on America's most-watched TV show. This is a big deal, a little bit of pop history."[13]

—*MySpace.com* was the source of Bono's comments. It is one of the world's fastest growing social networking websites, with more than 100 million users around the world. In 2007, it agreed to partner with *Idol Gives Back,* (RED), and the ONE Campaign to use this outreach capacity in a joint effort to raise citizen awareness, funds, and activism to fight global poverty. Along with other social networking sites such as YouTube and Face-Book, MySpace is starting to put global issues and campaigns on the agenda in an accessible and engaging manner for millions of young people.

—*Life Makers and the Purpose Driven Network* are two of the world's other most popular websites and networks that have started to mobilize thousands of individuals through their faith communities to engage in a range of community initiatives and poverty alleviation efforts. The former is one of the projects of Amr Khaled, a Muslim layman preacher and activist who reaches an estimated 100 million Arab youth every week through his TV shows and has what is one of the most accessed personal websites in the world. His Life Makers program engages youth in practical action plans to transform their lives and communities, and encourages peaceful interaction between Islam and the West. The American pastor and philanthropist Rick Warren has inspired the Purpose Driven Network, which is a coalition of over 400,000 congregations in churches and synagogues from over 200 denominations around the world. This network also encourages faith-based community service, including advocacy and practical engagement in efforts to address poverty and HIV/AIDS, and to support initiatives such as the Global Fund.

These vignettes are a small sample of the emerging approaches to mobilize resources and advocacy for international development. They are facilitated by new types of activists, funders, technologies, and entrepreneurs, and in many cases leveraged by new models and/or sources of official development assistance. The vast majority of these approaches are relatively new and untested, but the opportunities and accountability challenges that they present are becoming too numerous and important to ignore.

New Opportunities and Accountability Challenges

The emergence of new players, models of engagement, and sources of official development assistance represents one of the most fundamental and rapid shifts in the history of international development. These emerging approaches do not, and this chapter argues should not, replace the responsibility of donor and recipient governments in ensuring the security and prosperity of citizens. Yet they can supplement, leverage, and in certain cases improve the role of government.

Some of these players, for example, have the potential to fill governance gaps, tackle market failures, improve public accountability frameworks, and strengthen public institutions. Others offer potential to mobilize untapped financial, technical, and human resources for development, and to seed innovative new products and processes for serving, and in many cases working directly with the world's poor. Furthermore, the focus of a number of these new models on more market-oriented and demand-driven approaches, and on local capacity building and asset accumulation by the poor themselves, offers hope for greater sustainability than has been the case with many development efforts to date. In the case of "new" official donors, such as China and India, there is also the potential to increase the amount and variety of official assistance available to developing countries.

At the same time, these new players and approaches represent unfamiliar challenges related to their own accountability and effectiveness in terms of their governance, impact, stakeholder participation, legitimacy, and scalability.

They may undermine or "crowd out" more effective existing development activities, for example, or make less efficient use of scarce resources. They may increase dependency on external sources of support rather than build in-country capacity. Some have been challenged for distorting local market incentives or national development priorities by going around official processes, favoring single issues and vested interests, or focusing on "quick-win" media-friendly but unsustainable successes. There are concerns in certain quarters about the influential role that individual celebrities and philanthropists are playing in shaping global and national public policy agendas when they are neither elected nor appointed officials. Few of these high-profile new models have achieved national or global scale to date, and in many cases their methodologies are still being tested and their impact evaluated.

To be fair, it is still early days for the vast majority of these new approaches, and similar criticisms can be made of most long-standing official development assistance programs and humanitarian agencies. Indeed, in many cases it has been the high operating costs, and the growing inability of more traditional approaches to tackle increasingly complex and interdependent global challenges that have spurred the emergence of new models. This is not to suggest that nongovernmental and private sector approaches are a panacea or even a better alternative to traditional official development assistance, but it illustrates the need to be increasingly rigorous in analyzing the costs and effects of different development models and funding mechanisms—both new and traditional.

Good or bad, the growing impact, influence, and potential of these new players and models, and their relationship to more traditional development actors and approaches, cannot be ignored by anyone who is serious about alleviating global poverty. Their implications for improving governance and ensuring greater accountability for development outcomes can be viewed from four main perspectives:

—*First, increasing the accountability of governments, official donor agencies, and large corporations.* What role are new players and models playing in monitoring and advocating for greater accountability of donor governments, developing country governments, and large corporations, all of which continue to have enormous influence on the quality of poor peoples' lives and the nature of development outcomes?

—*Second, ensuring the accountability of civil society organizations.* Given that many nonstate and noncorporate actors are increasingly global and influential in their own right, what public responsibility do they have and should they have for their own organizations' governance, operations, and impact?

—*Third, enhancing the accountability of public-private partnerships and multistakeholder alliances.* In the case of increasingly complex and global multistakeholder alliances and networks, what is their responsibility to ensure that their beneficial impact outweighs the high transaction costs often associated with building such partnerships? Or at a minimum, what is their responsibility to ensure that they do not waste scarce resources or create more obstacles to alleviating poverty than would have been the case in their absence?

—*Fourth, encouraging the accountability of "new" official resource flows.* What are the accountability implications of the emergence or more accurately in some cases, the reemergence of "new" official donors and investors such as those from China, India, and oil-rich nations in the Middle East?

The Harvard University scholar David Brown identifies three different but not mutually exclusive models of accountability that have applicability across these different public, private, and civil society sectors, and for a range of development challenges and situations:[14]

—*Agency accountability,* which focuses on an agent's accountability to a principal whose goals that agent has been contractually hired and/or funded to accomplish. Examples include relations between corporate boards and management teams, or NGOs having to account for use of funds and program results to their donors.

—*Representative accountability,* which usually focuses on the accountability of elected officials and public bureaucrats to the people who have elected them or whom they claim to represent. It is also relevant for advocacy NGOs and campaigners who seek to influence public policy and corporate standards, and/or who claim to speak on behalf of the poor.

—*Mutual accountability,* which Brown defines as "accountability among autonomous actors committed to shared values and visions, and to relationships of mutual trust and influence that enable renegotiating expectations and capacities to respond to uncertainty and change."[15] This approach is increasingly relevant for the multistakeholder alliances and public-private partnerships that are starting to play a prominent role in tackling some of the most complex and multidimensional development challenges. They usually lack hierarchical and clearly defined relationships between participating parties, and often change over time in terms of their goals, participants, and activities.

Despite these different approaches and definitions, most assessments of institutional or organizational accountability cover the following issues, which are as relevant for public institutions as they are for corporations and civil society organizations:

—*Governance:* ownership and governance structures.

—*Financial integrity:* sources of funds, methods of fund-raising, use of funds, book-keeping and auditing systems.

—*Administrative reliability, competence, and credibility:* policies, process, and management systems. Discipline and consistency in implementation.

—*Performance effectiveness:* the level of benefits and types of effects experienced by targeted beneficiaries or the general public. The ability to deliver on commitments made to stakeholders. Performance relative to alternative approaches.

—*Performance evaluation:* quality, independence, integrity, and disclosure of evaluation mechanisms, methods, indicators, and results.

—*Advocacy credibility:* veracity, accuracy, authority, fairness, and representative nature of public statements and/or advocacy campaigns.

—*Transparency:* access by stakeholders to information about the organization.

—*Dispute resolution mechanisms:* responsiveness to stakeholder complaints. Independence, confidentiality, and enforceability of dispute resolution mechanisms.

—*Level of stakeholder participation:* the degree to which stakeholders are actually involved in the organization or institution's governance, strategic planning, policymaking, implementation, evaluation, and learning processes.

The following sections review these issues in relation to the four sets of questions posed on pages 161–62.

Increasing the Accountability of Governments, Official Donor Agencies, and Large Corporations

From the abolition of slavery two hundred years ago to the American civil rights movement, social movements and civil society organizations have long played a vital role in promoting human rights and advocating for better governance and accountability from their governments and other powerful actors and elites. Despite the advent of democracy in many nations, this role is arguably more important and feasible than ever. The emergence of information technology, global media, and new activists has the potential to empower many more citizens to take action to promote better governance and greater accountability by governments, official donor agencies, and large corporations. New models of public sector interaction also offer the potential for increasing the accountability of these key actors.

Notable examples include these four modes of engagement, which are often interrelated and are driven by both civil society organizations and public sector entities:

—Initiatives to monitor government policies, budgets, and performance;
—Initiatives to strengthen public sector capacity;
—Initiatives to increase public advocacy for international development;
—Initiatives to promote corporate responsibility.

Initiatives to Monitor Government Policies, Budgets, and Performance

Civil society organizations are playing an increasingly effective role in monitoring, communicating, and in some cases ranking the performance and accountability of governments. International NGOs and donors, and in a few cases corporations, are also building the capacity of locally based citizen groups and journalists in developing countries to undertake this role. In some cases, these "watchdog" advocacy and capacity-building initiatives are also leading to the establishment of new types of on-the-ground collaborative governance and accountability mechanisms. Some notable examples are summarized in box 9-2.

The examples summarized in box 9-2 have been initiated and led primarily by civil society organizations and citizens. There are also some interesting new models emerging that are led by donor and developing country governments aimed at either holding each other to account or creating multistakeholder accountability mechanisms.

The *African Peer Review Mechanism* offers one new and potentially important government-led approach to increasing public accountability for development outcomes. Established in 2002 by African leaders, this aims to serve as a voluntary mechanism for assessing and publicly reporting on the performance of participating governments. While its effectiveness is clearly limited by its voluntary nature, and the fact that nations such as Zimbabwe and the Sudan refuse to participate and are not required to do so by their peers, this mechanism is still a model that offers interesting lessons for greater South-South cooperation, monitoring, and capacity building.

Over the past decade, a number of donor governments have also established new mechanisms in consultation with developing country governments and other actors aimed at ensuring better governance and more accountable, pro-poor development outcomes.

One such example is the *Extractive Industries Transparency Initiative* (EITI) initiated by the U.K. government in 2002 partly in response to growing public awareness of the "resource curse" and to the Publish What You Pay campaign outlined in box 9-2. EITI has evolved into an unprecedented model for improving governance, which aims to build multistakeholder accountability mechanisms within resource-rich developing countries between the national governments, donor governments, extractive industry companies, and major investors. To date, some twenty countries have committed to implement the principles and criteria developed by EITI.

It is still early days and numerous obstacles remain in terms of EITI achieving its ultimate objective of ensuring that oil, gas, and mining revenues contribute more effectively to economic growth and poverty reduction instead of exacerbating corruption, conflict, and poverty. Yet, the model offers one of the most interesting advances toward a new era of more collaborative governance and mutual accountability. It is financed through a Multi-Donor Trust Fund and governed by an independent International Advisory Group, which has representation from implementing countries, supporting countries, civil society organizations, industry, and investment companies. Similar transparency initiatives are being established in the construction and pharmaceutical sectors, again with leadership from the U.K. government, but with a strong emphasis on multistakeholder consultation and governance structures.

A well-known bilateral example aimed at increasing government accountability has been the establishment of the *Millennium Challenge Corporation* (MCC) by the U.S. government in 2004. This aims to reduce poverty in some of the poorest countries in the world through working cooperatively with recipient governments in the promotion of sustainable economic growth and good governance. To become eligible for funds and other forms of assistance from MCC, governments in these countries formally agree to be assessed against the following set of sixteen independent and transparent policy indicators: civil liberties; political rights; voice and accountability; government effectiveness; rule of law; control of corruption; immunization rate; public expenditure on health; girls' primary education completion rate; public expenditure on primary education; costs of starting a business; inflation rate; days to start a business; trade policy; regulatory quality; fiscal policy; and supplemental information on natural resource management and land rights and access.

Countries that qualify for assistance then enter into a time-limited public Compact with MCC aimed at mutual accountability for an agreed set of deliverables by both parties. Others with potential are designated for Threshold Program assistance, to support them in improving their performance against these indicators. As of May 2007, MCC was working with forty countries and had provided $3 billion in grants to eleven partner countries.[16]

Clearly, the question of establishing conditionality and good governance criteria for the provision of donor funds is a complex and contentious issue

BOX 9-2
Civil Society Monitoring Mechanisms
to Promote Better Governance

The Open Society Institute (OSI) is playing a crucial leadership role in this area as a private operating and grant-making foundation with the explicit goal of shaping public policy to promote democratic governance, human rights, and economic, legal, and social reform. In 2004, for example, it worked with national partners and civil society groups to establish the Africa Governance Monitoring and Advocacy Project (AfriMAP). This aims to monitor the compliance of member states of the African Union with standards of good governance. Starting in five countries in 2005, with a focus on the justice sector, rule of law, political representation, and the civil service, AfriMAP is using a standardized framework to compile publicly available country reports on these issues. These reports will enable comparison and learning between countries, as well as opportunities to publicly highlight both good and bad practice. In addition, they provide a useful framework for mobilizing citizen action, and for engaging with governments in a constructive and evidence-based manner.

OSI was also instrumental in creating the Revenue Watch Institute, which aims to improve democratic accountability in natural resource-rich countries. It does this by building local coalitions and enabling citizens in these countries to become more effective monitors of government revenues and expenditures through providing them with information, training, networks, and funding. It also advises governments on best practices in resource revenue management.

In 2002, OSI and the Revenue Watch Institute worked with Global Witness, Oxfam, CAFOD, Save the Children UK, and Transparency International UK to establish the Publish What You Pay campaign. This has been one of the most effective civil society led campaigns for better governance and accountability in resource-rich developing countries. It now involves a worldwide coalition of over 300 NGOs calling for the mandatory disclosure of payments made to governments by oil, gas, and mining companies for the extraction of natural resources. It also calls for resource-rich developing country governments to publicly disclose details of their natural resource-related public revenues.

The Brookings Transparency and Accountability Project is another example that was established by the Brookings Institution and the William and Flora Hewlett Foundation to strengthen the mechanisms by which the public can hold governments in developing countries accountable. It is doing so by building the capacity of local civil society organizations to monitor and analyze public expenditure processes and to advocate for more effective use of scarce resources that can lead to better development outcomes—similar to the role the Brookings Institution was initially established to play in the United States more than ninety years ago.

Two other new entrants to the important work of monitoring, ranking, and communicating government performance are the International Budget Project and the Mo Ibrahim Foundation. The International Budget Project was established in 1997 to build the capacity of civil society organizations around the world to analyze and influence government budget processes, institutions, and outcomes. In 2002 it developed the Open Budget Index, a survey tool that currently ranks the transparency of central government budgets in fifty-nine countries. The 2006 survey concluded that 90 percent of countries covered do not meet the standard of accurate, timely, and comprehensive provision of information during each stage of their budget cycles. Indeed, only six countries surveyed—France, New Zealand, Slovenia, South Africa, the United Kingdom, and the United States—scored particularly well (data from Center on Budget and Policy Priorities, International Budget Project, *Open Budget Initiative 2006*). It is notable that several of these countries and others that ranked well in the index are developing countries—demonstrating that good governance and accountability are not the preserve of developed nations.

The Mo Ibrahim Foundation has supported the development of an independent ranking of the governance performance of African governments by Harvard's Kennedy School of Government. It is also awarding an annual prize for good governance to the retired African leader who has achieved the best governance performance for his or her citizens as determined by the ranking process and evaluated by an internationally recognized, independent panel chaired by former UN secretary-general Kofi Annan.

In all these and similar civic-led initiatives to improve government accountability, the role of the media is essential. It is often seriously undermined by repressive and corrupt governments, and by logistical and financial obstacles faced by the poor in accessing reliable information. The emergence of new media, such as the Internet and wireless enabled access to information, as well as basic radios that can be operated without batteries, such as the *Freeplay* wind-up radios, are playing an important role in getting information to low-income and remote communities and helping to raise public awareness about governance and accountability issues. Emerging online networks and social networking initiatives include global user-driven websites such as YouTube, MySpace, and PoliticsOnline. Other notable examples include Afrigator, allAfrica.com, and Pambazuka News, which focus on Africa and between them aggregate hundreds of bloggers and news services.

beyond the scope of this chapter. Apart from long-standing and ongoing debate within the OECD donor nations themselves, there is the rapidly evolving political and operational challenge of "new" official donors that do not require the same performance standards from recipient governments. Despite such challenges, the new government-led and civil-society-led models that are emerging to monitor and encourage more transparent and accountable government policies, budgets, and performance offer great potential for ensuring better development outcomes.

Initiatives to Strengthen Public Sector Capacity

In a growing number of cases, developing country governments are committed to being more responsive and accountable to their citizens, but despite their best intentions they lack the institutional, administrative, and research capacity to achieve this. In short, their problem is weak governance rather than bad governance. Even when they want to provide their citizens with transparent and readily accessible information and with reliable and efficient services, they are all too often constrained by a lack of human capital, a lack of modern technology, and a lack of administrative capability. They lack capacity when it comes to gathering and analyzing data, evaluating different public policy options, consulting with key stakeholder groups, assessing development effects, planning for emergencies, and improving the efficiency and administration of judicial, legislative, regulatory, and economic institutions.

In such cases, a much greater and more creative role could be played by official development agencies, foundations, philanthropists, universities, and corporations in helping to strengthen public institutions. More needs to be done, for example, to develop a new generation of scholars, researchers, public policy institutes, universities, research institutes, and evaluation programs within developing countries themselves rather than relying on expensive external experts. Increased efforts are also needed to help developing country governments harness the benefits of new information technologies for more effective and accountable delivery of services ranging from education and health, to social welfare and enterprise support. Public and private donors can also support economic capacity-building efforts in areas such as trade negotiations and improving local investment climates.

Interesting models are beginning to emerge in all these areas, led by a combination of both new and more established players, often working in partnership with each other. In some cases, they build on a long tradition of private foundation support for strengthening public institutions and systems. The Ford Foundation and Rockefeller Foundation, for example, have a long-standing track record in this area. New multi-billion-dollar foundations such as the Bill and Melinda Gates Foundation, which has invested substantial sums in strengthening public health systems in developing countries, and the recently created Mohammed Bin Rashid Al Maktoum Foundation, which has committed $10 billion to build capacity in public education, research, science and technology throughout the Middle East region, offer great potential for an era of renewed and more technology enabled efforts to build public sector capacity.

Three other public-private efforts are summarized in box 9-3. These and others like them are playing a unprecedented—and as yet untested—role in strengthening weak public institutions and systems in the areas of research, public health, education, and economic management.

Initiatives to Increase Public Advocacy for International Development

Within donor countries, there has also been a burgeoning of new activists and engagement models over the past five years aimed at mobilizing citizens, voters, and consumers in efforts to advocate for greater leadership and accountability from their own governments in the areas of aid, trade, and debt relief.

Well-known initiatives include the Make Poverty History campaign and the ONE campaign, which are both advocating for increasing the quantity and improving the quality of aid from donor governments. They are also providing citizens with the information, tools, contacts, and networks needed to have a multiplier effect, whether it is campaigning on a particular issue or raising financial and in-kind resources to send to developing countries. The Initiative for Global Development is another example established in 2003 that aims to mobilize corporate and civic leaders toward similar goals. One of its main campaigns aims to rally these leaders behind efforts to advocate for agricultural trade reform. Between them, these initiatives have made effective use of the media, Internet, social networking websites, and high-profile events to mobilize the support of a growing number of citizens, celebrities, civic leaders, and corporate executives to call for greater government resources and accountability in the fight against global poverty.

Initiatives to Promote Corporate Responsibility

Over the past decade, an important role has been played by human rights, environmental, labor, and development NGOs in both campaigning against, and increasingly working with, multinational corporations to improve the rigor and industry-wide implementation of corporate codes of conduct and standards.

BOX 9-3
Alliances to Strengthen Public Sector Capacity

The Global Development Network (GDN) offers one emerging model that aims to share and apply development research that is locally generated and more relevant to local policy conditions and constraints. It is a network of public and private research and policy institutes, with a growing number based in developing countries. The GDN was launched initially in 1999, with support from the World Bank and a group of donor governments and academic associations, and GDN's secretariat is now based in India with an affiliated office in Cairo. Though its donors remain mostly governments and multilateral agencies, the Ford Foundation, the Bill and Melinda Gates Foundation, and Merck are also supporting GDN.

The Business Coalition for Capacity Building (BCCB) offers another interesting new model, which aims to support capacity building efforts in developing countries in the areas of public policy, economic development, and rule of law. Founded in 2003 by major corporations such as AIG, ExxonMobil, Gap, Limited Brands, Microsoft, Pfizer, and Procter & Gamble, BCCB advocates for capacity building to be integrated into international economic and trade agreements, and it leverages the work being undertaken by its corporate members to strengthen economic institutions and trade capacity within selected developing countries.

The African Investment Climate Facility is a new public-private vehicle that aims to apply business principles to creating more attractive investment conditions in Africa. Launched in 2005 as a formal partnership between African and donor governments, and a small number of private sector companies, the facility is based in and run from Africa. Its public-private composition is reflected in its governance, funding, and operational structures, with a former African president and corporate chief executive acting as co-chairs. It has set a target of $100 million for its first three-year phase with results to be assessed annually by an independent board.

Examples of civil society activism and engagement in this area are numerous and multifaceted. They range from the sweatshop campaigns that beset the apparel and toy industries in the 1990s to campaigns against the extractive sector, banks, pharmaceutical, and food companies. In many cases, confrontational campaigns have evolved into multistakeholder and collective industry-wide initiatives aimed at developing common accountability standards, auditing processes, and sanctions. Examples include the Fair Labor Association in the apparel sector; the Ethical Trading Initiative in the apparel, food, and retail sectors; the Equator Principles for project finance; the Forest Stewardship Council; the Partnership for Quality Medical Donations; and the Extractive Industries Transparency Initiative—to name just a few.

More broadly, the United Nations Global Compact has become the largest corporate citizenship initiative in the world, with almost 5,000 corporate participants from more than 120 countries, many of them developing economies. Its participants commit to implementing a set of ten principles in the areas of human rights, labor rights, environment, and anticorruption in their business activities, and it has an independent multistakeholder governance structure, which includes leaders from business, civil society, trade unions, and government.

Most of these multistakeholder accountability mechanisms are less than five years old, and it is still too early to judge their efficacy and effectiveness. There are obvious free-rider problems given their voluntary nature and questions relating to the independence of auditing and evaluation mechanisms. Critics also question the rigor or lack of sanctions for bad performance. Despite these concerns, these accountability mechanisms suggest a hopeful way forward for ensuring that large corporations contribute to more accountable and sustainable development outcomes, and at the minimum do not seriously exacerbate poverty.

Ensuring the Accountability of Civil Society Organizations

As civil society organizations gain influence and extend their global reach, their own accountability has obviously become an emerging issue. Kumi Naidoo, secretary-general of CIVICUS, the World Alliance for Citizen Participation, which has over 1,000 members in some 100 countries, comments, "The debate over civil society accountability is gaining momentum, and more and more civil society actors are entering the discussion and engaging with accountability challenges head-on. While negative criticism from external actors has helped to fuel the debate, it's important not to underestimate the internally generated drive toward accountability on behalf of many in civil society."[17]

Naidoo lists three key levels of civil society accountability that need to be considered: *upward accountability,* to funders and meeting the formal requirements of regulatory provisions where they exist; *downward accountability,* to the people who are being served or the constituency in whose name the rationale for existence is achieved in the first place; and *horizontal account-ability* or peer accountability, failure of which can lead to unnecessary dupli-cation, failure to forge the appropriate synergies, and wastage of resources.[18]

Although these issues are relevant to most civil society organizations, there are also specific accountability challenges depending on the goals, gover-nance, and modus operandi of the players in question. Antiglobalization and anticorporate activists, for example, will face some different accountability challenges to proglobalization and promarket philanthropists. Likewise, advocacy or campaigning NGOs will face different accountability issues compared with operational NGOs delivering services on the ground in devel-oping countries.

Some of the emerging accountability questions faced by operational organizations include issues related to project selection, and whether these players are distorting local market incentives, undermining government and public institutional capacity, advancing individual vested interests, or hiring scarce skilled workers away from local NGOs and government bodies. Advo-cacy NGOs, conversely, face accountability questions relating to who they represent, their legitimacy to talk on behalf of the poor, and the level of par-ticipation and consultation they have with their stated beneficiaries. Another accountability concern for such organizations is whether well-intentioned campaigns can sometimes harm the most vulnerable people they are aiming to support rather than helping them. The challenges faced by campaigns to eliminate child labor in global supply chains, while at the same time ensuring that children are not forced into even less desirable occupations, is one such example.

Another set of accountability issues gaining attention relates to situations where there is a lack of alignment, inconsistency, or conflicts of interest between different programs or policies undertaken by individual civil society organizations and foundations—for example, foundations that are deemed to have inconsistent policies in the way they allocate their program funding and how they invest their endowments, or that place unduly onerous reporting and accountability requirements on their grantees, without adhering to simi-lar standards of transparency and accountability for their own operations; or NGOs that are undertaking a monitoring or watchdog role, while raising funds from the same organizations they are monitoring.

The massive growth in cross-border remittances also raises new account-ability challenges for the NGOs and financial and telecommunications enter-prises that are facilitating these resource flows. Though there is compelling evidence that these remittances are largely beneficial and often directly meeting social needs and supporting enterprise development in recipient countries, they raise a variety of accountability challenges. According to the World Bank, these challenges include a potentially negative economic impact, such as currency appreciation and adverse effects on exports, in addition to the creation of dependency, and the misuse of remittance channels for money laundering and financing terror.[19] This raises a growing need for greater disclosure, monitoring, and management of these resource flows, while at the same time reducing their costs and increasing their access and effectiveness in alleviating poverty.

A variety of both mandatory and self-regulatory mechanisms are emerging in response to these and other accountability concerns associated with NGO activities. The following three subsections describe mechanisms that are of particular note and relevance for most civil society organizations.

Legal and Regulatory Accountability Mechanisms for NGOs

Research by the Center for Civil Society Studies at Johns Hopkins University and the International Center for Not-for-Profit Law identify the following legal and regulatory mechanisms as being essential for both enabling an active and open civil society, and calling it to account:[20]

—The basic legal standing of civil society organizations
—Establishment and registration procedures
—Capital, asset and/or membership requirements
—Tax treatment and benefits
—Disclosure and public reporting requirements.

There is clearly a balance that must be achieved in ensuring that the legal and regulatory framework in which civil society organizations operate holds them to account without undermining or even destroying them. Recent legal developments in countries such as Russia and Zimbabwe illustrate how draconian restrictions and requirements can have a severe impact not only on specific organizations but on the openness and vitality of civil society more generally.

Independent Monitoring and Ranking Systems

A number of independent watchdog organizations, rankings, and information providers have emerged in response to growing interest in the accountability of civil society organizations. In the United States, these include initiatives such as GuideStar, Charity Navigator, CharityWatch, NGOWatch, and

ForeignAID Ratings LLC. GuideStar, for example, provides data on more than 1.5 million nonprofit organizations, and it claims that its information is accessed by about 20,000 people a day. ForeignAID Ratings LLC, as another example, uses a patented system for rating development NGOs based on their socioeconomic impact; transparency; self-monitoring and evaluation; institutional development; and financial efficiency and growth.

Self-Regulatory or Voluntary Accountability Mechanisms

In a growing number of cases, just as has happened in the corporate world, civil society organizations are voluntarily establishing their own internal codes of conduct and approaches to organizational accountability. Alnoor Ebrahim at Harvard's Hauser Center for Nonprofit Organizations identifies five categories of accountability mechanisms being used by these NGOs: reports and disclosure statements; performance assessments and evaluations; participation by beneficiaries; self-regulations; and social audits.[21]

Collective NGO accountability mechanisms are also of growing relevance. These include voluntary certification or accreditation schemes, peer review and learning networks, and collective codes of conduct, ombudsmen mechanisms, and accountability charters. Three notable collective initiatives aimed at defining principles and standards for NGO accountability are summarized in box 9-4.

Enhancing the Accountability of Public-Private Partnerships and Multistakeholder Alliances

The emergence of public-private partnerships and global multistakeholder coalitions and networks has been referred to throughout this chapter. As has been illustrated, in a number of cases these initiatives are themselves a response to governance and accountability gaps on the part of governments and/or multinational corporations—the Extractive Industries Transparency Initiative and Fair Labor Association being examples. Others have been established to mobilize new resources, technologies, and skills for specific development challenges—the emergence of global public-private health partnerships being a good example. In all cases, these new multisector and multi-participant initiatives face their own governance and accountability challenges—over and above the accountability of the individual, often very diverse organizations that participate in them.

To date, relatively little analysis has been undertaken on these "networked or collaborative" accountability challenges, or indeed even on the development

BOX 9-4
Collective NGO Accountability Initiatives

One notable collective NGO accountability initiative is the Humanitarian Accountability Partnership (HAP), the humanitarian sector's first international self-regulatory body. Officially established in 2003, HAP grew out of an interagency research initiative in response to lessons learned and accountability gaps identified in the international response to the Rwandan genocide. Its mission is to make humanitarian action more accountable to its intended beneficiaries through an independently governed process of self-regulation, compliance verification, quality assurance certification, research and capacity building of NGOs in developing countries.

A second notable initiative is the International Non-Governmental Organizations Accountability Charter. In June 2006, a group of eleven international NGOs signed a ground-breaking charter based on nine core principles and aimed at enhancing accountability and transparency, encouraging stakeholder communication, and improving organizational performance and effectiveness. It is the first ever set of international and cross-sector guidelines for the NGO sector, encompassing human rights, environmental, and international development NGOs. The charter's founding members are ActionAid International, Amnesty International, CIVICUS World Alliance for Citizen Participation, Consumers International, Greenpeace International, Oxfam International, International Save the Children Alliance, Survival International, International Federation Terre des Hommes, Transparency International, and World YWCA.

A third notable initiative is InterAction's Private Voluntary Organization Standards, which aim to promote responsible standards in the areas of governance, finance and communications with the U.S. public, management practice, human resources, and program and public policy. Compliance is a requirement for admission to InterAction, which constitutes the largest alliance of U.S.-based international development NGOs, currently numbering over 160 with operations in all developing countries.

impact of these cross-sector alliances. In part this is due to the fact that most of them simply did not exist ten years ago. In one of the most comprehensive impact assessments undertaken to date, the World Bank reviewed its portfolio of about seventy global programs, all of which involve a variety of different public, private, and civil society participants in their funding, governance, or program delivery activities.[22] It carried out in-depth analysis of twenty-six of these programs, which represented 90 percent of all the World Bank's global program expenditures in 2004. Only six of these twenty-six programs are more than ten years old.

The World Bank's evaluation concluded that while most of these public-private partnerships have been innovative and responsive to addressing selected development challenges, and several have added measurable value, there are weaknesses that need to be addressed. These include accountability challenges in terms of their governance, management, and financing, and particularly the level of participation in decisionmaking by developing country governments and intended beneficiaries. The establishment by the World Bank of a Global Programs and Partnership Council to address some of these issues illustrates another new approach to improving the impact and accountability of new development players and models.

In another comprehensive study focused on twenty-three global public-private health partnerships, the Overseas Development Institute also concluded that though these partnerships add significant value in tackling diseases of poverty, this contribution is undermined by some common and soluble accountability challenges.[23] These include insufficient participation in decisionmaking by recipient countries and beneficiaries, inadequate use of critical governance procedures, failure to compare the costs and benefits of public-versus-private approaches, high transaction costs for managing the alliances, lack of partnership building skills, and wastage of resources through inadequate use of existing country systems.

The Partnership Governance and Accountability Project (PGA) was initiated by AccountAbility in 2006, in collaboration with a variety of academic, development and civil society organizations, with the aim of addressing some of these challenges.[24] It views accountability as consisting of three layers: being held to account (compliance); giving an account (transparency); and taking account (responsiveness to stakeholders). The project has undertaken a comprehensive governance and accountability analysis of nine diverse multisector alliances, some of which are global and others national or local in scale, and which address a range of development challenges and sectors. It is also developing and testing a systematic framework, including a diagnostic rating tool to enable better analysis and communication of a partnership's governance and accountability structures, processes, and norms. It is envisaged that over time this tool will be helpful to both participants and stakeholders in improving the performance of multisector partnerships and coalitions.

Encouraging the Accountability of "New" Official Resource Flows

Few changes in the flow of resources to developing countries over the past five years have been more dramatic or are more likely to have long-term strategic impact, than the growth in aid, trade, and investment between rapidly emerging economies such as Brazil, Russia, India, and, most notably, China, and other developing countries in Asia, Africa, and Latin America. There has also been a growth in resource flows from oil-rich nations in the Middle East and the Organization of the Petroleum Exporting Countries (OPEC) more widely (in particular Venezuela) to neighboring developing countries.

In many cases, these flows are driven by either the quest for energy assets and other commodities, as is the case of many Chinese activities in Africa, or as a result of high energy and commodity prices, as is the case in the outflow of resources from the oil-rich nations. In most cases, they are government driven, although a growing number of companies from these countries are also starting to invest internationally. Numerous commentators have noted that although these resource flows are often referred to as "new" sources of finance, there is a well-documented history of engagement between China, India, Russia, the Middle East, and other developing countries.[25] The scale of the recent increase in such flows, however, is substantial and has major implications for the global economy and financial system, international development, and the alleviation of poverty.

Attention has been focused in particular on Sovereign Wealth Funds from emerging economies, particularly those from China, the Middle East, and Russia. Though such funds date back to the 1950s, their size and influence have exploded in recent years. One estimate by Morgan Stanley predicts that these funds "could grow from $2.5 trillion now to nearly $12 trillion by 2015."[26] The chief economist at Standard Chartered Bank has commented, "State capitalism and resource nationalism are set to become two of the main economic issues of our time. Across Asia, Russia and the Middle East, governments look set to use their countries' currency reserves and savings to acquire overseas assets. The concept of using official savings is not new. . . . The difference now is that the number of countries pursuing such a strategy has soared, the funds at their disposal are huge and targets are more controversial."[27] Though these funds currently focus most of their cross-border investments on mature markets and global corporations, they have implications for all economies, and there are growing calls for greater transparency and accountability with respect to their size and management strategies.

In the case of "new" official aid flows and donor assistance, according to Richard Manning, chair of the OECD's Development Assistance Committee (DAC), "We are seeing not so much a sudden or unprecedented fall in the DAC share of aid, but rather the consequences of the much increased range of options that many developing countries now have to finance their development. This has been evident for years in the case of the stronger middle-income countries, mainly as a result of increased access to private capital. . . . The more interesting question may be whether for low-income countries the options are not also widening."[28]

Manning identifies four emerging or reemerging groups of donors: OECD members that are not members of the DAC (such as Turkey, South Korea, and Mexico); new members of the European Union that are not members of the OECD; Middle Eastern and OPEC countries and funds; and others that fall outside these three categories, such as China, India, Malaysia, Thailand, Brazil, Chile, Israel, and South Africa.[29]

China is clearly the "elephant in the room" in terms of aid, trade, and investment in developing countries. Opinions vary widely on whether its rapidly emerging role in international development will benefit developing countries and their citizens or not. This is particularly the case in Africa, where Chinese trade increased from an estimated $12 million in the 1980s to more than $50 billion in 2006, and foreign direct investment increased from less than $5 million a year in 1991 to an estimated $2 to $6 billion in 2006, with some 800 Chinese companies now estimated to be operating on the continent.[30]

As a recent report by the United Kingdom's Institute for Public Policy Research stated, "Managed well, China could bring real development benefits to Africans. For example, China could be a major new source of investment and development assistance, and contribute to higher levels of trade and growth. There are also important lessons that Africa might learn from China's remarkable development success of recent years. . . . Managed badly, however, China's role in Africa may lead to worsening standards of governance, more corruption and less respect for human rights."[31]

The accountability implications are enormous, and the levers to ensure accountability and transparency are limited without the active leadership and commitment of recipient governments and of the "new" official donors and investors themselves.

Several concerns have been expressed by a number of development practitioners, scholars, and commentators:[32]

—New resource flows (whether in the form of aid, natural resource exploitation, or other investment) that place few or no conditions on recipient governments in terms of good governance, human rights, and the environment will benefit corrupt and repressive regimes and elites at the expense of ordinary citizens—Sudan and Zimbabwe being two current examples;

—No conditionality or low conditionality aid will encourage recipient governments to postpone necessary policy reforms and improvements in governance standards and administrative performance, even if it does not directly exacerbate conflict or worsen existing poor standards of governance and accountability;

—Access to new sources of capital, whether private funds, export credit, or low-concession loans, could increase borrowing on inappropriate terms and reverse recent improvements in debt obligations and dependency;

—Large amounts of new resources could usher in another era of inappropriate tied aid and wasted resources on unproductive or unnecessary projects that have no or little benefits for citizens and do not make any contribution to the Millennium Development Goals;

—Foreign companies, both large and small, that are supported by government funds and guarantees back home, could further displace local enterprises and undermine fragile and fledgling private sectors in Africa.

These issues are obviously not only relevant to "new" official donors. They continue to be of concern to traditional DAC donors and investors, and are the focus of ongoing reform efforts within the OECD donor community, but they are of even greater magnitude when one considers the impact of "new" official donors.

Growing dialogue and cooperation between members of the DAC and non-DAC donors, both at the global level and between country-level offices and government officials within developing countries themselves, will be essential to ensuring a mutually beneficial way forward. So too, will be efforts by public-private initiatives such as the Extractive Industries Transparency Initiative and the Equator Principles to engage with major state-owned corporations and financial institutions, as well as government bodies, in countries such as China and Russia. Opportunities also exist for increased dialogue, shared learning, and the development of common standards between export credit agencies. In addition, there is potential for greater programmatic cooperation between "new" official donors, members of the DAC, and major corporations in areas such as health, training, infrastructure, and local enterprise development.

BOX 9-5
New Models of Public and Private Sector
Cooperation between China and Africa

Four new models of public and private sector cooperation between China
and Africa are illustrated by the examples that follow.

The China-Africa Development Fund, initiated by the China Development
Bank and launched in June 2007, plans to commit $5 billion in several stages.
According to the Xinhua News Agency, "The business scope of the fund
mainly includes equity and quasi-equity investment, fund investments, fund
management, investment management and consulting services. The fund will
be used to support African countries' agriculture, manufacture, energy sector, transportation, telecommunications, urban infrastructure, resource
exploration, and the development of Chinese enterprises in Africa" ("China
Approves China-Africa Development Fund," Shanghai, June 14, 2007).

The China Guangcai Program, established in 1994 by a small group of
about ten Chinese entrepreneurs with support from the government and
Chinese Communist Party, is now coordinated by the All China Federation of
Industry and Commerce and supported by more than 20,000 enterprises. It is
estimated to have invested over $16 billion in some 15,000 development proj-
ects, mostly in rural parts of China, and helped to create jobs for an estimated 5 million people (according to Li Hejun, chair of FarSighted Group, in
a speech at UN Global Compact Summit, Geneva, July 5, 2007). The program
serves as a key partner of the UN Global Compact in China, and it has initiated a China Guangcai Abroad initiative that is currently working with the
United Nations Development Program and the Chinese government on business-led development projects in Africa.

The China-Africa Business Council (CABC) was launched in 2005 with its
joint founders being the China Society for the Promotion of the Guangcai

In the case of China and Africa, emerging public-private partnerships
deserve further analysis and engagement by donors, NGOs, scholars, and
investors with interests in Africa; four of these are profiled in box 9-5. It is far
too early to tell whether these new initiatives will be instrumental in ensuring
that China's growing engagement in Africa is beneficial to Africa's citizens or
not, but they offer interesting new models of South-South cooperation that
are worth watching and engaging with.

Program, the United Nations Development Program, the Chinese Ministry of Commerce, and China International Center for Economic and Technical Exchanges. It has been established as an NGO and views nonstate owned businesses as its key participants. CABC's stated aim is to build direct business linkages and technical cooperation between Chinese and African companies, including the sharing of business standards embodied in the UN Global Compact's ten principles for human rights, labor, the environment and anticorruption. It is initially focusing on Cameroon, Ghana, Mozambique, Nigeria, Tanzania, and Kenya. According to the United Nations Development Program, "Driven by the private sector with strong public sector support, CABC is believed to be the first public-private partnership initiative between China and Africa under the South-South Cooperation Framework" (see www.undp.org/china [July 2007]).

The Centre for Chinese Studies at Stellenbosch University is the first academic center devoted to the study of China on the African continent. It is housed in South Africa's oldest Afrikaans-language university, which has a charter dating back to the 1880s. This may seem like an unlikely combination. Yet it is symbolic of the emergence of new alliances and models in the international development arena. The center—which was established in 2004 as a joint undertaking by the governments of South Africa and China, and is supported by a growing number of private donors and corporate partners—is becoming a key hub for African and Chinese research institutes and universities, as well as a source of analysis and dialogue for the public, private, and civil society sectors.

Conclusion

This chapter has attempted to capture some of the dynamism and diversity of new development players, models, and sources of official assistance, some of the opportunities and accountability challenges they are creating, and some of the evolving relationships between them that aim to leverage these opportunities and address accountability challenges.

It is a period of enormous flux. The pros and cons of these new approaches to development, especially relative to those of the past, are still being evaluated and debated. There can be little doubt, however, that some of the changes are needed and many of them are irreversible.

Achim Steiner, executive director of the United Nations Environment Program and former director-general of the International Union for the Conservation of Nature, sums up the central challenge: "We are struggling, with globalization, in a framework of national governments and international organizations, to define how we create accountability for the big challenges of our time, such as poverty, health, education, gender issues or human rights. We are facing a vacuum, as the systems that we have at our disposal are simply unable to cope with a globally-networked society in terms of information, capital, and environmental impacts. How do we establish norms and standards as the baseline of accountability, which are more legitimate in today's world? We have to redefine who sits at the table because, without this, these norms and standards lose their legitimacy. Societies, individuals, and communities are less and less controlled by government so the emergence of the private sector and civil society in shaping public discourse and creating public pressure has to be reflected."[33]

Many of the multistakeholder partnerships, alliances, and networks that are starting to emerge at the global, national, and local levels are a response to this challenge. In particular, they are a response to the need to redefine how we can most legitimately shape governance and accountability frameworks, and how we can most effectively mobilize and deploy resources for development and poverty alleviation. And they are an initial attempt at creating models for mutual accountability—be it between developed and developing countries, between donors and beneficiaries, or between public and private players.

Whether it is multisector ranking initiatives such as the Global Accountability Project, learning networks like the UN Global Compact, consultation processes like the UN secretary-general's special representative on business and human rights, dialogue structures such as the Helsinki Process, South-South cooperation such as the China-Africa Business Council, or joint accreditation and accountability mechanisms such as the Extractive Industries Transparency Initiative, we are seeing the dawn of a new era of multistakeholder institutions and networks.

As this chapter has explained, these multistakeholder initiatives are not a panacea, and they face their own challenges of governance and accountability. There is an ongoing need, for example, to balance efficient and timely results with the need for more participatory processes. There is a need to ensure rigorous evidence-based evaluation while allowing space for innovation, risk taking, and innovation. A need to remain focused on results and measurements, while keeping in mind Einstein's adage that "not everything that counts can be measured, and not everything that can be measured counts." And there is a need to encourage long-term local capacity building and empowerment, while being able to respond effectively to short-term crises and constraints. These are the types of dilemmas and trade-offs that lie at the heart of the accountability challenge. They can be summarized as accountability for impact; accountability for consultation and inclusion of all relevant stakeholders including the poor; and accountability for local capacity building, institution building, and empowerment.

There are no easy solutions and no perfect players and models. Simple comparisons of "old" versus "new" are often not helpful or insightful. Many "old" players are adapting creatively and accountably to this new world, be they the 94-year-old Rockefeller Foundation, the 100-year-old Shell corporation, the 126-year-old University of Stellenbosch, or the 60-year-old UNICEF. And some "new" players are creating as many operational and accountability challenges as the models they are replacing. Regardless of the types of players or models that are being adopted, however, there does appear to be growing consensus on these areas:[34]

—*The centrality of economic growth.* Economic growth, which ensures participation of the poor and takes measures to protect environmental sustainability, is increasingly recognized as an essential and powerful force in the fight against global poverty—both in terms of its potential to generate direct improvements in standards of living and to support broader social progress.

—*The foundation of good governance.* There is recognition that good governance, supported by effective institutions, forms another fundamental pillar for sustained development and poverty reduction. Equally, there is recognition that good governance is a challenge that needs to be addressed at the global, national, local, and organizational levels—and that it is an issue not only for governments but also for major corporations and civil society organizations.

—*The shared responsibility of governments as development partners.* There is greater acceptance that both developing country governments and donor governments must share responsibility and take mutual leadership for creating the necessary enabling environment—at both national and global levels—for achieving development goals.

—*The active participation of the poor.* The assets, capabilities, and voices of the poor themselves are now accepted as being essential in creating effective approaches to poverty reduction, with civil society organizations often playing a key role as interlocutors and advocates.

—*The importance of private sector development, especially small enterprise.* There is now strong evidence of the crucial importance of a diversified, productive, profitable, and responsible private sector—ranging from large multinationals and domestic corporations, to small firms and microenterprises in both rural and urban communities. The vital role of small enterprises as key producers, employers, distributors, innovators, and wealth creators is especially recognized.

—*The potential of new types of multistakeholder partnership and mutual accountability models.* There is a growing recognition that new and traditional development players need to work proactively together to develop more effective, efficient, and equitable solutions for complex and interdependent development challenges. They also need to work together to build accountability mechanisms that are not only compliance driven but also led by a commitment to shared learning and responsibility, and more participatory and performance-driven approaches to development.

All these factors should be taken into consideration in the drive toward greater accountability for development outcomes. The challenges we face as a global community are daunting, from climate change to high levels of poverty, inequality, and insecurity. Tried and tested solutions remain elusive, especially those that have achieved a large-scale impact and sustainability. There is no option but to keep experimenting with new approaches, evaluating and learning from what works and what does not, engaging key stakeholders in decisionmaking, advocating for greater accountability, and building bridges between different sectors, perspectives, and cultures. Above all—whether as individual voters, consumers, investors, or citizens, or as governments, corporations, foundations, universities, and other civil society organizations, in both developed and developing countries—we need to recognize that we are all mutually accountable for effecting change and for working toward a more equitable, just, and sustainable world.

Notes

1. Global Development Alliance, U.S. Agency for International Development, *Guide to the 2005 Resource Flows Analysis: US Total Flows to Developing Countries* (Washington:. U.S. Agency for International Development, 2007).

2. For a detailed analysis of the concept of "mutual accountability," see David L. Brown, "Multiparty Social Action and Mutual Accountability," in *Global Accountability*

and Moral Community, ed. Alnoor Ebrahim and Edward Weisband (Cambridge University Press, 2004).

3. Moisés Naim, "The Five Wars of Globalization," *Foreign Policy,* January–February 2003, 30.

4. Lester M. Salamon, speech made to the International Association of Volunteer Effort Conference, Amsterdam, January 2001

5. See www.rockfound.org.

6. Ibid.

7. See www.cleantechnetwork.com.

8. "Economic and Financial Indicators," *The Economist,* December 15, 2007.

9. Bill Gates, speech at Harvard University commencement, Cambridge, Mass., June 7, 2007.

10. See www.one.org.

11. See www.joinred.com.

12. Ibid.

13. See www.americanidol.com/idolgivesback.

14. Brown, "Multiparty Social Action."

15. Ibid.

16. See www.mcc.gov.

17. Kumi Naidoo (secretary-general of CIVICUS), "Civil Society Accountability: 'Who Guards the Guardians?'" address delivered at UN Headquarters, New York, April 3, 2003.

18. Kumi Naidoo, *The End of Blind Faith? Civil Society and the Challenge of Accountability, Legitimacy and Transparency,* AccountAbility Forum 2, NGO Accountability and Performance (Sheffield, U.K.: Greenleaf Publishing, 2004).

19. Dilip Ratha (World Bank), "Economic Implications of Remittances and Migration," presentation at Global Consumer Money Transfers Conference, London, October 30, 2006.

20. Lester M. Salamon, "The Scale of the Nonprofit Sector and the Enabling Legal Environment Required to Contribute to It," presentation at Turkish Third Sector National Conference, Istanbul, June 6, 2001. See also "Toward an Enabling Legal Environment for Civil Society," statement of Sixteenth Annual Johns Hopkins International Fellows in Philanthropy Conference, Nairobi, 2005.

21. Alnoor Ebrahim, "Accountability in Practice: Mechanisms for NGOs," *World Development* 31, no. 5 (2003): 815.

22. Operations Evaluation Department, World Bank, *Addressing the Challenges of Globalization: An Independent Evaluation of the World Bank's Approach to Global Programs* (Washington: World Bank, 2005).

23. Overseas Development Institute, *Global Health: Making Partnerships Work,* Briefing Paper 15 (London: Overseas Development Institute, 2007).

24. AccountAbility, *Partnership Governance and Accountability: Reinventing Development Pathways–The PGA Framework* (London: AccountAbility and U.S. Agency for International Development, 2006).

25. The articles, speeches, and publications that address this question include Richard Manning, "Will 'Emerging Donors' Change the Face of International Cooperation?" lecture at Overseas Development Institute, London, March 9, 2006; Akwe Amosu, *China in*

Africa: It's (Still) the Governance, Stupid, Foreign Policy in Focus Discussion Paper (Washington: Foreign Policy in Focus, 2007); Leni Wild and David Mepham, eds., *The New Sinosphere: China in Africa* (London: Institute for Public Policy Research, 2006); and Sanusha Naidu, *China and Africa's Natural Resource Sector: A View from South Africa* (Stellenbosch, South Africa: Centre for Chinese Studies, University of Stellenbosch, 2006).

26. Morgan Stanley Research Global, *How Big Could Sovereign Wealth Funds Be by 2015?* (New York: Morgan Stanley, 2007).

27. Gerard Lyons, "How State Capitalism Could Change the World," *Financial Times,* June 8, 2007.

28. Manning, "Will 'Emerging Donors' Change the Face."

29. Ibid.

30. Amosu, *China in Africa.*

31. Wild and Mepham, *New Sinosphere.*

32. This is drawn from the works cited in note 25.

33. Achim Steiner, "Accountability in a Globalized World," *World Conservation,* January 2007.

34. This section draws on *Building Linkages for Competitive and Responsible Entrepreneurship: Innovative Partnerships to Foster Small Enterprise, Promote Economic Growth and Reduce Poverty in Developing Countries,* by Jane Nelson (Cambridge, Mass., and Vienna: John F. Kennedy School of Government, Harvard University, and United Nations Industrial Development Organization, 2007).

10

Collaborative Governance: The New Multilateralism for the Twenty-First Century

SIMON ZADEK

A N ERA OF globalization, international development, and multilateralism as practiced for over half a century is over, for both better and worse. As we bid it a fond farewell, we might reflect for a moment on four emergent challenges we face in reinventing our global community to effectively address the imperative of sustainable development:

—*Fractured multilateralism:* a fracturing, perhaps fatally, of an inherited twentieth-century multilateralism and associated institutional arrangements. Visible is the decline in effectiveness of the United Nations, including its once-powerful cousins, the World Bank and the International Monetary Fund, in sustaining a reasonable universal consent over what constitutes acceptable state behavior and how best to steward the global commons. Confronting it is a new geopolitics underpinning a resurgent economic nationalism and mercantilism and associated with emerging economic and political powerhouses.

—*Globalization losers:* increasing income inequalities within developed as well as developing countries stemming from our inherited approach to market liberalization and global economic integration. The demise of the current Doha Round of multilateral trade negotiations exemplifies the need for a "development" deal and the likelihood that one will either not be done or else will achieve far less than needed. The despair of a growing rump of relative "losers" in wealthy nations is driving a new, largely democratic, politics fed by xenophobia and racism mixed with a fearful realism about the threats to livelihoods and economy.

—*Development's last round:* recent increases in public resource commitments for development, along with new and enlarged philanthropic ventures, provide an extraordinary "development bonus" from the immense wealth creation process of the last half century. But this is likely to be the "last development round" in anything like the form we have hitherto experienced, that is, driven by an international community dominated by the West's narrative of a universalist, liberal project.

—*Environmental resurgence:* the reemergence of "environment" as a critical development issue, in macro terms in the form of climate change and energy security, and consequentially in terms of affordable access to the basics: water, food, and safe shelter. These factors are reshaping our understanding of development drivers, with new imperatives for investment in technology, and people and institutional capacities. Taken together, we can surmise that the ways in which the world is run is up for grabs, and that tomorrow's dominant leaders, values, and institutions are unlikely to resemble what has gone before.

Defining the New Actor

In this context, *new and transitioning actors* take on increased importance—indeed, are the most likely drivers of the paths we will ultimately take us through our current historical moment. Three specific transitions seem particularly relevant to international development:

—*Engaged business.* In every sense, business is becoming a key development actor. Most obviously, business is the key to economic prosperity through investment, product innovation, and production. But business is also becoming increasingly central in the delivery of public services and infrastructure, and in the broader evolution of public governance, both nationally and internationally.[1]

—*Activist states.* This includes the reactivism of the state, globally but very particularly in the United States and key emerging economies, notably China and Russia, whether because of their military and economic significance, energy resources, ethnic and religious leadership, and/or physical and geopolitical location.

—*Bipolar civil society.* Civil society is evolving in two distinct directions. One track is maturing into structural governance roles, engaging with business and the state, and it is often influential over considerable resources. Another track is both more radical and reactionary, rooted in despair, anger, and disillusionment with the dominant governing players.

Developments across each of these actors are critically important, driven by new sources of economic strength, resurgent cultures and civilizations, technology shifts, and largely tactical responses by all three to their changing circumstances. However, the *most significant new actor on the development scene is, paradoxically, none and all of these. It is their complex combination into blended forms of collaborative organization that is already becoming, and will increasingly be, the really extraordinary new actor.* This emerging organizational form needs to be understood as an actor in its own right rather merely than as an ad hoc combining of existing actors. This development will challenge us to abandon long-cherished distinctions in the purposes and modus operandi of commercial, private nonprofit, and public institutions as we grapple with the practical realities of institutions that combine all three in creating a distinct "fourth estate."

Whether collaborative organization as the new actor is good or bad news is not so much a principled issue as, unsurprisingly, a matter of the "small print." Above all, it depends on whether this new actor can be effectively held to account by those affected by its decisions and actions, the single most important litmus test of all institutions. Governance is of course a contested issue for any institution, but it raises particular challenges for collaborative organization. Because this form of organization profoundly reconfigures the basis on which public goods and private gains are related in their creation and exploitation, these new actors will catalyze a reassessment and reinvention of our practice of governance and accountability.

Today's governance and accountability of collaborative organization are poorly understood, and are often viewed in exemplary or even unique **terms** rather than as common practices forming the basis for agreed-on standards. AccountAbility, with its partners, has undertaken some early work on a codified set of principles for good collaborative governance akin to the now well-developed body of work on corporate governance, but much remains to be done.[2] The importance of collaborative governance will become all the more important if, as predicted here, collaborative organization itself becomes a key element in the makeup of tomorrow's broader societal governance—for example, through its influence on, and stewardship of, standards. In this case, the governance of collaborative organization will become a key element of the DNA of our broader societal approach to governance, the essence of a new multilateralism for the twenty-first century.

Our Accountability Moment

Accountability is today's fashionable topic. It is splashed across our media, debated in bars, and is the topic of learned conferences and papers. It is the "preferred currency" in globally spotlighted topics as diverse as the failed response to Hurricane Katrina, the endemic profiteering from the war in Iraq, and the ghastly spectacle of Robert Mugabe's Zimbabwe. But beyond such high notes in our global media, a simple World Wide Web search reveals that accountability figures in practically every topic of interest to the reasonable citizen, from the provision of basic public services like garbage collection to our changing roles and responsibilities as parents, from the terms on which we can consume with a conscience to our sense of civic responsibility to those who are old and disabled.

Shaping effective accountability is a prerequisite to acceptable and sustainable forms of development. And today, accountability is therefore rightly acknowledged as the lingua franca of "international development." It dominates the center stage in most robust diagnoses of the problem, and it is key to most thoughtful insights into desperately needed solutions. Corruption is the most obvious form of unaccountability. It is not just that it is the illegal privatization of resources allocated to investment for the public good. Corruption rips the very heart out of societies' institutions, destroying citizens' trust and indeed their very imagination of the good society. Sadly, the Western-dominated development era, which is now almost over, has catalyzed and embedded modern forms of "development theft" linked to a perversion of development assistance and globalizing markets. But what is to come at present offers little source of hope, as increasing commodity prices combined with new forms of patronage and associated access to capital provide a basis for political and business regimes to maintain their destructive and hugely profitable habits.

The most pervasive causes and consequences of inadequate accountability are, however, perfectly legal. Our greatest failures are enacted *within* the law because our institutions are no longer fit for their purpose, responding to outdated and often toxic forms of accountability:

—There is a deepening unease among traditional *public development agencies,* with doubts being cast over their own accountability and effectiveness.

—This is mirrored by painfully slow progress in attempts to strengthen *national public institutions,* despite decades of extensive investment.

—*Business's* traditionally unqualified "homage to finance" is under siege as its development effects become more visible and contested, including new *investment actors,* notably derivatives traders but also private equity, which demonstrate a disinterest in long-term business success let alone broader development outcomes.

—*Civil society organizations,* traditionally the quintessential "accountability agents," find themselves under the spotlight of legitimacy and in many instances are found lacking in their own accountability.

Globally, we have created a generation of international institutions intended to foster interdependence and mutuality. But instead, we see horse trading between nations, the worst forms of economic nationalism, and rotten domestic politics. Witness the weakened World Trade Organization in its efforts to mediate a successful "development round." How much more difficult will it be to enjoin xenophobic, mercantilist-minded governments to address the problems of climate change, water scarcities, energy security, and the needs of tens of millions of migrants? Awarding the Nobel Peace Prize to Al Gore rightly celebrates someone who has contributed to creating a global debate about climate change, but it is equally a condemnation of most of our political representatives, and business and spiritual leaders, who have chosen to remain inactive or, worse still, hostile to addressing this profound challenge.

Accountability centrally concerns the manner in which power is exercised. Societies cannot function without effectively defining the rights and responsibilities of those who legitimately make an impact on others. At its core, accountability concerns the manner in which societies seek to "civilize power," establishing an accommodation, albeit often temporarily, between the needs of power and the claims of justice.[3] We recognize in this the tenets of democracy, arguably global civilization's greatest-ever accountability innovation. And it is through this lens that we can see the magnitude of the threat. One recent survey of political attitudes in Latin America reported that barely half of respondents agreed that "democracy was the best system of government," with affirmative scores as high as 35 percent, in the one country case when answering the question "Are there circumstances when an authoritarian government can be preferable to a democratic one?"

Arguably, there has never been a period in modern history where the credibility of every category of our most familiar institutions has been simultaneously challenged because of visible and significant accountability failures. As Anwar Ibrahim, AccountAbility's president and formerly deputy prime minister of Malaysia, concludes: "There is no obvious island of integrity from which to point the finger. Governments, businesses, and civil society in every part of the globe face profound challenges in meeting their obligations."[4]

Accountability as Development

Reinventing accountability is *the* development challenge for the twenty-first century. But while there is an abundance of information and debate about the consequences of failures in accountability, there is far less about what might be the "right" accountability needed to create healthy societies over the coming century. To say "more participation" is not helpful or even necessarily right in an era where populist outcomes can be ghastly. To demand "more transparency" is understandable, yet many of the most outrageous instances of unaccountability are played out in full view of the global community. Enforced compliance against unacceptable behavior must be right, of course. Yet we all know that mitigating the downside will not be enough to overcome poverty or prevent climate change.

To envision good health, it is not enough to understand illness or even how best to mitigate it. We need to have a vision of accountability, not just a sense of its absence.

One way of understanding the healthy side of accountability, moving beyond what people should *not* do, is as a mirror image of Amartya Sen's elegantly framed insight that development concerns peoples' freedom to be active agents of their own destiny. A great impediment to this freedom, and so also to development, is the exercise of power in ways that are unaccountable to those affected. Freedom and accountability are not in this sense equivalent. Yet if freedom without accountability is unattainable, development is then fundamentally a matter of accountability. It is in this sense, that we can talk meaningfully about "development as accountability."[5]

Meaningful accountability must deliver the conditions that unlock people's potential and our ability to invent, steward, and sustain ourselves indefinitely into the future. It must nurture the "right" relationships between people, establishing the basis on which the dangers and opportunities of our interdependencies can best be managed. From this perspective, accountable development does not just mean more layers of compliance-based systems to ensure that money is accounted for, or to feed philanthropists' craving for instant, and perfectly measured, results. Accountability is not just a toolbox of metrics and mechanisms, a bolt-on to existing development projects, designed to reduce corruption and inefficiency at the margin. Indeed, this one-way, bottom-to-top orientation is too often part of the problem—accumulating power, dispersing responsibility, dampening innovation, and disempowering collaboration.

"Development as accountability" requires that we reimagine and reinvent the social contract, and in particular the deal between those with and those without power. Nothing less will do, because without reciprocity, essentially an embedded mutual accountability, no number of noble principles or independent auditors will enable development to progress. "Empowering the poor and marginalized" is the right demand from enlightened members of the development community. But it is too often romanticized by a liberal elite, rather than penetrated as a matter of accountability. The bottom line is that empowerment means nothing unless it means more effective accountability for those with power. Yesterday's "development community" has not and might not ever be able to deliver on this. Development agencies and practitioners are themselves largely without significant power, and they are often compromised by their relationships with those who count. New actors will only make a difference if their entrance enables the matter of accountability to be more effectively addressed. Resources can be mobilized, but without radical innovations that drive forward the accountability agenda, we must be prepared to be disappointed, to the cost of many without voice in this debate. As the U.K. government's own Commission on Africa concluded, "Without progress in governance, all other reforms will have limited impact"—so true, although perhaps with a wider application than the commission intended in the light, for example, of the growing revelations associated with U.K. government's complicity in the trading practices of BAE Systems.

Collaborative Governance

Multistakeholder or public-private partnerships—essentially collaborative initiatives between state and nonstate, commercial, and nonprofit actors—have been born out of their participants' pragmatism. Said simply, these initiatives have been founded on participants' views of potential synergies in capacities in leveraging improved outcomes for all concerned. This is quite unlike the grand ideological visions of earlier generations of institutional utopias, such as nationalization and privatization. But this lack of any overarching narrative to date should not fool us into missing the fact that lurking beneath the surface of this ad hoc collection of activities are the most exciting new ventures along new accountability pathways for development. Indeed, new forms of collaborative governance are likely to represent the most radical shakeup of our understanding and practice of accountability in modern times.

Collaborative initiatives have become the preferred institutional form through which diverse forms of development initiatives are designed and implemented. Global development partnerships and collaboratively governed standards initiatives are the institutional pathway of choice for a new generation of initiatives dealing with everything from global health to the marginalization of so-called blood diamonds to the role of telecommunications in empowering peasant farmers in global markets. Classical public-private partnerships are increasingly seen as the only way in which public services and infrastructure are going to be provided in both developing countries with weak public sectors and mature economies with an eye on reducing or deferring costs to the public purse. For business, new forms of collaboration are becoming key in realizing business opportunities, in addressing public goals, and, critically, in exploiting the growing interconnections between the two, whether it concerns Coca-Cola's need to secure access to business-critical water or GE's efforts to improve its competitiveness by lobbying for increased carbon prices in the United States. At the macro level, similarly, reaching agreement on key trade issues and shaping a global response to climate change will depend on the collective and often collaborative efforts of business and civil society as much as the assertion of public authority at national and global levels.

The number, scope, and effects of such collaborations have dramatically increased in recent years. In fact, such initiatives, collectively, are graduating from an initial "experimental zone" for leveraging more resources and cross-sector synergies *to becoming the single most important new actor* in development.[6] Collaborative initiatives are, in short, *the* institutional innovation of the period, the "new actor" as such, that can drive creative and disruptive innovation across all other actors (for example, the nature of business or government bodies) and configurations (for example, the shape of cross-border relationships and rule-making processes).

Collaborative Standards Initiatives as a Case in Point

The role and effectiveness of rule-setting or "collaborative standards initiatives" (CSIs) exemplifies the opportunities and challenges of collaborative initiatives as a powerful force on the development stage (box 10-1). CSIs, deliberately or by virtue of their actions and importance, establish standards for private and often also public agents. Over the last decade, many dozens of such initiatives have become globally significant, from the Equator Principles (project finance) to the Forest Stewardship Council (sustainable forest products) to the Global Reporting Initiative (sustainability reporting) and Social Accountability International's SA8000 (labor standards) (box 10-2). At the next tier, hundreds more are emerging at national and regional levels (for example, sector-level black economic empowerment standards in South Africa based on collaborative agreements), and sector initiatives from gambling (for example, the World Lottery Association's newly agreed-on "Responsible Gambling" initiative) to access to pharmaceuticals.

Collaborative standards initiatives are, in short, emerging as a powerful engine for building cross-border standards of behavior by business, but also

---

BOX 10-1
Primary Categories of Collaborative Initiatives

Category	Description
Commercial	Public services and infrastructure (for example, water management, transport infrastructure) delivered by business in pursuit of profit, drawing in diverse partners to enable effective delivery, contractual obligations and business interests to be realized
Resourcing	Delivering resources to address public goals (for example, combating HIV/AIDS, road safety), involving mobilization of public and private resources; assessment, awarding, and evaluation; issue-focused advocacy; and capacity development
Rule setting	Evolution of rules-governing behavior of targeted adopters (for example, business and human rights, anticorruption codes), involving their development, advocacy, and stewardship

---

increasingly of governments themselves. The *development opportunities* are considerable, and include:[7]

—the creation of mechanisms to ensure the compliance of private and public institutions with agreed-on environmental, economic, and social norms;

—the ability to reshape markets to value environmental and social performance;

—the ability to fill public governance gaps, as well as enhancing the development of effective, accountable, and legitimate public governance; and

—the opportunity to give voice to stakeholders and communities in the development of markets that affect their lives.

The *challenges and risks* are, however, also imposing and could if unchecked actually damage pro-poor development. They include:

—the governance, accountability, and transparency of CSIs and the participation of developing countries in their decisionmaking procedures;

—the connection between CSIs and national governance, including the potential for CSIs to weaken national regulatory systems, and the opportunity

BOX 10-2
Examples of Collaborative Standards Initiatives

Ethical Trading Initiative	multisector	www.ethicaltrade.org
Equator Principles	financial services	www.equator-principles. com
Extractive Industry Transparency Initiative		www.eitransparency.org
Fair Labor Association	textiles	www.fairlabor.org
Forest Stewardship Council		www.fsc.org
Global Reporting Initiative	all sectors	www.globalreporting.org
International Council on Minerals and Mines		www.icmm.com
Commodity Roundtables	agriculture	www.bacp.net/
Kimberley Initiative	conflict diamonds	www.kimberleyprocess. com
Medicines Transparency Alliance		www.dfidhealthrc.org/ MeTA
Construction Sector Transparency Initiative		www.dfid.gov.uk
Marine Stewardship Council fisheries		www.msc.org
PACI	anticorruption	www.weforum.org/en/ initiatives/paci/index. htm
MFA Forum	textiles	www.mfa-forum.net
Responsible Care Initiative	chemicals	www.responsiblecare.org
Social Accountability International	multisector	www.sa-intl.org

Source: A. Litovsky, S. Rochlin, S. Zadek, and B. Levy, *Investing in Standards for Sustainable Development*, Working Paper (Washington: World Bank, 2008).

and related challenges for states to align national regulation and statutes to support the effectiveness of CSIs;

—the free-rider problem and the evolution of a governance model for CSIs that avoids free riding and strengthens inclusion;

—the compliance and enforcement mechanisms of CSIs, as well as how roles, responsibilities, authorities, and resources are distributed between global and national players for monitoring and sanction mechanisms;

—the technical barriers to trade that some CSIs may impose on poor countries, thereby hindering their competitiveness and increasing the dependency of small producers on foreign aid;

—the challenge of managing CSIs as they mature and the multistakeholder processes core to their governance design grows more complex and, often, inert; and

—the lack of a "capital market" to support the investment in CSIs and the associated failure of most CSIs to develop a viable revenue model.

Governing Collaborative Governance

Collaborative organization is a new reality in development, offering huge opportunities for technical synergies, resource mobilization, and innovative design and implementation approaches. It is delivering and might increasingly deliver more effective operational design and associated outcomes. Equally, it could provide a new lens and practice for establishing the broader rules of the game, acting as a replacement or transition bridge for gaps in effective national and intergovernmental deal making, regulation, and enforcement.

Collaborative organization as the new development actor does, however, poses important public policy questions that go well beyond simple matters like securing operational efficiencies. Fundamentally, the policy issue revolves around matters of governance and accountability, which we can understand to reside at three distinct levels, so the approaches taken to collaborative governance ensure

—the efficient and effective blending in practice of participant's capacities in securing the desired outcomes;

—the accountability of the collaborative organization to those it affects rather than the current, often "fudged," norms of confused accountabilities; and

—the legitimacy and effectiveness of collaborative organization in underpinning new forms of governance of markets and communities.

From a development perspective, shortfalls at one or more of these levels might reduce or even reverse their positive impact on poverty alleviation, by, for example,

—reducing aid effectiveness (that is, poor orientation and inefficiencies);

—raising the costs and reducing the appropriateness of, and access to, public services and infrastructure (for example, wrong services, driving poor investment decisions, high pricing); and

—distorting the design and implementation of social and environmental standards (for example creating impediments to, rather than enabling, trade).

These negative pathways are practical and immediate options that need to be avoided before their pursuit and practice become embedded norms. For example, one report by the World Economic Forum and the United Nations Financing for Development Initiative presented at the UN General Assembly in September 2005 concluded, with encouragement through inputs from AccountAbility, that "effective partnership is problematic, not least because of ambiguity in the concepts of good governance: accountability, transparency, legitimacy, disclosure, participation, decision-making, grievance management and performance reporting." Similarly, a review of a major global health partnership criticized it for lack of effectiveness and cost-efficiency, citing accountability failures as the primary cause. More broadly, reviews of collaborative approaches to providing public services have repeatedly concluded that partnerships' lack of public accountability explain a great deal of why they have failed in most instances to provide the goods.

AccountAbility is now entering the fourth phase of its work on this matter. At the end of 2005, it launched a "beta" version of the world's first "collaborative governance" framework, comprising principles, criteria, and guidelines developed over two years engagement from the experience of dozens of collaborative initiatives on the ground.[8] More recently, AccountAbility has joined forces with partners in Brazil, India, and South Africa to advance national and regional debate on collaborative governance. In addition, it has recently completed the current phase of a peer-to-peer learning network involving ten global collaborative initiatives exploring their governance experience, on the back of which a second version of the framework is due to be published in early 2008, targeted particularly at the growing numbers of public and private investors in these new forms of collaborative organization.

Ensuring the effective governance of new forms of collaboration involves high stakes when their potential scope of application is fully appreciated. The bulk of the United Kingdom's health system now relies on partnerships between private and public actors, and many developing countries are being encouraged by international development agencies to follow a similar pathway for many public services as well as the provision of public infrastructure. In a decade or less, many developing countries will have embedded such partnerships at the heart of their approach to the provision of public goods. Without the right deals and associated approaches to governance, such arrangements might prove highly problematic, involving decades and enormous costs to unravel, as has been the case with previously advocated approaches such as nationalization.

Collaborative standards initiatives' very survival depends on their own governance. Most have been developed by coalitions of Western companies, governments, and civil society organizations, and these origins are reflected in their current governance approach and incumbent players. Yet their success depends on the engagement of new economic and political actors, for example, from China, Russia, and India. Initiatives such as the Equator Principles and the Extractive Industry Transparency Initiative will only be able to effectively corral the market if they open themselves to being governed in part by these new actors.

Last, there are competing views of what constitutes good collaborative governance. Collaborative governance recombines economic and political power, threatening their "best practice" separation across what we would consider to be relatively well-governed states. Such recombinations can deliver on development in innovative ways, but they could just as easily become a deeply rooted problem as we move beyond the exciting avant-garde in mainstreaming such approaches. Indeed, we can point to this very problem in the emergence of old-style collaborative governance at the very heart of today's geopolitical shifts. This is true whether we look at the Chinese and Russian governments joined at the hip with their emerging business powerhouses or at the resurgent activism of the Atlantic states working to preserve their power and influence by seeking to serve the interests of their all-too-mobile multinational business communities and their all-too-nonmobile electorates.

Conclusions

Collaborative organization is the new development actor, bringing with it the potential to overcome many of the inertias and inadequacies of our traditional institutions. Over time, collaborative organization is likely to challenge the very existence of its component parts, thereby opening the way to the most dramatic institutional transformation of modern times. But the contribution of this emerging actor will depend, fundamentally, on the effectiveness of the new forms of governance that are developed to ensure that it is effectively held to account. The realm of collaborative governance will be the laboratory and, in all probability, the battleground that determines the legitimacy and impact of this new actor, and thus its contribution to development. This will be true at the micro and increasingly at the macro levels. It is in this latter sphere that collaborative governance is likely to emerge as contending DNA for our approach to multilateralism in the twenty-first century.

Notes

1. World Economic Forum, in association with Business for Social Responsibility, AccountAbility, Harvard University, and International Business Leaders Forum, *Business Roles in Public Governance* (Geneva: World Economic Forum, 2008).

2. S. Zadek and S. Radovich, *Governing Partnership Governance: Enhancing Development Impacts through Improved Partnership Governance,* Working Paper, Corporate Social Responsibility Initiative (Cambridge, Mass.: Center for Government and Business, John F. Kennedy School of Government, Harvard University, 2006).

3. J. Sabapathy, S. Zadek, and P. Raynard, *A Short History of Accountability,* Working Paper (London; AccountAbility, 2006).

4. T. Burgis and S. Zadek, *Accountability 21: Reinventing Accountability for the 21st Century* (London: AccountAbility, 2006).

5. Litovsky and McGillivray, *Accountability as Development.*

6. S. Zadek, *The Logic of Collaborative Governance: Corporate Responsibility, Accountability and the Social Contract,* Working Paper, Corporate Social Responsibility Initiative (Cambridge, Mass.: Center for Government and Business, John F. Kennedy School of Government, Harvard University, 2006).

7. A. Litovsky, S. Rochlin, S. Zadek, and B. Levy, *Investing in Standards for Sustainable Development,* Working Paper (Washington: World Bank, 2008).

8. Zadek and Radovich, *Governing Partnership Governance.*

11

Aid: From Consensus to Competition?

JOSEPH O'KEEFE

AID IS MORE fragmented today than ever before. Bilateral and multilateral aid agencies have proliferated in recent years: The average number of donors per recipient country rose from about 12 in the 1960s to about 33 in the 2001–5 period, according to World Bank research. In addition, there are currently more than 230 international aid organizations, funds, and programs. This growth has been accompanied by ever more earmarking of aid resources for specific, narrow uses or special purpose organizations, including global programs or so-called vertical funds. In fact, about half the official development assistance (ODA) channeled through multilateral channels in 2005 went through some degree of earmarking by sector or theme.[1]

The result of these two trends has been the duplication of aid efforts, high transaction costs for recipient nations, and significant opportunity costs as efficiencies from collaboration are lost. In response, aid agencies have championed coordination and harmonization efforts. Such initiatives aim to benefit both aid donors and recipients by sharing financial and strategic information, creating a consensus on aid objectives, and collaborating on project or program implementation.

The Consensus Model

In recent years, a loosely tiered system of coordination—or, rather, coordination attempts—known as the "Consensus Model" has evolved from these efforts by aid agencies. At the highest tier is the Millennium Development Goals (MDGs), which both the United Nations and the World Bank adopted in 2000. The MDGs provide a set of specific measurable development goals to which both aid donor and aid recipient nations are nominally committed. For example, the MDGs include a goal for the international aid community to reduce by half the proportion of people living facing extreme hunger by 2015. Another MDG aims to eliminate gender disparity in primary and secondary education at all levels by 2015.

At the next tier of coordination is the Paris Declaration on Harmonization, which 108 nations, 24 development organizations, and about 12 civil society organizations signed in March 2005. The declaration sets forth 56 "partnership commitments" based on five principles: ownership, alignment, harmonization, managing for results, and mutual accountability. The declaration also sets forth 12 indicators of aid effectiveness to encourage and track progress against the partnership commitments. The Organization for Economic Cooperation and Development–Development Assistance Committee (OECD-DAC) Working Party on Aid Effectiveness is the lead agency for helping both developed and developing nations implement the Paris Declaration. Efforts at this tier are intended to ensure coherence of aid activities across donor nations and among donor and recipient nations, as well as establishing tracking mechanisms to determine whether programmatic aims and MDGs are being reached.

The third tier of the aid coordination system is the consultative group meetings that are held at the country level. Consultative group meetings, often chaired by the World Bank, convene donors, country officials, and in some cases civil society and private sector participants in order to reach an accord between donor goals and the development goals of a particular recipient nation. In a parallel vein, the United Nations Development Program holds roundtable meetings to reach country-level accords on development goals and implementation.

The fourth tier of the coordination system is represented by Poverty Reduction Strategy Papers, first adopted in 1999, which low-income recipient countries prepare for the World Bank and the International Monetary Fund based on each country's development goals, input from the Bank and IMF, and feedback from civil society and the private sector.

Historically, there has been a backlash by aid recipients against the plethora of donor-driven initiatives that conflicted with one another, imposed onerous or unrealistic "conditionality" requirements, or were at odds with country-level priorities. (According to one survey, for example, in 2005 donors fielded 10,453 missions in thirty-four countries—an average of 307 missions per country per year.)[2] Many aid recipients are increasingly vocal about their discontent. According to one recent study, "Many [aid recipient] countries in regional workshops and elsewhere are voicing concerns about the high transaction costs of managing foreign aid and the slow pace of change in donor practices. They see a strong disconnect between headquarters policies and in-country practices, as illustrated by continued donor-driven technical co-operation and lack of visible progress on untying aid."[3] One indication of this growing discontent and shifting balance of power between aid agencies and recipient countries is illustrated by the fact that several African nations are reported to have declared "mission-free" periods, during which official visits from aid agencies (traditionally known as "missions") have been officially prohibited.[4] As a result of such tensions, under the current Consensus Model, aid-receiving countries are supposed to be put "in the driver's seat," and their national development priorities are supposed to take precedence over those of donors. The tie binding the interests of donors and recipients is a grand bargain of sorts: Donor nations agree to honor their pledges to provide aid funds on time, while recipient nations agree to honor their pledges to make policy and programmatic reforms, integrate aid flows into their budget planning processes, and track the outcomes of aid programs.

The Results to Date

The Consensus Model has proceeded haltingly and is beset with fundamental problems. More than fifty low-income developing nations have developed Poverty Reduction Strategies (PRS), and some have taken practical steps to align their annual budgeting process with donor flows. However, middle-income developing countries have largely opted out of the PRS process. This omission is glaring, because middle-income countries account for 80 percent of the developing world's population and 90 percent of its gross domestic product.[5]

No sooner had the grand bargain of aid coordination been struck than donor nations walked away from fulfilling their aid pledges. Indeed, as the World Bank's managing director, Graeme Wheeler, noted in discussing aid coordination in 2007 that "donors need to urgently enhance the quality and quantity of their development assistance or risk falling well short of the [aid] commitments made in Paris and Gleneagles. In 2006, [official development assistance] fell by 5 percent. It's simply not viable to backload increases in aid to 2009 or 2010 since relationships of mutual trust only develop in time."[6] This comports with historical research showing that "commitments by donors consistently exceed disbursements and that aid cannot be predicted reliably on the basis of donors' commitments alone."[7]

Meanwhile, about half the bilateral contributions channeled through multilateral development banks are still earmarked for specific trust funds, sectors, or aid themes, which constrains a recipient's ability to allocate such resources in keeping with national development priorities (box 11-1).[8]

Last, would-be aid coordinators in the developing nations face a conundrum: In instituting the budgetary and tracking systems necessary to track aid harmonization and improve efficiency, they face significant expenses. Thus, rather than enjoying lower transactions costs through aid coordination and harmonization, they find that such costs are actually higher in the short run. One of the biggest practical obstacles to better aid coordination is the capacity of planning and budgeting agencies within the developing nations.[9]

Factors Driving Further Change

Supporters of the Consensus Model will have to contend with several challenges in the coming years. Foremost is the degree of fragmentation and competition that will occur as donor channels proliferate and existing channels handle greater volumes of aid. The sheer number of players is already daunting:

—Within the U.S. federal government alone, about fifty federal agencies and offices play a role in international aid and development.[10]

—Outside the United States, the number of bilateral donor nations has grown from a handful at the end of World War II to more than fifty-six today, raising the political and, in some cases, market-like competition for aid and development projects.[11] As in the United States, many of these bilateral organizations use nongovernmental organizations (NGOs) for aid and development services, further complicating efforts to streamline administration. The World Bank now estimates that the average number of donor nations for each developing nation has risen from twelve in the 1960s to about thirty-three in the 2000s.[12]

—U.S. private foundations provide relatively little development assistance directly to recipient governments, preferring to provide financial support to nongovernmental institutions with well-developed capabilities for delivering aid effectively in specific program areas. However, the number of foundations with international programming is continuing to grow. About $3.8 billion of these foundation disbursements went to international initiatives, most of which was channeled through sector-specific organizations and global funds

BOX 11-1
Successful Aid Coordination:
Budget Planning Reform in Low-Income Nations

An innovative and—by early accounts—successful approach to building capacity, ownership, and incentives at the core of government has been applied in Madagascar in the form of a Leadership and Management Program. Albania's work points to the importance of increased PRS ownership developed under that country's integrated planning system for budget formulation and implementation. Tanzania's initiative to harmonize planning and budgeting instruments demonstrates sensitivity to the goal of integrated reforms. Mozambique's efforts to avoid duplicating reporting instruments for donors and domestic stakeholders have helped to strengthen domestic processes and to promote integration. Last, relatively informal approaches to results-oriented budgeting in Mali and Uganda have arguably enjoyed more success than more formal approaches, because they have been in step with, rather than ahead of, the level of sophistication of the budget.

Source: World Bank and Deutsche Gesellschaft für Technische Zusammenarbeit, "Minding the Gaps: Integrating Poverty Reduction Strategies and Budgets for Domestic Accountability," April 2007, xiv.

(for example, the Global Fund to Fight AIDS, Tuberculosis, and Malaria); NGOs; and public-private partnerships (for example, the GAVI Alliance—formerly known as the Global Alliance for Vaccines and Immunization).

—Globally, a rough approximation of the number of civil society secretariats (that is, NGOs) with transnational operations is 18,000,[13] some 4,100 of which operate from the United States.[14] Private sector aid contributions totaled $11 billion in 2006, an amount equal to 13 percent of the aid provided by DAC donors (excluding debt relief), up from 9 percent in the 1990s. Government funding of NGOs still predominates; in general, about 6 percent of all reported official aid to developing nations has been provided through civil society organizations, NGOs, and public-private partnerships.[15] However, the actual amount of development assistance provided by NGOs is difficult to quantify.[16]

A second challenge facing the Consensus Model is the shifting center of gravity in global aid. By various accounts, the member nations of the DAC have provided roughly 95 percent of aid since the 1990s. However, in recent

BOX 11-2
Non-DAC Donors and Emerging Donors

Non-DAC donors and emerging donors are becoming increasingly important as ODA providers. New donors bring with them more resources to help developing countries reach their MDGs. At the same time, new challenges for harmonization and alignment are being created. Non-DAC donors are a fairly heterogeneous set of countries, which can be broadly classified into four groups: (1) OECD countries which are not members of the DAC, such as South Korea, Mexico, Turkey, and several European countries; (2) new European Union countries that are not members of the OECD; (3) Middle Eastern and countries belonging to the Organization of the Petroleum Exporting Countries, particularly Saudi Arabia; and (4) non-OECD donors that do not belong to any of the previous groups, including Brazil, China, India, and Russia. Two of the most important policy challenges as regards non-DAC donors and emerging donors are (1) the limited availability of data regarding their aid volumes and terms; and (2) their diverse approaches to harmonization and alignment.

Insufficient data on non-DAC ODA make it difficult to accurately assess aid volumes and prospects from these sources. Non-DAC OECD countries alone are expected in aggregate to double their current ODA levels to over $2 billion by 2010. The available information suggests that non-DAC donors have been particularly involved in humanitarian aid. In response to the Indian Ocean tsunami in early 2005, for example, seventy non-DAC donors responded with pledges of support. A recent Overseas Development Institute study found that non-DAC donors focused their efforts in a few countries (that is, Afghanistan, Iraq, North

---

years, non-DAC nations have started to increase their aid. Net ODA disbursements provided by the fifteen non-DAC donors that report their aid activities increased from about $1 billion during the period 1995–2001 to $4.2 billion in 2005 (the most recent year for which data are available).[17]

According to World Bank research, the composition of non-DAC flows has shifted substantially over the past few years as ODA provided by the Arab countries declined (from $2.7 billion in 2002–3 to $1.7 billion in 2005), while ODA provided by other non–DAC donors increased (from $0.5 billion to $2.5 billion in 2005). The increase was led by South Korea, which provided $0.75 billion in assistance in 2005, and Turkey, which provided $0.6 billion.[18]

ODA provided by non-DAC donors has increased over the past few years, but it has risen by less than ODA from DAC members. In 2002 ODA by

Korea, and the occupied Palestinian Territories), preferred bilateral aid over multilateral routes, and accounted for up to 12 percent of official humanitarian
financing in the period 1999–2004 (based on data from the United Nations Office
for the Coordination of Humanitarian Affairs' Financial Tracking System).

Although a number of non-DAC donors signed the Paris Declaration, harmonization challenges remain present. The degree to which DAC approaches and
norms as regards the provision of aid finance applied by different non-DAC
countries varies across the four country groupings described above. There are
three main risks for low-income countries (LICs) associated with insufficient
harmonization between DAC and non-DAC donors: (1) LICs, particularly those
with enhanced "borrowing space" in the wake of the Multilateral Debt Relief
Initiative, might find it easier to borrow on inappropriately nonconcessional
terms; (2) LICs may also have increased opportunities to access low-condition-
ality aid that could help postpone much-needed reforms; and (3) if good practices in project appraisal are not followed, increased aid could translate partly
into more unproductive capital projects in LICs. These risks could be mitigated
by means of a strong, coordinated effort to implement the principles and targets
of the Paris Declaration.

Source: International Development Association, "Aid Architecture: An Overview of the Main Trends
in Official Development Assistance Flows," February 2007, available at http://web.worldbank.org.

non-DAC donors totaled $3.2 billion, an amount equal to 5.5 percent of the
ODA provided by DAC donors (5.9 percent, excluding debt relief). In 2005
non-DAC donors provided $4.2 billion, equal to just 4 percent of the ODA
provided by DAC donors (5 percent, excluding debt relief). However, one
variable that should not be discounted is China's Africa Policy, introduced in
January 2006, which provides substantial amounts of capital both within and
outside the traditional definitions of ODA. Estimates of the size of China's
development aid lending and grant flows vary widely but could significantly
alter the non-DAC figures (box 11-2).[19]

A third variable likely to pose a challenge to operation of the Consensus
Model is the role of private capital in developing nations. Developing nations
are increasingly able to access bank lending or achieve credit ratings that
allow them to access capital markets for their long-term development needs.

According to World Bank research, 90 percent of the world's 135 developing nations have now accessed the syndicated loan market, and 40 percent have issued sovereign bonds.[20] Such access is already being viewed as a destabilizing factor for harmonization. Indeed, the World Bank noted in a recent report: "Uncertain whether donors will meet their commitments to enhance development assistance, some low-income countries may opt to meet their financing needs by borrowing on nonconcessional terms. Doing so could erode debt sustainability over the long term and erase the benefits of recent debt-relief initiatives. Because such borrowing is not reported in a comprehensive and timely manner, creditors and policymakers have difficulty assessing its potential impact on debt sustainability."[21] In addition, developing countries are continuing to privatize significant numbers of assets responsible for water, telecommunications, and other types of services that have previously been classed as "developmental."[22]

Revolution or Evolution?

In 2007, the Group of Eight took official note of the increasing volumes of development aid coming from countries such as China, India, Brazil, South Africa, and Mexico, warning that these up-and-coming donors should have to meet higher standards for governance and transparency. However, the potential consequences reach much further. There are dangers that low-income countries could borrow from these new donors on inappropriate terms and reverse years of hard-won gains on debt relief, and that easy access to aid money would create an incentive to delay necessary policy adjustments.

The worst-case scenario for the Consensus Model would be to see ever more low-income countries taking the path of such nations as Venezuela, which has rejected its World Bank and IMF ties on the crest of its petrodollars. In Latin America, Argentina, Bolivia, Brazil, Nicaragua, and Venezuela have paid off their IMF debts in recent years and begun distancing themselves somewhat from the Bank and IMF. As of 2007, Argentina, Bolivia, Brazil, Ecuador, Paraguay, and Venezuela were toying with the idea of opening a "Bank of the South" development bank as an alternative regional development bank.

Are we witnessing the first stage of a revolution in aid, or merely the latest step in a gradual evolution? At first glance, there would appear to be an unprecedented amount of capital available within former aid recipient nations to fuel the rise of a radically different multipolar aid system, one that would operate apart from Western aid agencies. Foreign exchange reserves among developing nations increased by $630 billion in 2006 alone, up from about $400 billion in 2004 and 2005. Brazil, Russia, India, and China accounted for 70 percent of the increase, with reserves rising by $247 billion in China, $120 billion in Russia, $39 billion in India, and $32 billion in Brazil. International reserves held by all developing countries have increased from less than 10 percent to almost 25 percent of their gross domestic product during the past ten years. China's reserves are now in excess of $1 trillion—its share of all developing nations' reserves rose from 25 percent in the late 1990s to 40 percent in 2006—while Russia's share increased from under 2 percent to 11 percent.[23] Given the scale of such reserves, one could imagine China, India, and Russia surpassing ever more countries in aid donations and tempting recipient nations to bypass the conditionality of DAC relationships. China, for example, already provides aid amounting to $2 billion a year, a figure higher than that of Belgium, Switzerland, or Australia. India's estimated total of about $1 billion exceeds that of Finland and Ireland.[24]

There are several reasons why this will not happen on a wholesale basis. From an aid recipient's perspective, it makes little sense to reduce the number of nations in one's donor base. Dealing simultaneously with two to three dozen aid donors poses administrative headaches, but it also provides a hedge against the fickle nature of individual donors. Some donors honor their pledges; some do not. Some disburse their funds on time; some do not. Some donors are genuine partners; some are not. Thus, a broad, diversified donor base serves an aid recipient's long-term interests better than reliance on a single donor or small group of donors.

Some nations, of course, do not have the option of accessing a wide base of donors. Countries such as Sudan, Zimbabwe, and Angola have such poor records on human rights and corruption that many aid agencies eschew doing business with them. However, as the case of Sudan demonstrates, this does not entirely exhaust their options. Sudan, like several other African nations, has been able to bargain away access to its natural resources in exchange for financial, trade, and military support from China. China attaches its own strings in the form of geopolitical conditionality and project-specific conditionality. At the geopolitical level, China has succeeded in getting several nations to drop diplomatic recognition of Taiwan in favor of relations with Beijing. And when nations cooperate, China reciprocates. China, for example, has opposed UN sanctions against Khartoum over its behavior in Darfur, defended Sudan from any external criticism of its human rights, and denied complicity in fueling the ongoing violence there. The Chinese deputy foreign minister, Zhou Wenzhong, explained that "business is business. We try to separate politics from business. Secondly, I think the internal situation in the Sudan is an internal affair, and we are not in a position to impose upon them."[25] Sudan, meanwhile, has granted wide-ranging access to Chinese arms dealers, companies, contractors, and government-owned banks. At the project level, China has insisted that Chinese companies be awarded contracts for projects funded by Chinese aid agencies or Chinese government-owned banks. Nonetheless, there are two limiting factors to such an aid model. First, it is overwhelmingly associated with the development of oil, gas, timber, and other natural resources that are of critical importance to the growth of the Chinese economy. Second, the Chinese model dispenses with global standards—environmental, social, labor, and human rights—that many developing nations now recognize as essential to participating in the mainstream global economy. Thus, although China is likely to penetrate a handful of nations deeply with its aid, it is unlikely to have the broad, multinational, and multisectoral reach of established multilateral aid agencies (box 11-3).

One must also remember that many low-income nations have significant sunk costs associated with participation in the Consensus Model. Preparing PRS papers and retooling bureaucratic systems to integrate aid planning, budgeting, and forecasting is a laborious and time-consuming process. Moreover, soliciting and assimilating the views of civil society and the private sector—as required by the PRS process—are likely in many cases to change political norms regarding participation. Thus, to reverse years of participation, even partial participation, in the Consensus Model could be costly, both financially and politically.

Aid increases by non-DAC nations will take place against a backdrop of aid increases by DAC members. Collectively, DAC members have committed themselves to a roughly 60 percent increase in aid from 2004 to 2010, reaching a level of $130 billion by 2010. Even if only a portion of this commitment is honored (and history suggests that backsliding is likely), the increase will be substantial. With the proportion of DAC aid to global aid already at 95 percent, there is unlikely to be a dramatic change in the proportion of DAC aid to non-DAC aid.[26]

Technical expertise and effective standards based on global experience are often critical to the effective use of aid funds, and the bilaterals and multilaterals within DAC are the repositories of that experience. Thus, the rejection of DAC donors carries a risk that an aid recipient will repeat mistakes that have been made in other nations.

BOX 11-3
Types of Aid Conditionality

Conditionality is a pliable term, and commentators often mean very different things when using the term. As non-DAC donors increase their aid in the coming years, several types of gaps in conditionality could emerge:

—*Geopolitical conditionality.* When recipient nations are engaged in human rights abuses, repressive behavior, or cross-border aggression, donor nations often withhold aid as a sanction. However, if new non-DAC donors are willing to provide aid funds to the regime—concessional or non-concessional—they can help sustain it in power. China, for example, has continued to provide military aid to both Sudan and Zimbabwe despite their horrific human rights records.

—*Structural adjustment conditionality.* Multilaterals and bilaterals often attach policy reform conditions to lending for donor nation government programs. For example, concessional financing will be predicated on trade liberalization, freeing of agricultural prices, reforms of the national financial system, or other wide-ranging changes in economic or budget policy.

—*Sector-specific conditionality.* Certain sectors, such as the extractive industries sector, generate tremendous revenues for national, state, and local governments. Often, these revenues are illegally diverted for personal use, bribes, the purchase of paramilitary weapons, or other illicit uses. About twenty countries have now agreed to join the Extractive Industries Transparency Initiative, which seeks to improve governance in resource-rich countries by verifying and publishing company payments and government revenues from oil, gas, and mining.

—*Project-specific conditionality.* Many of the major infrastructure, energy, and water projects in developing nations are financed as free-standing project finance deals rather than government initiatives. In recent years, the World Bank has increased the conditions it places on its project finance deals, including for example labor, social, health, and environmental standards. These conditions have gained more force as they have been adopted by about fifty project finance banks, including some of the world's largest, such as Citigroup, ABN Amro, and the Royal Bank of Scotland.

Market-Like Competition

The lure of accepting money from non-DAC donors may be significant for some aid recipients in isolated instances. For most recipient nations, however, this will not entail a simultaneous rejection of DAC aid across the board. Rather, aid recipients will simply look to diversify their portfolio of donors. Uganda is a prime example. A recipient of substantial and increasing amounts of aid from China, it is also fully engaged with DAC donors and midway through its PRS paper process.

A more powerful force in the aid industry will likely be the force of competition among all donors. Evidence of such competition is already apparent. As early as 2005, well ahead of the rise of non-DAC donors, the World Bank, among others, was already keenly aware of the competition it faced from rival development banks. The Bank cut its loan fees and raised its lending limits, pointing out that "the World Bank lends to middle income countries on terms that are financially competitive when compared with other multilateral development banks."[27] In 2007, the Bank cut interest rates on loans to middle-income countries by about 0.25 percent.[28] In the same vein, a Bank consultant told the *Washington Post* that "the market is [driving reform]. We are desperate for clients" and ready to adapt in order to secure and keep them. "The middle-income countries know how to use us. We can no longer go with the recipe of the month of what is supposed to lead to development [because] they are defining their own development paths."[29]

Viewed as a quasi-market, the aid industry is now maturing. For most of the postwar years, transactions were supply driven by a handful of agencies. In the second phase of the market evolution, significant numbers of agencies entered into the industry but product type and price were still determined by dominant suppliers. Consumers, meanwhile, lacked the ability to compare and contrast the products or to affect prices.

We are beginning to see, in some cases such as nonconcessional aid, the third stage of market development: consumers—in this case, the aid recipients—beginning to have a modest influence on the pricing and products of suppliers (aid donors). An interesting trend to track in the coming years will be to see whether concessional aid suppliers begin to compete with one another on the basis of brand and other nonprice attributes, just as competitors in mature private industries do.

The Road Ahead

The odds of the aid industry becoming more centralized (that is, dominated by a small club of agencies sharing an agenda) or more realpolitik (that is, powerful nations dictating the development agenda) are vanishingly small. The preponderance of evidence indicates that we will be living in a world where the aid industry is more crowded, fragmented, pluralistic, and competitive.

At the political level, considerable progress has been made in incorporating non-DAC donors into the high-level discussions of the DAC. Indeed, in 2007 the OECD Council made a landmark decision to offer enhanced engagement programs, with a view to possible membership, to Brazil, China, India, Indonesia, and South Africa. However, substantial gaps remain at the lower tiers of the Consensus Model—such as the extent to which many donor nations are participating fully in the Paris harmonization process and how well recipient nations are effectively integrating aid flows into their national development planning.

Several reforms would be helpful. First and foremost, a concerted effort to increase the reach of sector-specific and project-level standards in the developing world—such as the Extractive Industries Transparency Initiative and the Equator Principles—would have a far-reaching developmental impact and would help to diminish the performance gaps between DAC and non-DAC initiatives.

Second, country "ownership" of aid programs is strongest in instances where local and national development goals and processes mirror those of donors. However, disparate line agencies within a recipient government often have sketchy and incomplete information about the aid programs being proposed across their country. Thus, targeted interventions that provide technical capacity so that recipient governments can gather comprehensive information about donor operations in their country and compare and contrast donor performance would be helpful. In 2006, two nongovernmental organizations, Oxfam GB and Debt Relief International, held workshops in twelve aid-receiving nations and asked local aid officials to evaluate the strengths and weaknesses of various aid agencies. The findings were illuminating.[30]

Third and finally, independent impact assessments are very rare among donor agencies. Pooling funds at the DAC level or allowing cross-agency assessments of aid impact would markedly increase the credibility of such studies and enable aid recipients to be much more effective consumers of aid projects.

The Consensus Model is an imperfect process and a partially fulfilled aspiration. However, proponents of the model need to appreciate that aid recipients will have ever more choices with each passing year, and those choices will bring something akin to market power. In this environment, providing credible information about the performance of aid programs and agencies, both within and across developing nations, will be essential to improving aid's developmental impact.

Notes

1. See International Development Association, "Aid Architecture: An Overview of the Main Trends in Official Development Assistance Flows," February 2007, 19; available at http://web.worldbank.org.

2. Organization for Economic Cooperation and Development, "2006 Survey on Monitoring the Paris Declaration: Overview of the Results," 55.

3. Ibid., 10.

4. Ibid., 33.

5. OECD-DAC Working Party on Aid Effectiveness, "Harmonisation, Alignment, Results: Report on Progress, Challenges, and Opportunities," February 2005, 18.

6. Wheeler's broadcast remarks were made during the World Bank seminar "Countries in the Driver's Seat: Making Poverty Reduction Strategies Work," April 13, 2007.

7. Ales Bulir and A. Javier Hamann, "Aid Volatility: An Empirical Assessment," *IMF Staff Papers* 50, no. 1 (2003): 66.

8. International Development Association, "Aid Architecture," ii.

9. David Booth and others, "Incentives for Harmonisation and Alignment in Aid Agencies," Overseas Development Institute, June 2005, vii.

10. Janelle Kerlin, "U.S. Government Funding for International Government Organizations," in *Nonprofits in Focus: Urban Institute Policy Brief* (Washington: Urban Institute, 2006).

11. International Development Association, "Aid Architecture," 12.

12. Ibid., ii.

13. Helmut Anheier, Marlies Glasius, and Mary Kaldor, eds., *Global Civil Society 2004/5* (London: Sage, 2004), 302.

14. Kerlin, "U.S. Government Funding," 2.

15. International Development Association, "Aid Architecture," 16.

16. World Bank, *Global Development Finance 2007: The Globalization of Corporate Finance in the Developing Nations* (Washington: World Bank, 2007), 57.

17. Ibid.

18. Ibid.

19. Ibid.

20. Ibid., 59.

21. Ibid., 37.

22. Amit Burman and Sunita Kikeri, "Privatization Trends: Near Record Levels in 2005," *Public Policy for the Private Sector,* no 314 (February 2007): 1. The authors note that "in 2004–2005, 62 developing countries carried out nearly 400 privatization transactions worth $90 billion."

23. World Bank, *Global Development Finance,* 21, 39.

24. Hugh Williamson, "G8 Calls for Increased Scrutiny of Aid," *Financial Times,* March 28, 2007.

25. Quoted by Howard W. French, "China in Africa—All Trade, with No Political Baggage," *New York Times,* August 8, 2004.

26. Richard Manning, "Will 'Emerging Donors' Change the Face of International Cooperation?" lecture at Overseas Development Institute, London, March 9, 2006.

27. World Bank, "World Bank Cuts Loan Fees, Raises Lending Limit for Big Borrowers," Press Release 2006/051/S, August 9, 2005.

28. Krishna Guha, "World Bank Reduces Interest Rate to Middle-Income Countries," *Financial Times,* September 28, 2007.

29. Quoted by Marcela Sanchez, "IMF, World Bank Face Irrelevance," *Washington Post,* May 11, 2007.

30. Overseas Development Institute, "Reform of the International Aid Architecture: A Role for the Commonwealth," paper prepared for Commonwealth Secretariat, London, August 2006, 7–8.

12

Philanthropy, Aid, and Investment: Alignment for Impact

MARK R. KRAMER

THE RECENTLY RELEASED United Nations 2007 *Update on Africa* offers a sobering conclusion: "At the midway point between their adoption in 2000 and the 2015 target date for achieving the Millennium Development Goals, Sub-Saharan Africa is not on track to achieve any of the goals."[1] This conclusion is especially discouraging in light of the unprecedented level of attention that major philanthropists, celebrities, academics, corporations, and governments have in recent years focused on Africa's urgent and crushing needs. Why has so much money, publicity, and goodwill produced such limited effects?

One reason, I suggest, is the lack of collaboration, or even coordination, among these different kinds of actors. Philanthropy, international aid, and foreign direct investment are three entirely separate sources of funding that operate in very different ways. The institutional cultures, staff expertise, and incentive structures are largely dissimilar, as are the channels of communication, the conferences they attend, and even the terminology they use. Yet the lack of cooperation among these three separate flows of capital limits the impact that could be achieved either independently or in the aggregate.

Despite their different practices, the goals of each sector overlap and reinforce each other to a surprising degree. The humanitarian objectives that government and philanthropic assistance serve—such as fostering a well-nourished, healthy, educated, and peaceful society—are also the preconditions necessary for businesses to flourish. And the economic development that results from a strong and growing economy can reduce armed conflict, improve health conditions, and raise the standard of living throughout a region. In short, business, philanthropy, and government aid all contribute to—and are strengthened by—a healthier society.

This is not to suggest that the three sectors have identical goals. Philanthropic donors often bring personal values or religious convictions, whereas government aid may be linked to political objectives and corporate investment aims to make a profit. Yet problems for one are often problems for all: The lack of basic infrastructure impedes commerce, as well as access to health care and the distribution of humanitarian aid. Corruption may siphon off aid, but it also obstructs corporate investment and the efforts of social sector organizations.

The widespread acceptance of the Millennium Development Goals among all three sectors further demonstrates this overlap in objectives. Yet the resources and capabilities of each sector differ markedly. And, when it comes to evaluation, each sector—indeed, each actor within the three sectors—often struggles to arrive at a separate and unique set of performance measures.

The challenge, then, is whether this commonality of goals can be leveraged to build collaboration across sectors, with each sector drawing on its own unique capabilities, in order to accelerate social progress and increase the impact of current expenditure levels.

Although the figures tend to dance around, depending on definitions, all three sectors contribute substantial amounts of funding to the developing world. Using Africa as an example, foreign direct investment amounted to $30 billion in 2005.[2] International aid was reported at $32 billion, although a substantial amount ($10 billion) of this sum was in the form of debt relief, which, though valuable in the long run, frees up little immediate funding for development. Thus, a more realistic figure for aid to Africa would be in the range of $22 billion, although Homi Kharas's thoughtful analysis in chapter 3 of the present volume suggests that only $12 billion of this can truly be counted as development aid. Using Kharas's estimates, Africa might receive an additional $25 billion from private philanthropists.[3] In sum, despite the differences in the sources and motivations of funding, it seems likely that corporate investment, official development aid, and philanthropy each contribute roughly $20 to $30 billion annually to the neediest regions of the developing world.

Despite the dramatically different capabilities that corporations, governments, and private donors bring, they tend to act in a similar fashion by pouring funds into a range of projects that advance their independent agendas rather than working together in a division of labor that maximizes the value of the unique contributions each might make to a common agenda. This lack of differentiation means that the flow of funds among these sectors is largely overlapping. Philanthropic contributions typically flow through nongovernmental organizations (NGOs), but so does a significant amount of aid money. Corporate investment follows a very different path, but government aid programs in many countries provide investment capital for business enterprises or major construction projects as a form of development assistance. And corporate royalty payments to local governments are a substantial source of revenue. The decisionmakers behind these allocations may operate in isolation from each other, but the support they provide is often commingled in ways that disregard the different tools and objectives that each brings.

It is only by understanding the differences and interdependencies among these sectors that a more strategic alignment can be developed. Rather than commingling funds through overlapping channels, each sector could achieve a greater impact through a division of labor that utilized its different capabilities. In other words, the greatest impact will be achieved when each sector directs its funding to projects that it can undertake more efficiently or effectively than the other two sectors, but which simultaneously help support the developmental needs of those other sectors. This shift in thinking is precisely what is needed for each sector to accomplish its agenda more effectively.

At the same time, the overlapping nature of their goals suggests that a common set of evaluation metrics might be promulgated across all three sectors. Common evaluation processes could be a key leverage point to build collaboration: If each sector is working toward common ends, tracked by the same measures, then despite their many profound differences, the activities of the three sectors will inevitably begin to align.

Strategic Alignment

All three sectors exercise selectivity in deciding how to spend their money, practice conditionality by imposing requirements on the recipients, and conduct evaluation by looking for results. Viewed strategically, however, each sector brings a very different set of tools to these activities. Among private donors, foundations can act with complete independence, support innovative and untested projects, fund research, and invest their capital at below-market rates of return. The funds at their disposal, however, are minimal compared with the other sectors, and their limited staffing means that they can provide little support beyond their cash contributions. They do, however, bring influence and the power to convene on neutral ground. Foundations are often more trusted than governments or corporations because they are viewed as being without ulterior motives. As such, they can sometimes enlist the cooperation of NGOs and local governments to a greater degree than other sectors.

The William and Flora Hewlett Foundation and the German Marshall Fund, for example, were able to assemble the International Food and Agricultural Trade Policy Council (IPC), a group of influential leaders in farming, agribusiness, government, and academia, to develop policy recommendations to end distorted agricultural subsidies. The policy papers were introduced into the Doha Development Round process of multilateral trade negotiations, and the recommendations were promptly integrated into the proposals from the Group of Twenty. The foundations played an important role in establishing contacts for IPC and in disseminating their work.

Other private donors, primarily individuals contributing to international NGOs, are most likely to target their contributions to disaster relief and humanitarian aid. The outpouring of support for the victims of the 2005 tsunami, as well as the steady annual growth in contributions to NGOs with humanitarian objectives, attest to the primacy of this motivation.

In contrast, corporations have extensive nonmonetary resources, specialized expertise, and a deep in-country presence that neither foundations nor government agencies can match. In the regions where they operate, they have the ability to employ people directly, train them, establish reasonable working conditions, provide access to global technology and distribution, and, through their supply chain purchasing, inject substantial income. The multiplier effect of their investment contributes broadly to sustainable economic development by creating wealth that is redistributed to employees and, through taxes, to governments. Unilever, for example, has calculated that every job it has directly created in India is responsible for indirectly creating sixty additional jobs.

The direct presence of global corporations serves as an important complement to the more attenuated role of private donors and aid organizations that fund others to manage and implement projects on their behalf. Despite the power and breadth of their resources, however, the competitive pressures under which they operate leave little room for them to dedicate any substantial portion of their resources to the altruistic ends that foundations and aid agencies more fully embrace.

Consider some of the effects of corporate investment. In developing countries, Coca-Cola distributes its products through a network of local kiosks and pushcarts, creating employment for more than 10,000 independent vendors. Nestlé similarly creates employment for more than 30,000 vendors.

Novartis has trained and paid East African farmers to grow the plants that produce Coartem, a key ingredient in its antimalarial drugs, and so has quadrupled the farmers' incomes. GlaxoSmithKline voluntarily licenses the production of antiretrovirals to a South African company, producing more than 120 million tablets a year. Starbucks has provided financing and techni- cal assistance through the Conservation Coffee Alliance in Latin America to enable farmers to increase the quality and scale of coffee production, and earning them a premium of up to 40 percent on the price of the coffee beans they sell. ICIC Lombard developed a new form of microinsurance that is tied to weather patterns and enables tens of thousands of small farmers in India to gain protection from crop failures. Aquas Argentinas, a major project by Suez, brought freshwater and sewage treatment to 500,000 inhabitants of the *favellas*.

These examples suggest the power of corporate investment acting alone. But consider the even greater humanitarian benefit provided by coordinating corporate, NGO, and government actions. In 2003, GE decided to under- take a philanthropic initiative to develop and equip hospitals in Africa. Unlike most corporations, GE took advantage of the expertise in aid and NGO organizations in planning its work, conducting more than a hundred interviews with experts from UNICEF, AfriCares, the European Union, the U.S. Agency for International Development, and the U.S. State Department. On the basis of this advice, GE decided to invest in building and equipping a health clinic in Ghana. The district they chose had a population of 100,000 people but no reliable power, clean water, or access to health care other than a single midwife.

Realizing that any solution required local ownership and participation, in Ghana GE developed a cross-sector partnership that included the state health ministry, local members of Parliament, the mayor of the city where the clinic is based, tribal leaders, and nonprofit organizations working in the region. Each partner contributed to the project. The government waived import fees on the equipment that GE donated; the ministry agreed to assign a doctor to the region and to complete a half-finished abandoned hospital building; and the nonprofits worked with tribal leaders and local residents to dig trenches for water pipes and construct a building to house the generator. Nine months after GE first selected the district, the clinic was complete, fully staffed, and functioning. GE now has eight similar projects under way in Ghana and is committed to opening clinics in all the twenty-two districts that currently lack them. In addition, it is extending its work to South Africa, Malawi, Tan- zania, and Uganda. GE's accomplishments depended on the expertise and direct investment of corporate resources but also on its willingness to engage local government and nonprofits as partners in its work. In many cases, cross-sector partnerships such as these enable the development of rapid and systemic solutions that no single player could bring about on its own.

Aid organizations bring yet a different mix of capabilities from foundations or corporations. They can respond to humanitarian needs on a scale that dwarfs the charitable contributions of philanthropists and corporations. Generally, they must operate with the cooperation of local governments, and in cases where local government is unwise or corrupt, it may be difficult for them to operate effectively. Their scale of operation also means that they cannot be as selective about the recipients of their aid, nor efficiently engage in small-scale experimental programs.

Aid efforts, however, have the scale to make an impact on societal conditions in a way that can pave the path for business. Corporations often cannot justify the massive investment required for infrastructure where societal conditions are inadequate to support profitable operations. The region may lack access to energy, stable capital markets, or a skilled labor force; transaction costs and traditional ways of doing business may be inconsistent with the usual corporate practices in more developed markets. Neither philanthropic dollars nor corporate investment can overcome these barriers; instead, governmental aid is required to help reshape local conditions.

In sum, by concentrating on their different capabilities and interdependencies, philanthropy, aid, and corporate investment could leverage each other to achieve a greater impact. Measuring that impact consistently across sectors, however, is equally important to sustained collaboration.

Coordinated Evaluation

If a common set of evaluation metrics and procedures were adopted across all three sectors, it would not only streamline the evaluation process for all players, but it would help forge a common language across these very different organizational cultures. Simply stated, the clarity of pursuing a common set of goals, tracked by common indicators, would lead to greater strategic alignment.

As yet, no generally accepted evaluation metrics cut across all three sectors and all types of projects. The United Nations, along with many other agencies, tracks macro data about progress toward the Millennium Development Goals, but this is at far too high a level to evaluate the results of specific interventions. What is needed is a common set of metrics that can be applied at the project, regional, and national levels, for all types of initiatives. Despite the wide variety of initiatives undertaken by different actors, all interventions create some or all of four types of impact:

—*Financial returns.* For corporate or government investors that expect a financial return, whether in the form of direct corporate investments, aid-related investments in small and medium-sized enterprises, or loan repayments, one measure of success is the money earned on the investment. This is not only important to the investor but is also an essential step in economic development. If investment capital earns a sound return, more will follow; if not, the investment may create short-term benefits but is unlikely to be sustained.

—*Socioeconomic benefits.* Socioeconomic benefits are improvements in the economic status of a target population as a result of the initiative. At the individual level, these benefits include job creation and increased earnings or cost savings, such as reduced time collecting fresh water or fuel. At the national or regional level, socioeconomic benefits include increased government tax revenues, decreased costs in providing public services, and increased regional investment and economic activity.

—*Social benefits.* Social benefits are improvements in the well-being of a target population as a result of the initiative, such as better health, education, or quality of life. Specific metrics are needed for each type of benefit, such as mortality rates by age as a measure of health, but a limited list of representative metrics can be developed.

—*Environmental benefits.* Environmental benefits are improvements in the natural environment resulting from the initiative, such as cleaner water, reductions in the emission of greenhouse gases, or reduced rates of deforestation. Again, a limited list of representative benefits can be developed.

Although these categories are quite broad, they can serve as the starting point for a set of quantitative and qualitative metrics that can be tracked against initial baselines for any initiative. Many different indicators can serve as valid proxies for progress. What matters is the consistency of metrics and data collection across different initiatives, enabling a common language to evolve that can facilitate collaboration and mutual learning.

Take, for example, an initiative called Renewable Energy Enterprise Development (REED) developed by the United Nations Environment Program, in partnership with the United Nations Foundation and E+Co. REED provides financing and business development support to small and medium-sized clean energy enterprises in Africa, Brazil, and China. Box 12-1 lists the indicators that REED uses to evaluate progress against its goals.

BOX 12-1
Performance Indicators Used by Renewable Energy Enterprise Development (REED) to Evaluate Progress toward Its Goals

Performance type	Performance indicator
Financial	Return on investment
	Financial performance of the investee enterprise (for example, sales, gross margin, net profits, increase in assets)
Social	Improved health of consumers from use of cleaner energy
	Enhanced quality of life for consumers from spending less time obtaining other sources of fuel
Socioeconomic	Additional jobs created by the enterprise
	Increased income of enterprise employees
	Customer cost savings from access to cheaper energy source
	Increased income for related industries
	Additional financing raised by enterprise as result of REED and E+Co's investment
Environmental	Greenhouse gas offsets (tons of carbon-dioxide equivalent), valued at the price of carbon credits traded on the global market
	Deforestation avoided or forest reclaimed (hectares)

REED's local program officers collect the financial and operational data from investees and enter it into a standard format as part of their regularly scheduled visits. REED staff and consultants also interview a wide range of stakeholders including local community residents and governmental agencies. This wide range of perspectives enables REED to take a broad view of effects, looking beyond the investee itself to the community and supporting industries.

During the interviews, REED's interviewers ask about the most important social or nonfinancial benefits that resulted from the investment. The responses are categorized, and REED reports the five qualitative effects that are most often cited as part of its summary, along with a one-page narrative about the enterprise and the results of the investment. The result is a concise but holistic report based on a methodology that could easily be translated across different projects.

Given the trusted independent status of foundations and their relatively small financial contribution, representing only 5 percent of the resources from the other two sectors, it may be that the best way for foundations to leverage their contribution to increasing the impact of aid and corporate investment is to facilitate strategic alignment, develop common metrics, and devise a consistent system for collecting them.

Conclusion

Private donors, governmental aid, and corporate investment together total nearly $100 billion to the world's neediest region. Each sector contributes roughly similar amounts of funding, and their goals largely overlap. Yet each pursues its own agenda independently of the other sectors, channeling funds through a confusion of overlapping intermediaries and evaluating outcomes in its own ways. Differences in culture, incentives, and even language keep the sectors from working together effectively. At the same time, each sector has a unique set of capabilities to bring to the needs of the developing world. Foundations are trusted partners to facilitate cross-sector collaborations, communication, and evaluation. Corporations bring technology, training, employment, and access to global markets. Governments alone have the scale and incentive to build out the infrastructure necessary for the other two sectors to function effectively. The power of these three sectors working in alignment—dividing their efforts in line with their unique capabilities, working toward common goals, and tracking progress on a uniform set of metrics—would enable them to have a far greater social impact and simultaneously improve their sectoral and mutual effectiveness.

Notes

1. United Nations, *Update on Africa* (www.un.org/millenniumgoals/docs/MDG africa07.pdf [January 2008]).
2. UNCTAD, "FDI Flows in 2006: The Global and Regional Pictures" (www.unctad.org/Templates/Page.asp?intItemID=4160&lang=1 [January 2008]).
3. See chapter 3 in this volume by Homi Kharas. I estimate this number from his sketches of the geographic focus of private aid organizations, as given in figure 3-3.

Contributors

Matthew Bishop is chief business writer/American business editor and New York Bureau chief of *The Economist*. He was previously *The Economist*'s London-based business editor. He is the author of *Essential Economics*, the *Economist*'s layperson's guide to economics. His book *Philanthrocapitalism: How the Rich Are Trying to Save the World*, coauthored with Michael Green, will be published by Bloomsbury in 2008. Before joining *The Economist*, he was on the faculty of the London Business School, where he coauthored three books on subjects ranging from privatization and regulation to corporate mergers. He was educated at Oxford University. He has served as a member of the Sykes Commission on the investment system in the twenty-first century. He was also a member of the Advisors Group of the United Nations International Year of Microcredit 2005.

Lael Brainard is founding director and vice president of Brookings Global Economy and Development, where she holds the Bernard L. Schwartz Chair in International Economics. She served as deputy national economic adviser and chair of the Deputy Secretaries Committee on International Economics during the Bill Clinton administration, where she was responsible for coordinating international financial and trade policies. As the U.S. sherpa to the Group of Seven and Group of Eight, she shaped the 2000 Group of Eight Development Summit, which included developing country leaders for the first time. Before coming to Washington, she served as associate professor of applied economics at the Sloan School of the Massachusetts Institute of

Technology. Previously, she worked at McKinsey & Company advising corporations on strategic challenges. She received an MA and PhD from Harvard University, where she was a National Science Foundation fellow, and a BA from Wesleyan University.

Joshua Busby is an assistant professor at the LBJ School of Public Affairs and is affiliated with the Robert S. Strauss Center for International Security and Law, both at the University of Texas at Austin. He teaches courses on international organizations, international development, and nonstate actors. His research looks at the role of transnational advocacy campaigns and the rise of new international challenges. He has been a research fellow at Brookings, Harvard University's Belfer Center for Science and International Affairs, and Princeton University's Woodrow Wilson School. His work has appeared in *International Studies Quarterly* and *Current History*, among other publications. He served in the Peace Corps in Ecuador from 1997 to 1999. He received his PhD and MA from Georgetown University and has bachelor's degrees from the University of North Carolina–Chapel Hill and the University of East Anglia, where he was a British Marshall Scholar.

Derek Chollet is a senior fellow at the Center for a New American Security. He is also a nonresident fellow in the Brookings Institution's Global Economy and Development program and an adjunct associate professor at Georgetown University. Previously, he was foreign policy adviser to former senator John Edwards, both on his legislative staff and during the 2004 presidential campaign. During the Clinton administration, he served in the U.S. State Department in several capacities, including as chief speechwriter for Richard Holbrooke, U.S. ambassador to the UN, and as special adviser to Strobe Talbott, deputy secretary of state. He also assisted former secretaries of state James A. Baker III and Warren Christopher with researching and writing their memoirs. He has been a fellow at the Center for Strategic and International Studies, a fellow at the American Academy in Berlin, and a visiting scholar and adjunct professor at George Washington University. He is a member of the Council on Foreign Relations and serves on the boards of the Woodrow Wilson House and the Truman National Security Project. He is the author, coauthor, or coeditor of five books on American foreign policy, including *America between the Wars: From 11/9 to 9/11* (PublicAffairs, 2008), cowritten with James Goldgeier; *Bridging the Foreign Policy Divide,* coedited with Tod Lindberg and David Shorr (Routledge, 2008); and *The Road to the Dayton Accords: A Study of American Statecraft* (Palgrave

Macmillan, 2005). His commentaries and reviews on U.S. foreign policy and politics have appeared in the *Washington Post, Los Angeles Times, Financial Times, National Interest, Washington Monthly,* and in many other books and publications.

J. Gregory Dees is professor of the practice of social entrepreneurship and nonprofit management and the founding faculty director of the Center for the Advancement of Social Entrepreneurship at Duke University's Fuqua School of Business. He has written extensively on the topic of social entrepreneurship, including two books, *Enterprising Nonprofits* and *Strategic Tools for Social Entrepreneurs,* with Jed Emerson and Peter Economy. He previously taught at the Yale School of Management, Harvard Business School, and Stanford University. Before his academic career, he was a management consultant with McKinsey & Company. He holds a PhD in philosophy from Johns Hopkins University, a master's degree in public and private management from Yale University, and a BA from the University of Cincinnati.

Homi Kharas is a senior fellow at the Wolfensohn Center for Development at Brookings. He was the chief economist for the East Asia and Pacific Region of the World Bank and the director of the region's Poverty Reduction and Economic Management Department from 1999 to 2007, and he has been following East Asian economies since 1982. He joined the World Bank in 1980 and has worked in its Research Department, Latin American and Caribbean Region, and Economic Policy Department. From 1990 to 1991, he worked as a senior partner with Jeffrey D. Sachs and Associates, advising countries in Central and Eastern Europe and the Soviet Union on transition issues. He completed his PhD in economics at Harvard University and his undergraduate studies at the University of Cambridge. He has published widely in the areas of external debt and developing countries' foreign borrowing, fiscal risks, and contingent liabilities.

Ashok Khosla is chairman of the Development Alternatives Group, a consortium of social enterprises based in India whose mission is to create technologies, businesses, and markets for the large-scale generation of sustainable livelihoods. He was previously director of the Office of Environment, Government of India, and director of Infoterra, part of the United Nations Environment Program. He is currently serving as president of the Club of Rome. He has been a board member of many government, industry, and nongovernmental bodies in India, including the National Security Advisory Board, the

Science Advisory Committee to the Cabinet, and the National Environment Council. He studied at Cambridge University and Harvard University.

Mark R. Kramer is the founder and managing director of FSG Social Impact Advisors. He is also the founder and initial board chair of the Center for Effective Philanthropy, and a senior fellow in the Corporate Social Responsibility Initiative at Harvard University's John F. Kennedy School of Government. He has published extensively on the development of effective practices in philanthropy, evaluation, mission investing, and corporate social responsibility in the *Harvard Business Review, Stanford Social Innovation Review, Chronicle of Philanthropy,* and other publications. He also serves on the jury of the annual Excellence in Corporate Philanthropy Award given by the Committee Encouraging Corporate Philanthropy. Before founding FSG, he was the president of the venture capital firm Kramer Capital Management. He received a BA summa cum laude from Brandeis University, an MBA from the Wharton School, and a JD magna cum laude from the University of Pennsylvania Law School.

Vinca LaFleur is a partner at West Wing Writers, a speechwriting and communications strategy firm. Previously, she served as a special assistant and foreign policy speechwriter for President Bill Clinton, and before that as a speechwriter for U.S. Secretary of State Warren Christopher. She has also served as a political and human rights analyst at the U.S. Commission on Security and Cooperation in Europe, and been a visiting fellow in the International Security Program of the Center for Strategic and International Studies. She holds a BA from Yale University and an MA from the Paul H. Nitze School of Advanced International Studies at Johns Hopkins University. She has been rapporteur for the Brookings Blum Roundtable since its inception in 2004.

Jane Nelson is a senior fellow at the Mossavar-Rahmani Center for Business and Government and director of the Corporate Social Responsibility Initiative at the John F. Kennedy School of Government, Harvard University. She serves as a director at the Prince of Wales International Business Leaders Forum and is a nonresident senior fellow of Brookings. During 2001, she worked in the office of the UN secretary-general, Kofi Annan, preparing a report for the General Assembly on cooperation between the United Nations and the private sector. She was previously a vice president of Citibank responsible for marketing worldwide securities services in the Asia-Pacific region. She has been a lecturer in agricultural economics at the University of Natal in South Africa and has worked at the Business Council for Sustainable Development in Africa. She has written a variety of books and publications on public-private partnerships and the changing role of business in society, especially in emerging markets.

Joseph O'Keefe is writer in residence at Brookings Global Economy and Development, where he is writing the forthcoming book *The Great Game for Good*, on competition, commercialization, and sector blurring in global aid, development, and philanthropy. From 2001 to 2006, he was senior manager of corporate relations for the International Finance Corporation, where he oversaw the dissemination of the Equator Principles, a set of environmental and social standards for project finance lending. Previously, he was a researcher at the *New York Times*, an associate editor of *Foreign Affairs*, a speechwriter for the U.S. trade representative and U.S. secretary of defense, and the editor and coauthor of *Science at Its Best, Security at Its Worst* (2000), a report on security problems at U.S. nuclear weapons laboratories. After his graduation in 1984 from Spring Hill College in Mobile, he worked as a newspaper editor and journalist covering local politics. He received a graduate degree in public administration from the John F. Kennedy School of Government at Harvard University in 1991.

Ngozi Okonjo-Iweala is presently managing director of the World Bank and a nonresident senior fellow of Brookings. From June 2006 to August 2006, she was minister of foreign affairs of Nigeria. From July 2003 to June 2006, she served as minister of finance and economy of Nigeria and head of Nigeria's Presidential Economic Team. Her achievements as finance minister garnered international recognition for improving Nigeria's financial stability and fostering greater fiscal transparency to combat corruption. In October 2005, she led the Nigerian team that negotiated the cancellation of $18 billion of Nigeria's external debt with the Paris Club. Previously, she pursued a twenty-one-year career as a development economist at the World Bank, where she held the post of vice president and corporate secretary. She was educated at Harvard University and has a PhD in regional economics and development from the Massachusetts Institute of Technology.

Darrell M. West is vice president and director of Governance Studies at Brookings. He was previously the John Hazen White Professor of Political Science and Public Policy and Director of the Taubman Center for Public

Policy at Brown University. He is the author of fifteen books, including *Biotechnology Policy across National Boundaries* (2007); *Digital Government* (2005); *Air Wars: Television Advertising and Election Campaigns* (2005); *Celebrity Politics* (with John Orman; 2003); *The Rise and Fall of the Media Establishment* (2001); and *Patrick Kennedy: The Rise to Power* (2000).

Simon Zadek is chief executive of the international nonprofit organization AccountAbility, which advances accountability innovations that support sustainable development. He is currently a senior fellow at the Center for Government and Business at Harvard University's John F. Kennedy School of Government and a professor extraordinaire at the University of South Africa's Centre for Corporate Citizenship. He was previously visiting professor at the Copenhagen Business School, development director of the New Economics Foundation, and founding chair of the Ethical Trading Initiative. His book *The Civil Corporation: The New Economy of Corporate Citizenship* (2001) was recognized by the Academy of Management with its award for the best book on social issues in 2006.

Index

Abacha, Sani, 102
ABN Amro, 211
Accountability: benefits of, 7; of civil society organizations, 171–74; collaborative governance and, 7, 189, 193–99; development and developing countries and, 34, 177–81, 190, 191–93; enhancement of, 35–39; factors and issues of, 6, 162–63, 182–84, 191, 193; of governments, official agencies, and corporations, 163–71; initiatives and modes of engagement, 163-171; legal inadequacies of, 190–91; models and layers of, 162, 176, 182; multistakeholder approaches to, 6–7, 174–76, 182–83, 184, 193; new approaches and, 160–63, 174–76, 177–84, 189–90, 193; of public-private partnerships, 174–76, 180–81, 182, 193–94, 198. *See also* Crime and corruption
AccountAbility, 176, 189, 198
Acquired immunodeficiency syndrome. *See* HIV/AIDS
ActionAid International, 175b
Acumen Fund, 15, 121, 157
Advanced Market Commitment mechanism, 19
Advocacy and advocacy groups: accountability and, 172; collaborative initiatives and, 195b; costs of, 74, 79; credibility of, 163;

exercise of influence by, 14–15, 20–22, 34, 39, 48–49, 63, 94–95; initiatives to increase public advocacy, 169; strategic context of, 70, 82, 87, 95, 160; success of, 86. *See also* Center for Global Development; Jubilee *2000* debt relief campaign; MoveOn.org; Purpose Driven Network
Afghanistan, 56, 206b
Africa: accountability in, 164, 166; aid and assistance to, 56, 64, 96–97, 155–56, 177, 216, 217, 220–21, 222; capacity building in, 170b; cellular networks in, 16, 18, 23; Chinese aid to, 29–31, 62, 72n13, 177, 178, 180–81, 207; debt relief for, 12, 81, 92; economies in, 122; equipment project for, 15–16; green lighting project for, 13; growth and development of, 23, 24–25b; HIPC initiative and, 112; leadership in, 34; Millennium Development Goals for, 216; Mo Ibrahim Prize for, 34; public perceptions of, 23; SMEs in, 17. *See also individual countries*
Africa Action Plan (G-*8*), 56
Africa Governance Monitoring and Advocacy Project (AfriMAP), 166
African Development Bank, 87
African Investment Climate Facility, 170b
African Peer Review Mechanism, 164